SOFTWARE PSYCHOLOGY

Human Factors in Computer and Information Systems

WINTHROP COMPUTER SYSTEMS SERIES

Gerald M. Weinberg, *editor*

SHNEIDERMAN

Software Psychology: Human Factors in Computer and Information Systems

GRAYBEAL AND POOCH

Simulation: Principles and Methods

WALKER

Problems for Computer Solutions Using FORTRAN

WALKER

Problems for Computer Solutions Using BASIC

CHATTERGY AND POOCH

Top-down, Modular Programming in FORTRAN with WATFIV

LINES AND BOEING

Minicomputer Systems

GREENFIELD

Architecture of Microcomputers

NAHIGIAN AND HODGES

Computer Games for Businesses, Schools, and Homes

MONRO

Basic BASIC

CONWAY AND GRIES

An Introduction to Programming:

A Structured Approach Using PL/I and PL/C, 3rd ed.

CRIPPS

An Introduction to Computer Hardware

COATS AND PARKIN

Computer Models in the Social Sciences

EASLEY

Primer for Small Systems Management

CONWAY

A Primer on Disciplined Programming Using PL/I, PL/CS, and PL/CT

FINKENAUR

COBOL for Students: A Programming Primer

WEINBERG, WRIGHT, KAUFFMAN, AND GOETZ

High Level Cobol Programming

CONWAY, GRIES, AND WORTMAN

Introduction to Structured Programming Using PL/I and SP/k

GILB

Software Metrics

GELLER AND FREEDMAN

Structured Programming in APL

CONWAY, GRIES, AND ZIMMERMAN

A Primer on PASCAL

CONWAY AND GRIES

Primer on Structured Programming Using PL/I, PL/C, and PL/CT

GILB AND WEINBERG

Humanized Input: Techniques for Reliable Keyed Input

SOFTWARE PSYCHOLOGY

Human Factors in Computer and Information Systems

BEN SHNEIDERMAN
Associate Professor
Department of Computer Science
University of Maryland

WINTHROP PUBLISHERS, INC.
Cambridge, Massachusetts

Library of Congress Cataloging in Publication Data

Shneiderman, Ben.
Software psychology.

Bibliography: p.
Includes index.
1. Electronic digital computers—Programming—
Psychological aspects. I. Title.
QA76.6.S543 001.6'4'019 79-17627
ISBN 0-87626-816-5

To Sara and Anna

17 Dunster Street, Cambridge, Massachusetts 02138

 Printed in the United States of America.

10 9 8 7 6 5 4 3 2

CONTENTS

PREFACE

If the point of contact between the product and the people becomes a point of friction, then the industrial designer has failed. If, on the other hand, people are made safer, more comfortable, more eager to purchase, more efficient - or just plain happier - the designer has succeeded.

Henry Dreyfuss, *Designing for People* (1955)

Six years ago while beginning to explore the relationship between computer science and psychology, I requested a computerized literature search for journal articles with keywords such as 'computers', 'programming', or 'programming languages' and 'psychology', 'cognitive psychology', 'linguistics', or 'experimental psychology'. The 61 documents produced by the search all described the application of computers to psychology. Not one document mentioned the application of psychology to computer science.

A psychological perspective would increase awareness of the distinctions between people and their machines. My experiences with controlled experimentation have repeatedly convinced me of the differences between human reason and computer power. I believe that fifty years from now people will look back on the latter part of the 20th century as a quaint era when computers were designed to act like humans and some people believed that computers would soon match human intelligence. Even as computer systems increase in sophistication, we will more clearly discriminate between human capabilities, needs, and aspirations and the computer's tool-like nature. We must remember that producing computer systems is not a goal in itself, but merely a means of increasing the kinship among people (Chapter 12).

It is my hope that this book will encourage controlled, psychologically-oriented experimentation on the problems of computer and information systems. The scientific method applied to the design and production of computer software can improve programmer productivity, terminal user effectiveness, and system quality. As in many marriages, this joining of psychology with computer science may involve conflict and compromise but offers substantial benefit to both partners. This book reviews current trends and experimental results which have immediate application in software engineering and offers a model of human behavior which may be useful for further research.

Rapid technological progress depends on a scientific understanding of basic principles, validated by experimentation. In an apocryphal story,

Aristotle claimed that large stones fall faster than small stones, and this basic falsehood was accepted for almost 2000 years until Galileo disproved it with his simple but dramatic experiment from the Tower of Pisa. Computer scientists and system developers often mimic Aristotle's informal, intuitive style. They make broad claims for the simplicity, naturalness, or ease-of-use of new computer languages or techniques, but do not take advantage of the opportunity for experimental confirmation. Application of the well-developed research techniques and enormous body of knowledge available from psychology could produce practical advances and insights to fundamental principles.

The audience for this book includes professional system designers, managers, and programmers. The experimental results, the psychological outlook, and the attention to human performance issues will be useful in improving programming languages and practices, information retrieval and database systems, text editors, control languages, and a variety of interactive systems.

This book is also intended for advanced undergraduate and beginning graduate students studying human factors in computer and information systems. Student projects for such courses should include the design, administration, analysis, and report of a small controlled experiment. Subjects for such a pilot experiment can usually be solicited from university courses or local industry. Programmers are often eager to participate in an experiment since it gives them a chance to demonstrate their skills and is a novel experience.

A third audience encompasses industrial and academic researchers with backgrounds in computer science, information systems, psychology, and human factors. This book reviews current trends in this developing area and hopefully it will stimulate further interest and research.

I wish to express my appreciation for the interest and effort of many personal and professional colleagues and friends. Detailed commentaries on portions of the manuscript, which helped reshape my thinking and improve this book, were provided by Michael L. Brodie, Jim Foley, John Gannon, Julie Good, Tom Love, Phyllis Reisner, G. Michael Schneider, Sylvia Sheppard, Norman Sondheimer, Glenn Thomas, John C. Thomas, and Jerry Weinberg. Chapter 5 and parts of Chapter 6 were written with Opal Reynolds.

The faculty of my former department, Information Systems Management, and the students in my seminars on Human Factors in Computer and Information Systems offered lively debate and intellectual stimulation. The monthly meetings of the informal Software Psychology Society provided another valuable forum for discussion. The National Science Foundation provided support for work related to database systems.

This book was phototypeset using the University of Maryland's text editor and document processing system. These tools were maintained by the Computer Science Center, which also provided financial support for use of the computer resources. Two members of the Computer Science Center staff were especially helpful in making the computerized phototypesetting possible: Ben Cranston and Andrew Pilipchuk. Carl Fosler and Jean Kvedar entered portions of the text in the early stages. Robyn Seaton performed diligently in entering the remaining portions and the innumerable changes. It's hard to express my full appreciation for the efforts of these five individuals.

My wife, Nancy, and daughter, Sara, provided more than acceptance of my struggle and absence. Nancy shared her training and experience as a psychotherapist giving me useful insights to psychological issues. Sara's birth heightened my awareness of the wonder of life and her growth taught me about developmental struggles. Both of them helped increase my understanding of the limitations of machines and of the blessed human qualities of wisdom, joy, and love.

ACKNOWLEDGEMENTS

Grateful acknowledgement is made to the publishers for use of the following material:

Section 3.6, pages 57–61: Quotation and Figures 3–5, 3–6, and 3–7 from Isabel Briggs Myers, *The Myers-Briggs Type Indicator Manual,* copyright © 1962. Reprinted by permission of Consulting Psychologists Press, Inc., Palo Alto, California.

Section 9.1, page 200: Poem by Margaret Chisman in *Creative Computing,* Sept.–Oct. 1976, p. 33. Reprinted by permission of Creative Computing, Morristown, New Jersey.

Section 9.1, pages 201–202: Quotation and Figure 9–1 from Terry Winograd, *Understanding Natural Language,* © 1972. Reprinted by permission of Academic Press, Inc., New York.

Section 9.1, pages 205–206; Chapter 12, pages 273 and 275: Quotations from Joseph Weizenbaum, *Computer Power and Human Reason: From Judgement to Calculation,* © 1976, p. 6, 208–209. Reprinted by permission of W. H. Freeman and Company, Publishers, San Francisco.

Chapter 12, pages 278–280: Quotations from Robert M. Pirsig, *Zen and the Art of Motorcycle Maintenance: An Inquiry into Values,* © 1974. Reprinted by permission of William Morrow and Company, Inc., New York.

Table of t values, page 309: Adapted from Table IV of R. A. Fisher, *Statistical Methods for Research Workers,* 14th edition (copyright © 1970, University of Adelaide), by permission of Macmillan Publishing Co., Inc., Hafner Press.

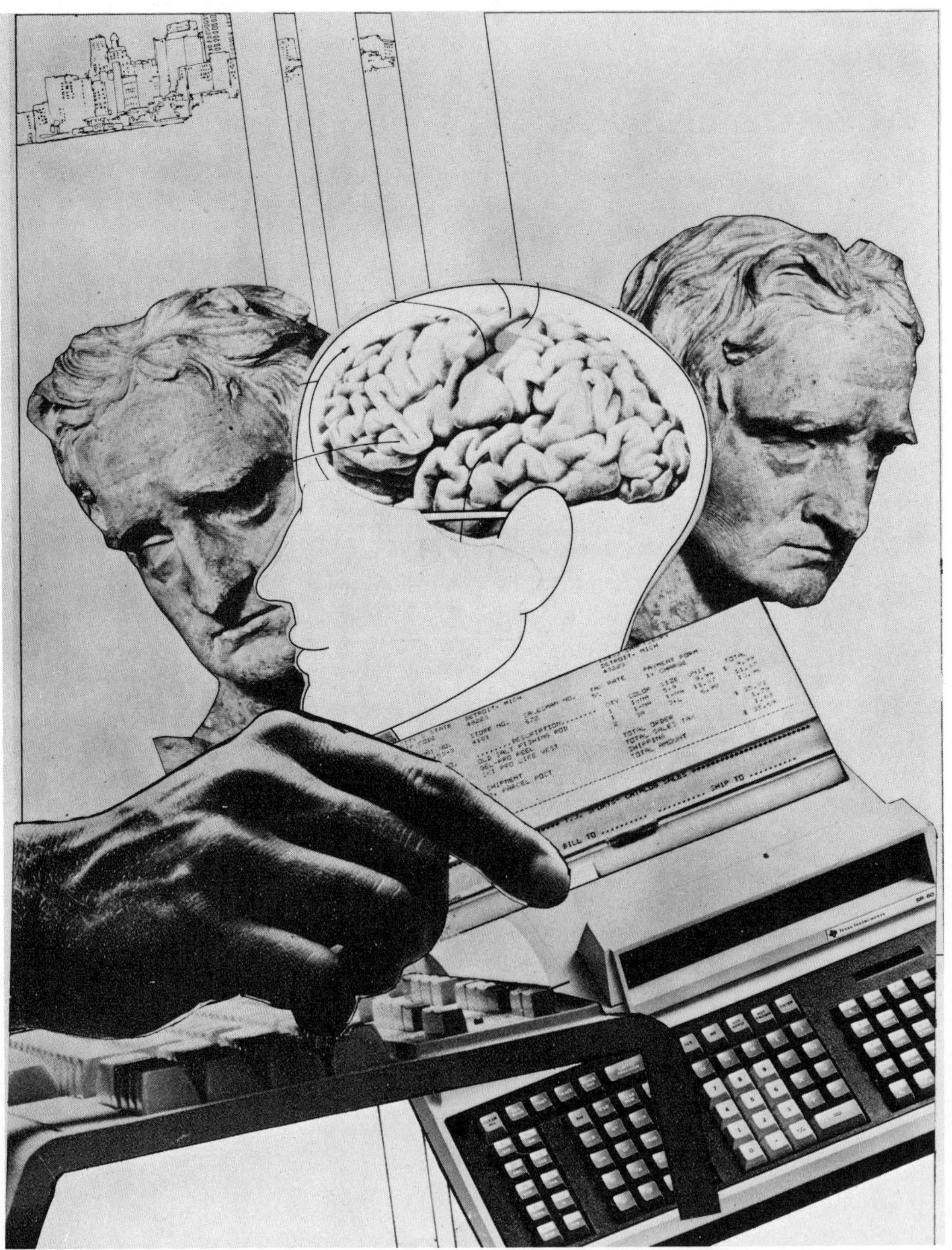
DETROIT, MICH
PAYMENT FORM
TOTAL ORDER
TOTAL SALES TAX
SHIPPING
TOTAL AMOUNT
BILL TO
SHIP TO

1

MOTIVATION FOR A PSYCHOLOGICAL APPROACH

Programmers constitute the first large group of men (and women) whose work brings them to those limits of human knowledge ... and which touch deeply secret aspects of the human brain.

Andrei Ershov, 'Aesthetics and the Human Factor in Programming' (1972)

Software psychology definition - scope - goals - programming languages - operating systems control languages - database query facilities - editors - terminal interactions - goals - programming environment, techniques, teaching and measurement - programmer aptitude and ability measures - review of sources

1.1 INTRODUCTION TO SOFTWARE PSYCHOLOGY

Programming has all the excitement and agony of making scientific discoveries, composing symphonies, designing buildings, and writing novels. Programming is an intensely human experience whose esthetics cannot be imitated or appreciated by mere machines.

In the first 35 years of computer history the emphasis has been on hardware developments, but now the emphasis is shifting toward human concerns. As late as the mid-1950's, 90 percent of application costs were devoted to hardware, but now 90 percent of the costs are for software. This reversal reflects not only the decline in hardware costs and the increase in programmer salaries, but also the recognition that systems must be carefully designed and developed to accommodate human users. The computer, like the artist's brush or novelist's typewriter, is the tool with which the programmer creates.

Programs cannot be produced on assembly lines like automobile engines, nor should productivity be measured by the number of lines of code produced per hour. Recognition of the high intellectual and creative skills required in software design and development will enable managers to provide proper environments for programmers to produce quality programs and computer users to have satisfying experiences. A deeper understanding of human cognitive skills, decision styles, information processing capacity, and personality variables will contribute to improved management strategies, performance metrics, programming aids, and coding techniques.

Controlled psychological experimentation will provide knowledge necessary to improve other computer uses such as sophisticated decision support systems for high level managers, inquiry systems for middle-level managers, supermarket terminals, banking terminals, computer-assisted instruction, and home computer systems. The intuition and experience of programming language and application system designers can and should be supplemented with experimental research to aid in producing high-quality 'user-friendly' interfaces, especially for nonprogrammers.

We need a new science which applies the techniques of experimental psychology and the concepts of cognitive psychology to the problems of computer and information science. This marriage of psychology and computer systems has been labeled *software psychology* by Tom Love, a General Electric psychologist working to improve software production methods.

Definition: Software psychology is the study of human performance in using computer and information systems. Understanding of human skills and capacity to design effective computer systems can be improved by application of the techniques of experimental psychology; the analysis of cognitive and perceptual processes; the methods of social, personnel and industrial psychology; and the theories of psycholinguistics. Software psychology is a new 'way of knowing' which complements current research and development practice while emphasizing human values. A more rigorous, psychologically based approach to systems may increase development costs and time, but long term savings result from improved system quality.

1.2 SCOPE OF SOFTWARE PSYCHOLOGY

Software psychologists focus on human concerns such as:

- ease of use
- simplicity in learning
- improved reliability
- reduced error frequency
- enhanced user satisfaction

while maintaining an awareness of

- machine efficiency
- storage capacity
- hardware constraints.

In its broadest sense software psychology encompasses all human uses of computers but concentrates on software development, query facility usage and interface design. Frequently mentioned topics for software psychology include programming languages, operating systems control languages, database query facilities, computer-assisted instruction, personal computing systems, editors, word processing, and terminal usage by non-skilled users.

1.2.1 Programming Languages

Procedurally oriented higher level programming languages have been a popular software psychology research topic because these languages play a critical role in developing valuable systems and their use is increasing rapidly. Sammet's (1978) roster of programming languages currently in use lists 166 for 1976–77. Commercial programmers emphasize COBOL while scientists, engineers, economists, and statisticians depend on FORTRAN or BASIC. More adventurous programmers seek out APL, PL/I, or Assembler, and academic researchers are heavier users of languages such as PASCAL, LISP, SNOBOL and ALGOL variants. Assembly language usage will be with us for a very long time, even though higher level machine independent languages are being used more frequently for systems programming.

These general-purpose problem-solving languages are supplemented by a variety of special-purpose languages for simulation (GPSS, SIMSCRIPT II.5, CSMP), statistical analysis (SPSS, CROSSTABS, SAS), engineering (COGO, STRESS, ICES), text handling (PAGE, SCRIPT), or formula manipulation (FORMAC, REDUCE).

In spite of the differences among these languages there are unifying principles which are candidates for research by experimental methods. Obvious issues include choice of meaningful variable names, data structures, documentation methods, modular design, control structures, input/output specifications, and syntactic form.

1.2.2 Operating Systems Control Languages

One of the most tedious tasks a programmer faces is using a control language to invoke operating system functions. Log-on procedures, password checking, file construction, compiler invocation, library usage, linkage editing, and device allocation require a special language which is rarely designed for easy use. Mention IBM's Job Control Language to a group of programmers and you will usually get a colleagial smile indicating recognition of shared anguish. What makes these programmers so angry? Is the JCL so bad, or is there something about it which produces unwarranted dissatisfaction? Can these languages be improved? Why have manufacturers persisted in using fixed or constrained formats with arbitrary and complex coding schemes?

1.2.3 Database Query Facilities

A rapid growth area is the development of database query facilities for use by nonprogrammers. A variety of proposals has been made, but none has emerged as dominant. This is an exciting opportunity for experimental research because language designs can be influenced before widespread usage makes major modifications difficult, as is the case with FORTRAN. Furthermore, experimental work on real users seems especially appropriate because the background of the potential nonprogrammer user is radically different from the background of programming or query language designers.

1.2.4 Editors

Interest in text editors is increasing as they become part of online terminal-based programming systems and word processing systems which are the basis of office automation and electronic mail projects. Editors are used in conjunction with document processors for producing neatly formatted reports and phototypesetting devices which are restructuring the newspaper and book publishing industries. Editor usage is characterized by higher typing rates than programming, numerous simple commands, and the need for short response time. Subtle problems such as long response time, awkward commands, and slow terminal display speeds can substantially decrease user satisfaction. Standardization of commands, based on experimental comparisons, would reduce the burden of those who use several editors and, for example, cannot remember whether 'K' means 'kill' or 'keep' a file.

1.2.5 Terminal Interactions

Computer terminals are rapidly becoming a part of banking, computer-assisted instruction, supermarket checkout, airline, and car and hotel reservation systems. Nonprogrammer clerks, middle-level managers, and the proverbial casual users outnumber programmers in computer terminal usage. The special needs of these diverse user classes are another obvious subject for experimental software psychology since it is difficult for a trained system designer to anticipate the problems of unskilled users. Since system designers still work largely from their own experience and often repeat the mistakes of others, guidelines for designing terminal interactions, testing them, and teaching them are needed.

1.3 GOALS OF SOFTWARE PSYCHOLOGY

In short, the goal of software psychology is to facilitate the human use of computers. This can only come from an understanding of human perceptual skills, information processing capacity, decision making ability, cognitive styles, and personality. These human characteristics have to be analyzed in the work environment and in the context of machine limitations.

Improvements in the use of computers could result from a deeper understanding of human cognition based on experimental studies. The improvements would manifest themselves through enhancement of programming practices, refinement of programming tools, improvement of teaching, development of software metrics, and accurate assessment of programmer aptitude and ability.

1.3.1 Enhance Programming Practice

Modest changes could be made in the way programming is done. These changes should be large enough so that programmers and managers will be able to perceive the improvement but not so large that they disrupt contemporary practice. Potential areas of improvement include:

- standards for programming language usage including commenting, formatting, mnemonic names, control structures, and data structures

- documentation guidelines covering internal comments, external writeups, and flowcharts

- team interaction patterns such as chief programmer teams, group testing, code reading, and structured walkthroughs

- programming environment features involving the physical space, hardware facilities, software tools, management, and morale

- guidelines for designing effective person–computer interfaces through online terminals.

1.3.2 Refine Programming Techniques

New programming language ideas may take many years to gain acceptance or they may never gain acceptance at all because of the *historical imperative*, the natural desire to keep things as they are. While revolutionary developments have met with skepticism, there is a sympathetic feeling for evolutionary change. Programmers and their managers like to believe that they are in a rapidly developing high technology discipline and that they are receptive to new ideas. However, in some ways, programming is a primitive one-at-a-time craft run in tribal fashion, and the young programmer who is enamored of today's new techniques may soon become the guardian of yesterday's fashion.

In spite of the fact that our first major high level languages, FORTRAN and COBOL, are still with us, much has changed in 20 years. Chaotic control structures are being replaced with more orderly and easier-to-follow program templates based on high-level control structures. Clever programming tricks and ad hoc data structures are giving way to more comprehensible and modifiable strategies. The ten thousand line subroutine is being superseded by well-defined, functionally decomposed modules.

There is hope that more changes can be made to popular older languages (for example, FORTRAN 77) and that newer languages (for example, PASCAL) will become more widely used. The new approaches in database management systems have taken hold in less than five years as programmers learned data manipulation and data description languages. More changes can be anticipated in database query languages and data communications languages as we move to distributed systems with multiple computers. Program design languages are in development and may become useful tools. New programming language control or data structures may emerge. Verification-oriented languages and unorthodox applicative languages (Backus, 1978) may inspire changes or replace contemporary languages.

All of these processes may be studied experimentally, but software psychology may play a more fundamental role than simply verifying the utility of new ideas. By providing an understanding of programmer behavior, software psychology may offer insights which suggest new programming language constructs. A theory of programmer behavior would be a valuable contribution.

1.3.3 Improve Teaching

Only recently have educational psychologists and computer scientists begun to study teaching methods specifically geared to programmer education (Mayer, 1976b). Much could be done to improve training of novice and experienced programmers by applying the principles of educational psychology. The spiral curriculum advocated by Bruner (1968) and the learning framework proposed by Ausubel (1968) have potential application to programming.

Techniques for testing programming skill have come under discussion with the development of the Computer Science Graduate Record Examination, the Association for Computing Machinery's (ACM) Self-

Assessment Test, and the Institute for Computers and Computer Programming's (ICCP) Certificate in Data Processing Test. In spite of these efforts no effective metrics for programming skills have been developed.

The ACM's Curriculum 68 (ACM, 1968) which has influenced University level courses for a decade has been revised (ACM, 1979) and graduate level curricula in information systems (ACM, 1972) have been proposed. The discussion of the contents, goals, and level of university and industrial training continues. An understanding of human learning and how to improve programming education would be a natural byproduct of research in software psychology.

Training manuals and online tutorial aids for terminal users could be improved by applying the results of educational psychology. The phased, layered, or spiral approach to teaching terminal users, depends on the step-by-step learning processes described by Bruner (1968), Ausubel (1968), and others.

1.3.4 Develop Software Metrics

In spite of the vast sums spent on programming and the importance of computer systems, there is no satisfactory and accepted method for evaluating program quality and programmer productivity. Number of lines of code is a simple and widely used measure, but unfortunately this measure encourages programmers to produce lengthy rather than lucid programs. Recent attempts by Gilb (1977), Halstead (1977), and Shneiderman (1977) are initial approaches to measuring program quality, but much remains to be done. Acceptable metrics could lend valuable guidance to programmers, managers, and experimenters.

1.3.5 Assess Programmer Aptitude and Ability

Programmer aptitude tests have been available from the earliest days of programming, but satisfactory demonstrations of their validity and reliability do not exist. Managers would like to know which employees are good candidates for programmer training, and college administrators, as well as students, would like to know what it takes to succeed in programming courses.

Reliable programmer ability measures are hard to come by, and managerial instinct has not been adequate. Researchers have found between 5 to 1 and 100 to 1 ratios in programmer performance. This means that programmers at the same level, with similar backgrounds and comparable salaries, might take 1 to 100 weeks to complete the same project. This staggering variability makes planning difficult and disrupts program development projects.

1.4 REVIEW OF SOURCES

Typically, human factors research has emphasized physical design of controls and displays in airline cockpits, automobiles, and electronic hardware. More recently, this literature includes cognitive issues, and the journal *Human Factors* occasionally carries articles about programming. The Human Factors Society has a Computer Systems Group which publishes a quarterly newsletter.

Behavioral research in programming goes back to the mid-1960's when comparative programming language studies and batch vs. time-sharing research were popular. Sackman's book on *Man-Computer Problem Solving* (1970) was the first extensive and experimentally sophisticated report on human factors experiments in the use of time sharing and batch processing. Weinberg's landmark text, *The Psychology of Computer Programming* (1971), provided a broad-ranging discussion of individual performance, social interaction, and programming tools. Weinberg offered engaging anecdotes and worthwhile insights, but rarely cited experimental results. He recognized the importance of personality and the utility of controlled experimentation. Weinberg's book is often quoted and has had a dramatic effect in elevating the consciousness of managers and programmers about the human aspects of programming. James Martin's *Design of Man-Computer Dialogues* (1973) was the first attempt to describe a variety of person-computer interfaces. His voluminous work provides a broad perspective, but much can be added about new hardware, experience with working systems, and experimental results.

The *International Journal of Man-Machine Studies* frequently publishes relevant papers. The *Communications of the ACM* and the *IEEE Transactions on Software Engineering* deal with human factors topics from time to time. Psychology journals such as the *Journal of Applied Psychology*, *Memory and Cognition*, *Journal of Educational Psychology*, as well as management science, operations research, and computer science journals contain related papers.

Conferences can also provide worthwhile research results. Large conferences such as the yearly National Computer Conference produce informative proceedings as do smaller meetings such as the the Annual Conference of the ACM Special Interest Group on Computer Personnel Research and the numerous meetings of other ACM Special Interest Groups.

Research is being conducted at an increasing rate at university and industrial research centers. There is a growing acceptance of the idea that psychologically oriented experiments on programmers and computer users can yield substantial intellectual and economic benefits.

1.5 PRACTITIONER'S SUMMARY

Help is on the way! By applying the techniques and resources of psychology to computer and information systems, we may be able to make the programmer's and terminal user's life easier, more productive, and more satisfying while reducing errors. By recognizing that computers are merely tools and that humans provide the creative energy to keep them moving, we focus attention on human effectiveness rather than machine efficiency. As the results of software psychology experiments are reported, you may discover ways of applying them to your work to enhance quality and reduce effort. By experimenting in your own environment, you can improve your product/performance and contribute to this emerging discipline.

1.6 RESEARCHER'S AGENDA

Computer and information scientists can complement current research practices by adding a psychological approach which includes controlled experimentation and an understanding of human cognitive processes. Experimental techniques provide an insight to human performance and guidance for improving programming practices, refining programming tools, improving teaching, developing software metrics, and assessing aptitude/ability.

Psychologists can extend the domain of application for their techniques and knowledge. Computer usage is expanding into every area of human endeavor, and a deeper understanding of cognitive processes and knowledge structures could yield significant performance improvements. Psychologists have an opportunity to shape computer systems, languages, training, and management thinking while contributing to their own discipline. Programs and terminal interactions provide concrete manifestations of human thought processes whose analysis can lead to progress in cognitive psychology. Software psychology is the study of individual and group problem solving at a level of detail and complexity that has previously been unexplored.

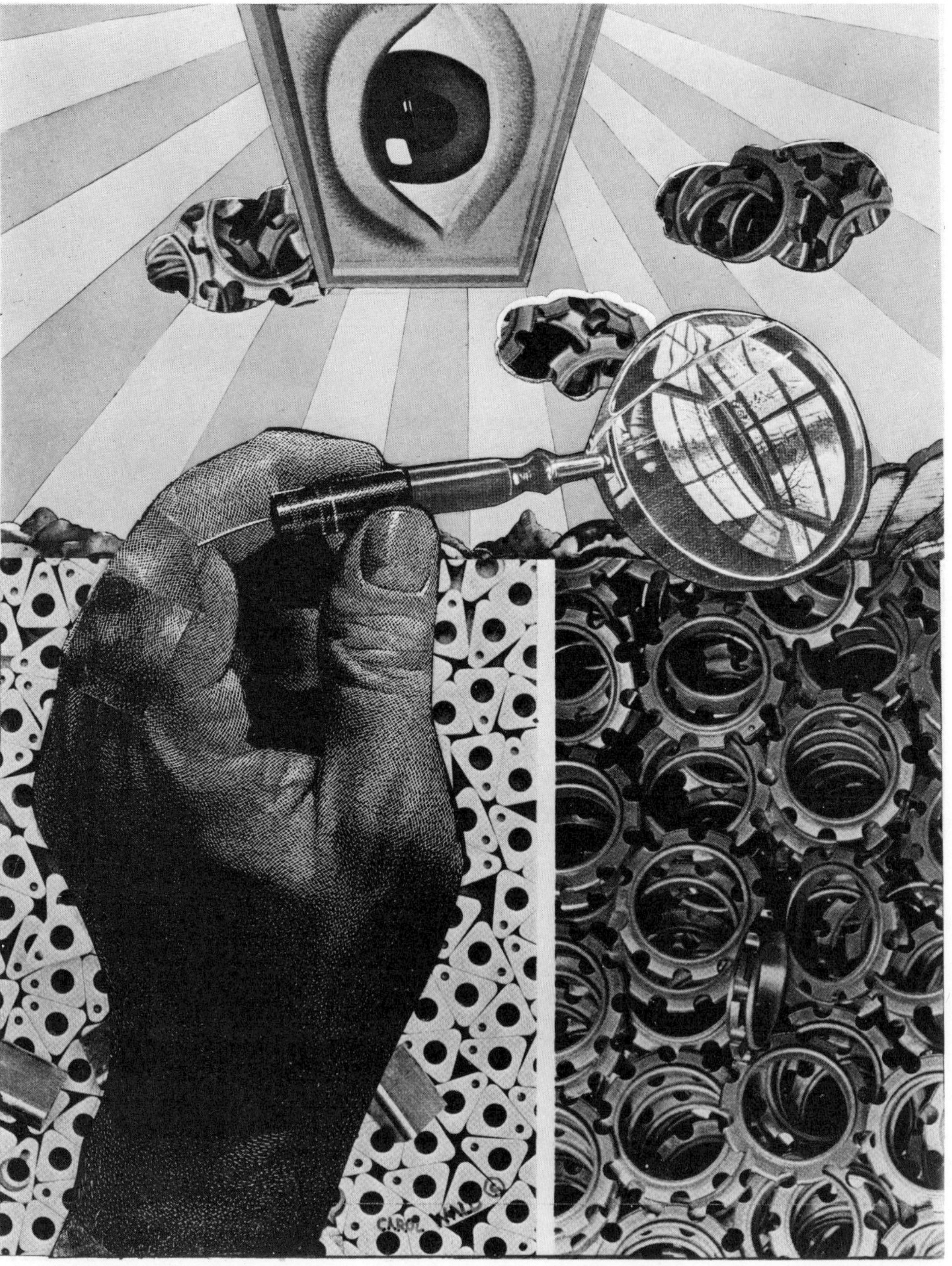
CAROL WALD ©

2

RESEARCH METHODS

We should bring the whole force of our minds to bear upon the most minute and simple details and to dwell upon them for a long time so that we become accustomed to perceive the truth clearly and distinctly.

Rene Descartes, *Rules for the Direction of the Mind* (1628)

Research methods – introspection – protocol analysis – case studies – field studies – controlled experimentation – experimental design – selection of subjects – statistical methods – factorial experiments – correlational studies – performance tasks – comprehension – composition – debugging – modification – timing – memorization/reconstruction – background data – subjective measures

2.1 INTROSPECTION AND PROTOCOL ANALYSIS

The simplest form of research in software psychology is *introspection*, in which the experimenters or the subjects simply reflect on how they write, study and debug programs or how they use terminals. This form of organized thinking often produces insights to the programming process or new ideas for improved syntax. Unfortunately, introspection is done differently by each individual, and the conclusions that one person reaches may not be shared by others. Folklore about the diverse idiosyncrasies of programmers should be enough to convince most people that introspection may not produce results which would be applicable to a wide range of users. Systems designers or computer-assisted instruction course authors are often surprised to find that not everyone understands the terminal interaction that they have designed. On the other hand, introspection is the way that most new ideas are discovered -- by an individual working alone in his or her office and thinking quietly. Introspective judgments based on experience in using, designing, and teaching systems play an essential role in generating novel ideas.

Introspection experiments might be conducted by asking a group of subjects to evaluate their use of indentation, commenting techniques, mnemonic variable names, flowcharts, modularity, debugging tools. Such forced thinking may compel subjects to understand their usage patterns for long or short variable names, for subscripts or statement labels, and for module or system names. As soon as one person makes his or her style explicit, it becomes possible to verify the utility of that rule and teach it to others. If the rule is widely accepted, old-timers will claim that they have been following it implicitly for decades, but, without an explicit rule, discussion is uncommon and teaching impossible.

A variant of introspection is *protocol analysis* in which the experimenter or the subject keeps a written or tape recorded record of his or her perceived thought processes. This permanent record or transcript can be reviewed at leisure and analyzed for frequency counts of certain words, first or last occurrence of a word or behavior, or clusters of behavioral patterns.

Standish (1973) produced some interesting protocols of his work on a few popular problems, such as the eight queens problem, with summary observations and hypotheses. Ruven Brooks (1977), following the techniques of Newell and Simon (1974), has performed extensive protocol analyses of program composition tasks using computer string processing facilities to help develop a model of the cognitive processes in program development.

These forms of introspection are worthwhile when the subject is a capable sensitive programmer, since important insights may be obtained. But, there is no guarantee that other programmers will behave in the same manner or even that the subject will repeat the same process tomorrow. Carrying out the tedious protocol analysis for substantial numbers of individuals is difficult, time-consuming, and expensive.

2.2 CASE STUDIES AND FIELD STUDIES

Case or field studies involve careful study of programming practices or computer usage at one or more sites. This approach has been used to compare management techniques, programming languages or error patterns and is effective in discovering how people actually use computer systems. Many researchers performing case or field studies collect voluminous amounts of data in the hope that 'something interesting' will emerge. Worthwhile insights may be gained but the lack of experimental controls means that there is no guarantee that results are replicable or generalizable. The same study conducted at a different time, by a different researcher, or at a different site may not give the same results. In spite of these problems, case and field studies are popular since they provide worthwhile data to compare performance against and can reveal unexpected usage patterns.

Knuth's famous 'Empirical Study of FORTRAN Programs' (Knuth, 1973) showed heavy dependence on simple forms of FORTRAN statements. Eighty-six percent of the assignment statements involved no more than one arithmetic operator, 95 percent of DO loops used the default increment of 1, and 87 percent of the variables had no more than one subscript. Similar studies have been repeated on PL/I (Elshoff, 1976b) and APL (Saal and Weiss, 1977). These studies were conducted by capturing samples of programs from program libraries. A similar set of studies using programs submitted for execution during normal production focus on errors that programmers make during program development (Young, 1974; Rubey, 1968; Boies and Gould, 1974; Gould, 1975). Studies of terminal usage provide data about use of interactive systems (Boies, 1976).

One of the most famous field studies was the IBM/New York Times

Information Bank Project in which the new Improved Programming Technologies such as chief programmer team, structured coding and open libraries were tested (Baker, 1972a, 1972b). This study showed dramatic improvements in productivity with reduced error rates when the new techniques were used, but it has been criticized for lack of experimental controls and exaggerated reporting. The project's high visibility and the dedicated work of expert programmers may have been as important as the new techniques.

Even if no initial hypothesis is advanced and no new technique is being 'tested,' data collecting case or field studies are useful in developing an image of actual computer usage and programmer performance. Often the statistical analysis, coupled with informal interviews of participants and experimenters, can suggest insights which are immediately useful or provide the basis for a controlled experiment.

2.3 CONTROLLED EXPERIMENTATION

Controlled experimentation is the fundamental paradigm of scientific reserch. By limiting the number of *independent variables*, controlling for external bias, carefully measuring *dependent variables* and performing statistical tests, it is possible to verify hypotheses within stated confidence levels. Controlled experimentation depends on a reductionist approach which limits the scope of the experiment, but yields a clear convincing result. Critics complain that controlled experimentation concentrates on minor issues, but supporters argue that each small result is like a tile in a mosaic: a small fragment with clearly discernible color and shape which contributes to the overall image of programming behavior.

2.3.1 Simple Experimental Designs

Controlled experimentation requires an initial hypothesis about performance, usually expressed in the negative: for example, 'Programmers given commented programs will do no better on a comprehension quiz than programmers given noncommented programs' or 'Terminal user satisfaction will not be improved by an increase in display rates from 10 to 30 characters per second.' In these two examples, commenting and display rates are the independent variables, and comprehension quiz score and user satisfaction are the dependent variables. Both of these experiments are *one-factor experiments*, since only one issue is being studied at a time. Both of these experiments have two *levels of treatment* for the independent variable: comments or no comments and display rates of 10 or 30 characters per second. By adding a 50 character per second display rate, we could make the second experiment a three treatment level experiment.

2.3.2 Subjects

To run these experiments, a group of *subjects* is needed. Getting subjects is often a problem in this kind of research since programming knowledge may be required and professional programmer's time is valuable. Even if professional programmers can be obtained for the necessary time, there are serious problems in assessing variations in the background and ability of subjects. A consistently reported result of programming experimentation is that the variability in subject performance often obscures the experimental issue. But, for the moment, assume that an adequate number of homogeneous subjects can be obtained for the necessary time. If the results are to be applied to a wide range of programmers or users, some argument must be made that these subjects are representative of the population. If the subjects are FORTRAN users, then the results may not be valid for COBOL users. As much as possible, the subjects should be representative of the typical class of users being studied.

Returning to the simple one-factor, two-treatment-level experiments, we might randomly assign half the subjects to one treatment level and the other half to the second treatment level. For the comprehension experiment, the subjects would be presented with the commented or non-commented forms and the comprehension quiz for equal lengths of time. For the terminal user experiment, subjects would carry out the interaction at the 10 or 30 character per second rate and fill out a user satisfaction questionnaire.

2.3.3 Statistical Methods: t-test

The quiz or questionnaire would be scored and the results tabulated, giving average and standard deviation for both groups. A higher average for one treatment level than for another does not necessarily indicate *statistically significant differences*. Since a few high or low scores in a group can distort the results, experimenters rely on statistical techniques such as the *t-test* to demonstrate significant differences between the means. This mathematical test takes into account the performance variation among group members at each treatment level, as indicated by the *standard deviation*.

The standard deviation measures how different the values in a group are from the group mean. The mean is computed by simply adding the values and dividing by the number of values. We use the following notation to describe M the mean:

$$M = \frac{\Sigma x}{N}$$

where x represents the set of the values and N is the number of values. The standard deviation, s, is derived by summing up the squares of the differences of the values and the mean. This summation is divided by N-1 and then the square root is taken:

$$s = \sqrt{\frac{\Sigma(x - \mathrm{M})^2}{\mathrm{N} - 1}} \tag{1}$$

If comprehension quiz scores are 8, 7, 6, 8, 9, 10 then the mean is

$$\frac{8 + 7 + 6 + 8 + 9 + 10}{6} = \frac{48}{6} = 8.0$$

and the standard deviation is

$$\sqrt{\frac{0^2 + (-1)^2 + (-2)^2 + 0^2 + 1^2 + 2^2}{5}} = \sqrt{\frac{10}{5}} = \sqrt{2.0} = 1.41$$

The square of the standard deviation, the *variance*, is often cited as an alternative measure of deviation from the mean.

Statistical significance is usually recorded as being at the .01 or .05 level; this indicates that there is less than a 1 percent or 5 percent chance that this difference between groups occurred by chance. The lower the significance level, the higher the confidence we have that the results are reliable. A 0.001 significance level (0.1 percent) is a strong indication that the independent variable treatment level produced meaningful differences in the dependent variable, while a 0.10 significance level (10 percent) is a weak indication. A significance level above 0.10 is not generally acceptable evidence of significant differences.

To compute the t-value and perform the t-test, use the following two formulas:

$$t = \frac{\mathrm{M1} - \mathrm{M2}}{\sqrt{\frac{s^2}{\mathrm{N1}} + \frac{s^2}{\mathrm{N2}}}} \tag{2}$$

where

$$s^2 = \frac{\Sigma(x - \mathrm{M1})^2 + \Sigma(x - \mathrm{M2})^2}{\mathrm{N1} + \mathrm{N2} - 2} \tag{3}$$

In these equations *M1* and *M2* are the means in the two treatment levels, *N1* and *N2* are the number of subjects in the two groups (usually we try to arrange experiments so that $N1 = N2$) and x represents the scores of the quiz or questionnaire.

If comprehension scores for the comment group were:

$$x = 5, 5, 6, 7, 7, 8, 9$$

then the number of subjects $N1 = 7$, the mean $M1 = 6.71$ and the standard deviation for group 1 is 1.50. If the scores for the noncomment group were:

$$x = 4, 4, 5, 5, 5, 7$$

then the number of subjects $N2 = 6$, the mean $M2 = 5.00$ and the standard deviation for group 2 is 1.10. Doing the calculations on equation (3) to get the standard deviation squared of the entire group yields:

$$s^2 = \frac{13.43 + 6.0}{7 + 6 - 2} = \frac{19.43}{11} = 1.77$$

and substituting into equation (2) for t gives:

$$t = \frac{6.71 - 5.00}{\sqrt{\frac{1.77}{7} + \frac{1.77}{6}}} = \frac{1.71}{\sqrt{.548}} = \frac{1.71}{.740} = 2.31$$

This t-value can be looked up in tables provided in standard psychological statistics texts.† The table will list the significance level (0.10, 0.05, 0.01 for example) and the *degrees of freedom*, usually shown as *df* or *n*. The degrees of freedom indicate the number of independent measurements in a sample. In a simple experiment with 8 measurements there are 7 degrees of freedom. For this experimental design the degrees of freedom are $N1 + N2 - 2$, that is, two less than the total number of subjects in the experiment. In our commenting experiment there are 11 degrees of freedom and we might choose a significance level of 0.05. Checking through a table we find that the t-value is 2.201. Since our t-value from the experiment, 2.31, is higher than the t-value in the table, we can claim statistical significance at the 0.05 level. Checking the table again, this time at the 0.01 level we find a t-value of 3.106. Since our experimental t-value is less than this, we cannot claim a 0.01 significance level.

†A table of t values appears on page 309.

	Mnemonic Variable Names	Nonmnemonic Variable Names	Group Averages
Commented	84.5	72.3	78.4
Noncommented	75.4	56.8	66.1
	80.0	64.6	72.3

Table 2-1: Mean modification scores for hypothetical two-factor experiment.

	Mnemonic Variable Names	Nonmnemonic Variable Names	Group Averages
Indented			
Commented	3.2	2.8	3.0
Noncommented	3.6	3.0	3.3
	3.4	2.9	3.2
Nonindented			
Commented	3.1	2.9	3.0
Noncommented	3.4	2.9	3.2
	3.3	2.9	3.1

Table 2-2: Mean number of bugs found in hypothetical three-factor experiment.

This basic one-factor, two-treatment-level experiment is easy to administer and evaluate. It can be used to study a wide variety of problems, where a comparison between two approaches is neccessary. Commented and noncommented programs might be compared for novice, intermediate, or expert programmers; for short, medium, and long programs, for simple, medium, and difficult problems; for any number of programming languages; for comprehension, modification, and debugging; and for a variety of application domains.

2.3.4 Two-Factor Experiments

After doing a few single factor experiments you may be interested in two- or three-factor experiments, because you can study two or three factors at once and observe *interaction effects*. A simple two-factor experiment might focus on commenting and mnemonic variable names. If each factor is presented at only two treatment levels, then there would be commented and noncommented programs, and mnemonic and nonmnemonic variable usage. The experimenter would prepare four program versions for this 2 by 2 (or 2 x 2) design:

1) commented with mnemonic variable names
2) commented with nonmnemonic variable names
3) noncommented with mnemonic variable names
4) noncommented with nonmnemonic variable names.

The subjects would be randomly assigned to one of the four groups and would perform the required task, such as, modifying the program. The modifications would be graded and group averages might be presented in a simple table, such as Table 2-1. The hypothetical results suggest that mnemonic variable names and commenting do improve modification performance for this group of subjects, but we cannot be satisfied with means alone. The original modification scores must be subjected to a statistical test called *Analysis of Variance* (often called ANOVA) which verifies the statistical significance of the differences between the means for the two *main effects*. The test also produces an analysis of the interaction effect between the two factors: Does the presence of comments reduce the impact of mnemonic variable names or does the absence of mnemonic names imply that comments are necessary for modification? These intriguing main and interaction effects can be studied by the *two-way analysis of variance* that is used in two-factor experiments. This statistical technique can show significance of the following effects:

Main effects
    Commenting
    Mnemonics
Two-way interaction
    Comments x Mnemonics

2.3.5 Three-Factor Experiments

If three-factor experiments are tried, then a three-way analysis of variance is used. We might study commenting, mnemonic variable name usage and indentation as aids in facilitating debugging. If each of the three factors were tested at only two treatment levels, there would be a 2 x 2 x 2 design with eight groups or cells, each having a different version of the program listing in which the experimenter had embedded a number of bugs. Subjects might be graded on the number of bugs found and a simple hypothetical tabular report (such as Table 2-2) might be produced.

The mean scores shown provide less clear-cut results than the previous sample experiment. We might 'feel' that mnemonic naming helps, commenting hinders, and indentation does not matter in the debugging task. Unfortunately, 'feelings' are not an acceptable replacement for statistical analysis. A three-way analysis of variance will indicate the significance of the differences for the three main effects, three two-way interactions and one three-way interaction.

Main Effects
- Commenting
- Mnemonics
- Indentation

Two-way interactions
- Commenting x Mnemonics
- Commenting x Indentation
- Mnemonics x Indentation

Three-way interactions
- Commenting x Mnemonics x Indentation

Higher than three factor experiments may be tried, but the complexity of administration and the high variance in subject performance, which tend to obscure significant differences, make it a dubious venture. A more worthwhile approach would be to increase the number of treatment levels for the factors. Three levels of commenting might be tried, producing a 3 x 2 x 2 design.

2.3.6 Correlation Studies

Another experimental approach is to investigate the correlation, that is the strength of the relationship, between two measures. For example, in a study of months of programming experience and performance on a program comprehension test we might get scores such as:

Months programming	15	12	43	33	21	17	22
Test score	65	57	89	75	75	70	77

Plotting these hypothetical scores produces Figure 2-1. The plot suggests that as experience, measured by months of programming, increases so does the comprehension test score. This implies that there is a *positive correlation* between experience and comprehension ability, but we should evaluate the *correlation coefficient* to get a numerical measure of the relationship. The correlation coefficient ranges from -1.0 to +1.0. The higher the correlation coefficient, the more directly related are the two measures; the lower the correlation coefficient the more inversely related are the two measures (as one goes up the other goes down). The closer the correlation coefficient is to zero, the less there is any relationship between the two measures. A plot of values with the points evenly scattered everywhere would have a correlation of zero.

Computing the correlation coefficient, usually referred to as r, can be done by using:

$$r = \frac{N\, \Sigma XY - \Sigma X\, \Sigma Y}{\sqrt{N\, \Sigma X^2 - (\Sigma X)^2}\, \sqrt{N\, \Sigma Y^2 - (\Sigma Y)^2}} \qquad (4)$$

where X is the value of the first measure, Y is the value of the second measure and N is the number of measurement pairs. In our example N is 7 and we might compute the following table:

	X	Y	XY	X2	Y2
	15	65	975	225	4225
	12	57	684	144	3249
	43	89	3827	1849	7921
	33	75	2475	1089	5625
	21	75	1575	441	5625
	17	70	1190	289	4900
	22	77	1694	484	5929
SUMS	163	508	12420	4521	37474

and plug into formula (4)

$$r = \frac{(7)(12420) - (163)(508)}{\sqrt{(7)(4521) - (163)^2}\sqrt{(7)(37474) - (508)^2}} = \frac{4136}{(71.26)(65.22)}$$

$$= 0.89$$

This high correlation coefficient suggests a strong connection between experience and test scores, but correlation never proves causality. It would be a false conclusion that more months of experience would

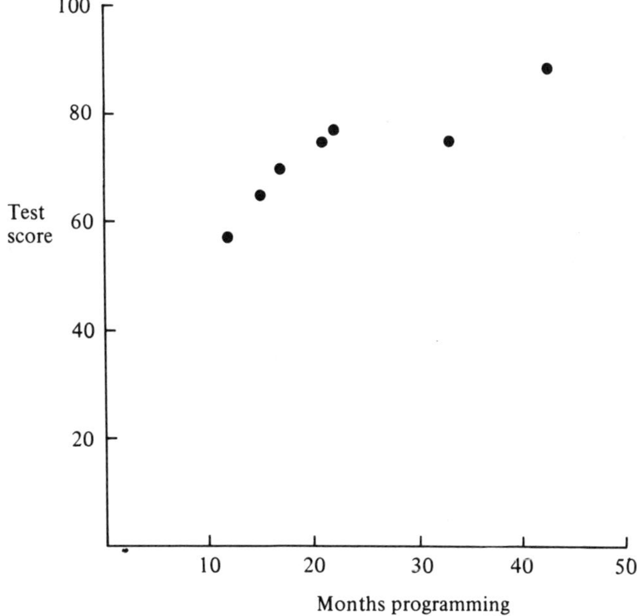

Figure 2-1: Sample plot.

guarantee improved test scores or even that it is the experience which improves test scores. It may be some other factor which is closely linked with experience, such as the number of programs written or the length of programs written. Analogously, the fact that smoking correlates with cancer death is no proof of the harm of smoking; it might be that the anxiety which drives some to smoke is the real villain. But looking at the correlation coefficient in a more positive way, high correlations are interesting because they suggest directions for further research and produce worthwhile rules of thumb. A correlation coefficient above 0.8 or below -0.8 is impressive evidence, above 0.6 or below -0.6 is important, above 0.4 or below -0.4 is interesting and worthy of future work. In behavioral research, the high variance in subject performance usually results in smaller correlation coefficients than in physical science research.

Correlation coefficients measure the strength of linear relationships only. If a different relationship exists among the variables then nonlinear statistical techniques are necessary. For example, programming performance might increase with mild increases in stress, but decrease beyond a certain level of stress. This parabolic of quadratic effect, usually visible if the values are plotted, can be evaluated with nonlinear statistical techniques.

In a typical experiment, a series of measures may be taken such as number of months of programming experience, number of lines in longest program written, score on comprehension quiz, score on modification task. It is usually worthwhile to do correlations between all pairs of measures and present them in tabular form as shown in Table 2-3. Notice that only the lower half of the table is filled in since the values in the upper half would be identical.

2.3.7 Counterbalanced Orderings

A serious problem in all the experimental designs presented thus far is that each subject is assigned to one group. It may just happen that a few of the most capable subjects are assigned to one group, even if some attempt at random assignment is made. This imbalance could produce biased results. To overcome this problem, experimenters may prefer *counterbalanced orderings* or *within subject* designs. Each subject performs two or more tasks, with task orderings permuted to account for the experience gained from the first task. The analysis compares performances for each subject on the two or more tasks.

For example, if modular and nonmodular programs are being tested for comprehension, half the subjects might work on the modular and then the nonmodular version. The other half would work on the nonmodular and then the modular version. Each subject is put in competition with him or herself. The statistical analysis would be a special form of the analysis of variance which is tailored to within subject designs. The main effects would be modularity vs. nonmodularity and the two orderings (modular/nonmodular vs nonmodular/modular). It might be interesting to see if the orderings made a difference in performance, that is, whether it is easier to study a modular version after seeing a nonmodular version or vice versa.

This approach requires each subject to do twice as much work, but only half the number of subjects are needed. The basic advantage is that the effect of diversity in programming ability is reduced.

2.4 STATISTICAL ANALYSIS BY COMPUTER

Performing these statistical procedures by hand or even with a calculator is tedious and error prone. Anyone contemplating a serious experiment should learn to use computerized statistical packages. Some of the packages have easy-to-use interfaces requiring minimal effort. Even small computers with BASIC programming facilities often have the fundamental statistical routines.

For more sophisticated analyses, the popular Statistical Analysis System (SAS) (SAS, 1979), Statistical Package for the Social Sciences (SPSS) (Nie et al, 1975), or Biomedical Statistics Package (BMD) (Dixon, 1977) can be used. These require training in control card use, but the variety of programs available make the effort worthwhile.

2.5 MEASUREMENT TECHNIQUES

The goal of experimental science is to measure and enable comparison. In software psychology we are interested in measuring human performance in the use of programming languages, query languages,

	Number of Months of Programming Experience	Number of Lines in Longest Program	Score of Comprehension Quiz	Score on Modification Task
Months of programming experience	1.00			
Number of lines in longest program	0.81	1.00		
Score on comprehension quiz	0.56	0.62	1.00	
Score on modification task	0.59	0.51	0.65	1.00

Table 2-3: Correlation matrix for hypothetical experiment.

or terminals. This is not an easy task because there are many interrelated variables which are difficult to separate. If we measure the time to compose a program, will subjects sacrifice quality? If we measure quality of work, won't we have to consider years of experience in comparing programmers? Won't programming ability be related to training and general intelligence? Can we compare two programming languages if subjects have had different amounts of training and experience with each?

These troublesome issues must be dealt with by proper experimental controls and statistical techniques. We hope to overcome them, but we must always remember that behavioral experiments on groups cannot be used to predict individual performance -- only group behavior.

Some critics complain that the results of group experimentation are used to confirm median behavior rather than to raise group behavior to the level of high performers. But, in addition to confirming or contradicting the experimental hypotheses, group experimentation with a range of programmers provides information about performance distributions, identifies high performance and reveals human cognitive processes. Group experimentation with a range of programmers should be complemented by detailed protocol analysis with highly skilled individuals and controlled experimentation with highly skilled groups. Studies of senior programmers could help set performance goals, reveal novel programming strategies, suggest educational practices, and provide clues to a theory or model of human behavior in programming.

2.5.1 Performance Tasks: Comprehension

Designers of program comprehension tests can benefit from linguistics and educational psychology research on reading, but approaches will have to be modified. In programming, comprehension must include low-level comprehension of the function of each line of code, mid-level comprehension structure of the algorithm and data, and high-level comprehension of the overall program function. The entire comprehension spectrum can be measured by presenting subjects with a program and a series of multiple choice or fill-in-the-blank questions. Multiple choice questions are easier to score, but more difficult to develop. Fill-in-the-blank questions are more difficult to score, but easier to develop. When fill-in-the-blank questions are used there should be several scorers.

Typical questions in programming language research might be for subjects to give the:

- value of a variable at a specific point in the program
- sequence of values assumed by a variable
- number of times a particular statement or procedure is executed

- sequence of statements or procedures executed
- output for a given input
- input required to produce a given output
- function of a variable, statement or the entire program, briefly described
- impact of an alteration.

Some subjects may follow the execution of the program, but not understand the high-level program structure. Other subjects may understand the program function but not comprehend the details. It is hard to say which is more important.

A second intriguing issue is that there seem to be two ways to look at programs: forward and backward (Sime, Green and Guest, 1977). *Forward comprehension* is the ability to discover the output for a given input; *backward comprehension* is the ability to discover the input necessary to produce given output.

2.5.2 Performance Tasks: Composition

Program composition is the fundamental programmer task and it must be studied directly, by requiring programmers to write programs according to either a hazy problem statement or a more precise design specification. Programmers can be required to write the program on paper, keypunch it, or enter it at a terminal. The experimenter might keep track of the sequence of executions to arrive at a working program or just accept the first version or the final version. Gannon (1976, 1977) and Dunsmore and Gannon (1977) emphasize the sequence of programs in the development process and concentrate on the 'persistence' of bugs.

Grading programs is a difficult task faced regularly by instructors, and, although cumbersome, it is possible. A written set of standards should be prepared in advance with precise point values assigned for portions of the program. Care should be taken to ensure that the grading is consistent and replicable. At least two graders should be used and the experimenter should keep a record of the similarity of the scores.

Query composition for database and information systems can be measured by the same techniques. For terminal interactions, the composition task will be to get the computer to perform a specified task or produce required information. While paper and pencil studies could be used to simulate an online situation, the actual hardware may be required for some studies.

An alternative composition task, which includes comprehension, is the 'cloze' procedure used in English comprehension studies. Subjects are preented a program listing with lines or portions of lines deleted and are required to fill in the missing material. Experimental material preparation and grading is substantially simplified and experimentation with longer programs is facilitated.

2.5.3 Performance Tasks: Debugging

Debugging is one of the more frustrating parts of programming. It has elements of solving puzzles or brain teasers, coupled with the annoying recognition that you have made a mistake. Heightened anxiety and unwillingness to accept the possibility of errors, increases the task difficulty. Fortunately, there is a great sigh of relief and lessening of tension when the bug is ultimately uncovered and corrected.

Debugging experiments are enjoyable to conduct, because subjects relish the challenge and opportunity to demonstrate their skills. Experimenters have added artificial bugs or natural bugs (which had earlier been removed) and required subjects to locate and/or correct the bugs. Multiple choice questions are inappropriate here since they probably give away the answer.

Subjects may or may not be provided with the output for the error-laden program. Although most programmers feel this is useful or even essential, an experiment by Gould (1975) found the output listing not as helpful as we might have expected.

Other supplementary materials might include:

- detailed specifications
- detailed or macro-flowchart
- samples of correct output
- machine generated trace of statement numbers executed or values of variables
- access to terminal for debugging runs
- clues to the type or location of the bug.

Subjects might be graded on how many of the bugs they located and how well they corrected the bugs. Points might be deducted if subjects found nonexistent bugs and additional points given if subjects found bugs which the experimenter was unaware of.

Debugging experiments suffer from the artificiality of laboratory experimentation. If the subjects are told that a single bug exists which can be fixed by modification to a single line, the situation is vastly different from reality where such information is not available. It would be interesting to study performance (and emotional reactions) when a single bug is included in a program but some subjects are told that a single bug exists, some are told five bugs exist and some are told an unknown number of bugs (possibly zero) exist.

2.5.4 Performance Tasks: Modification

Program modification, a common task in industrial programming environments, has been estimated to consume between 25 percent and 75 percent of all programming effort. Modification ease is an important measure of program quality. Success at a modification task may be used as a measure of program comprehension.

Subjects are provided with a program, instructions about the modification to be made, and supplementary materials such as external write ups, sample output, flowcharts or design specifications. After subjects perform the modification it can be graded in the same way as a program composition task. An alternative which simplifies grading would be to ask multiple choice questions about which modification would perform a required task.

2.5.5 Time

The amount of time required to perform a task appears to be a useful measure, but there are many difficulties in its use. If we tell subjects that they should work as quickly as possible, then exogenous personality variables become involved; some subjects will finish quickly even if it compromises the quality of the work. Professional programmers or students who finish first are not necessarily the best, since program quality is widely accepted as being more important than speed. Time-to-criterion, that is, time to reach a specified quality level or time to reach a specific answer, may be more acceptable, especially for simple tasks.

Setting a fixed time length for task performance not only simplifies administration of experiments but also focuses attention on correctness and quality. Subjects will probably stay till the end of a fixed time period, but given the option of leaving when they are done, they may do poorly and leave as soon as possible. This additional variance, produced by inter-subject differences in their attitude toward spending time in experiments can cloud experimental results. Subjects should be required to work for the full amount of time specified.

2.5.6 Memorization/Reconstruction

In an early study (Shneiderman, 1976a), we performed a variation on an experiment that Chase and Simon (1973) had conducted in chess board pattern memorization. Two short FORTRAN programs were keypunched from an introductory textbook and one of the programs was printed out on a line printer. The second program deck was shuffled and then printed. The proper program and the shuffled versions were given to a wide range of subjects from nonprogrammers to expert programmers. As experience increased, the ability to reconstruct the proper program increased rapidly, while the ability to reconstruct the shuffled program showed minimal change. Nonprogrammers did almost equally well on the two program forms but experts had dramatically different performances on the two program forms (Figure 2–2).

We hypothesized that as subjects gain experience in programming they improve their capacity for recognizing meaningful program structures, thus enabling them to recode the syntax into a higher-level internal semantic structure. When asked to reconstruct a program, the subjects applied their knowledge of the programming language syntax and reconstructed the statements as best as they could. Often the experienced subjects would write functionally equivalent but syntactically varying forms; replacing variable names consistently, replacing statement labels consistently, or changing the statement order when it did not affect the result. These variations were graded as incorrect in our experiment.

Our experience suggests that performance on a reconstruction task is a good measure of program comprehension. Memorizing complex material such as a computer program can not be accomplished by rote

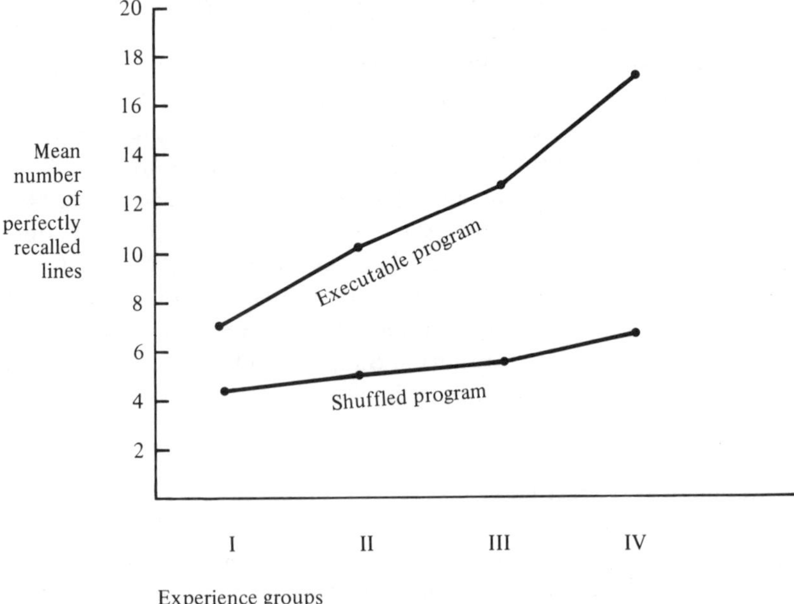

Figure 2-2: Recall scores for memorization experiment (Shneiderman, 1976).

memorization, but a knowledgeable programmer can successively recode program statement groups into ever higher-level semantic structures. Success at reconstruction indicates that the subject understands the low-level details of each statement, intermediate-level groupings, and the overall function of the program. This seems to be the best definition of program comprehension: the recognition of the overall program function, an understanding of intermediate-level processes including program organization, and comprehension of the purpose of each program statement.

Our work with program reconstruction parallels work done in memorization of English sentences. Sachs's study (1967) clearly revealed the difference in syntactic and semantic aspects of sentence memory and comprehension. Subjects read text passages and were asked if a test item sentence was identical to, a syntactic variant of, or a semantic variant (such as the negation) of the sentence in text. The results reveal that if the sentence appeared toward the end of the text, then subjects could accurately determine the relationship of the test item sentence to the text sentence. If the sentence appeared earlier in the text, then only semantic variants could be accurately identified; that is, the subjects recoded the text into an internal semantic form and forgot the precise syntax. Sach's results emphasize the utility of memory tests in measuring comprehension.

Bransford and Franks (1971) and Barclay (1973) carried out a series of ingenious experiments designed to reveal the importance of semantic recoding in memorization of English sentences. Barclay presented subjects with a series of sentences containing the expressions 'to the left of' and 'to the right of' in referring to five animals, for example 'The lion is to the left of the bear.' Subjects who were told about the situation, could acquire a mental image of the positions of the animals, other subjects who were simply told to memorize the sentences did not acquire an image. After acquisition, test sentences were presented and subjects were asked whether they had heard the test sentences during acquisition. Subjects who had formed a mental image, that is recoded the sentences and constructed a meaningful image, did better on this recognition test.

Bransford and Franks presented redundant portions of a complex idea such as 'The rock crushed the tiny hut' or 'The hut was at the edge of the woods.' The entire idea might have been 'The rock which rolled down the mountain crushed the tiny hut at the edge of the woods.' After a five minute break subjects were presented with sentences and asked if they had heard those sentences earlier. Subjects had a difficult time discriminating whether a sentence had been heard earlier or if it was new but semantically consistent. These results also suggest that the syntax of a sentence is retained briefly and only the underlying semantic structure is stored in long-term memory. Furthermore, sentence information is not stored one sentence at a time, but there is a recoding process to more complex higher-level semantic structures which capture the meaning of a group of sentences.

The relationship of these experiments to programming is clear. Programmers do not store the syntax of statements, but extract the semantic information and recode groups of statements into higher-level semantic structures which can represent the operation of a group of statements.

Simply asking subjects to memorize programs is a convenient and uniform approach but there are appealing alternatives. Subjects might be asked if a series of test statements appeared in a program they had studied. Subjects might be asked to give a verbal or written description of the program function and organization. Studies of this sort could reveal which parts were particularly easy to reconstruct or which section demanded additional study for complete reconstruction. We might expect that easily recognizable program structures would be easy to reconstruct, but unusual patterns would require more study before comprehension and memorization were accomplished. A third methodology would be to give subjects fragments of the program they had been asked to memorize and ask them to supply the missing statements. A final method would be to give multiple choice questions.

If the program is well organized and the problem domain familiar, we see no limit to the size of the program that can be committed to memory. Musicians can memorize thousands of songs or long symphonies and write down every note if required. The critical variables should be program organization and familiarity with the problem domains. Anecdotal evidence from blind programmers indicates that as long as they can comprehend the function of a group of statements and recode it into higher level semantic structures, they can recall details of programs whose length is in the thousands of statements. Sighted programmers who work with a large program for several months can recall details and make corrections to programs without a listing.

A longitudinal study of student programmers might reveal learning patterns which would lead to improved teaching techniques. We conjecture that as students learn programming the size of programs that they can commit to memory increases. A novice programmer might take several minutes to recognize that a group of statements computes an average; an expert would come to the same conclusion in seconds. This parallels learning to read natural language: Beginning readers carefully pronounce each syllable and eventually recognize words and phrases; experienced readers scan phrases and sentences quickly. Speed-reading courses start by flashing words, then phrases, then sentences on a screen.

Programmers might be taught to look for familiar statement patterns or templates (Shneiderman, 1978a), such as an IF statement in a DO loop to scan an array. Similarly, program composition should be taught by the development of templates which are organized into modules, analogous to paragraph formation. This approach generalizes the top-down modular design techniques proposed by structured programming advocates (Dahl, Dijkstra and Hoare, 1972; Wirth, 1971; Mills, 1971).

Another intriguing study would be to retest recall after 24 hours to determine which statements were retained. We conjecture that functionally graded reconstruction would deteriorate more slowly than lines perfectly recalled. Subjects can continue to reprocess the semantic structure but quickly forget the precise syntax. This last hypothesis could be tested by asking subjects to reconstruct the program that was memorized in another programming language with different syntax. We expect that if subjects were familiar with both languages, the functionally graded reconstruction scores would be similar in both languages.

As a result of these and other experiments we propose the following hypotheses:

1) Given two programs which perform identical tasks, the one which is easier to memorize/reconstruct is of better quality.
2) Given two programmers who study the same program, the one who does better on a memorization/reconstruction task has a better comprehension of the program.
3) Given a series of programs which are to be memorized by two programmers, if one programmer consistently scores better on the reconstruction tasks, then he or she is the better programmer.

It must be stressed that memorization/reconstruction is not necessarily an aid to comprehension or programmer education, it is merely a metric. Further validation and replication is necessary, but potential applications of these hypotheses can be envisioned. If new semantic structures or syntactic forms for programming are proposed, then one possible way of evaluating their usefulness is through the use of memorization/reconstruction tests. Of course, the testing of new language features, design techniques, or stylistic standards must be done with proper controls for experience in new and old forms.

Another application of these results is in measurement of programming ability. Instructors or employers might include a memorization/reconstruction task with other standard testing techniques. Reconstruction may seem irrelevant since it is rarely a required skill, but it does offer a rapid method of assessing an individual's skill in performing related complex cognitive tasks.

These conclusions are a byproduct of the syntactic/semantic model of programmer behavior (Shneiderman and Mayer, 1979). Reconstruction of a complex program can only be accomplished if an individual has a detailed knowledge of the programming language syntax and the ability to recode low-level syntax into semantically meaningful operations. The longer the program the more important is the ability to recode lower-level semantic structures into higher-level problem-oriented semantic structures. Without a knowledge of problem related concepts the subject's memory quickly reaches its limits. For example, a subject who understands the concept of a correlation coefficient would quickly recognize the section of program which performs the calculation and would easily recode this information. A knowledgeable programmer who is unaware of correlation coefficients would have difficulty in recoding the complex calculations of means, means squared, etc. into a simple higher-level concept.

2.5.7 Background

Experimenters are often interested in finding out effects of previous experience on performance, in using this information as a covariate in the statistical analysis, or in assigning subjects to experimental groups based on background. Unfortunately it is difficult to say what aspects of a person's background influence competency in programming. Programming aptitude or ability tests have not been resoundingly successful in predicting performance. Still, educators, researchers, employers and managers persist in collecting this information in the hope that they will be able to discover and take advantage of a pattern of behavior.

Subjects have been asked to provide the following information:

- number of months of programming
- list of programming languages they can use
- number of months with each programming language
- length of longest program written in each language
- subjective ratings of the ability with each language
- job experience
- educational background
- list of courses in computer science, accounting, engineering or mathematics
- Scholastic Aptitude Test Scores
- high school or college grade point average
- rank in class.

While each of these items may seem useful, none has been shown to be a consistently good predictor of programming aptitude or ability, performance on program comprehension tests, or scores on performance tasks. More experience and better performance on standard intelligence measures are useful guides, but none of the measures described is a reliable predictor of performance.

Two studies of COBOL programmers have sought to distinguish between the programming style of novices and professionals. Chrysler (1978a, 1978b) found that months of programming experience correlated negatively with data division source statements ($r = -0.37$) suggesting that experienced programmers are more cautious in the use of resources. Gordon, Capstick, and Salvadori (1977) report detailed statistics from a comparison of a group of 27 student trainees and a group of three professionals having an average of three years of COBOL experience. All subjects were monitored during the development of two COBOL programs. The students, on the average, used 6.8 times the number of runs and produced 2.8 times the number of diagnostics. In the first program the average number of source records coded by the professionals was 340 compared with 439 for the trainees; in the second program the contrast was smaller, 249 for the professionals compared with 260 for the trainees. The trainees used the GOTO construct four times as frequently as the professionals.

2.5.8 Subjective Measures

Performance and background data can be complemented by subjective measures of user satisfaction, preference, capability and confidence. Simply asking subjects which language style or feature they prefer can provide useful information which complements performance results. Unfortunately, subjective responses are easily influenced, vary with personality, and are not satisfactorily replicable. Subjects may try to please the experimenter by favoring a novel language feature, feel confident of their comprehension of a given program even when performance measure scores are poor, or may be generally optimistic and report being pleased with whatever is offered.

These potential flaws of subjective measures do not mean that they should be ignored, only that their validity must be questioned. If subjective measures correlate well with performance measures, then there is additional support. If subjective measures are favorable to a new programming technique, even if the performance measures are unfavorable, we might continue development, assuming that the users preferred the new method but had trouble learning it. Improved user and programmer satisfaction may be a goal in itself, even if performance is poorer, because this tends to reduce job turnover and improve morale. Finally, improved satisfaction may reduce anxiety and encourage better work habits.

Typical subjective questions that have been used in experiments are:

- Rate your programming skill (0 = none or poor, 4 = excellent)
- How well did you understand this program?

- How confident are you about your having found all the bugs?
- Rate your confidence in the responses to each comprehension question
- Evaluate the following features in this program (0 = bad, 4 = excellent):

  comments, mnemonic variable names, choice of algorithm, choice of data structures, modular design, modifiability, portability, neatness of program, neatness of output
- For specific tasks rate your preference for a particular programming language (e.g. PL/I, FORTRAN, COBOL) or interaction medium (time-sharing or batch)
- Compare the ease of studying the commented and noncommented versions of this program.

The subjective measures might be on a 3, 5 or 7 point scale ranging from bad to excellent, easy to hard, or simple to complex. To improve the reliability of the scores, the positive and the negative directions should be randomly assigned to the questions, that is, the higher values of the scale should alternate from favorable to unfavorable. A short description of the points on the scale is helpful, for example, 0 = no comprehension, 1 = poor comprehension, 2 = good comprehension.

Redundant, but differently worded subjective questions, may be inserted to test for reliability.

Experimental consent agreement

1. I have freely volunteered to participate in this experiment.

2. I have been informed in advance as to what my task(s) would be and what procedures will be followed.

3. I have been given the opportunity to ask questions, and have had my questions answered to my satisfaction.

4. I am aware that I have the right to withdraw consent and discontinue participation at any time, without prejudice.

5. My signature below may be taken as affirmation of all of the above, prior to participation.

Figure 2-3: Body of experimental consent agreement which subjects are asked to sign.

2.6 EXPERIMENTAL ETHICS

Experiment designers should make every effort to protect the integrity of experimental subjects. Since programming experiments rarely place subjects at physical risk, the more serious problems of medical experimentation are avoided. Emotional threats such as heightened anxiety, increased fear of failure, or decreased confidence; and personal threats such as the misuse of experimental data or invasion of privacy must be carefully reviewed and minimized. Experimental results should not influence a student's course grade and participation should be voluntary. Subject names or other identifying information should not be collected, unless absolutely necessary. Anonymous forms protect the subjects from invasion of privacy and experimenters from accusations that privacy has been invaded. Figure 2-3 contains the body of the experimental consent agreement which we ask subjects to sign.

2.7 PRACTITIONER'S SUMMARY

In reading software psychology results we need to be sensitive to experimental paradigms and the validity of introspection, case studies, or controlled experimentation. The selection, assignment, and number of subjects; the experimental tasks, controls, and design; the statistical techniques, and the conclusions should be carefully examined for sources of bias before accepting the results.

When confronted with a technical choice, consider carrying out a small experiment to provide supportive evidence. In designing programming languages, editors, operating system languages, or interactive facilities for novices, conduct experiments to verify your conjectures about user performance. Experimental evidence can improve your design, strengthen arguments for adopting your innovation, and support marketing efforts.

2.8 RESEARCHER'S AGENDA

This chapter offers only a taste of experimental design issues. Texts on experimental design should be consulted for more detailed discussions. The problems of conducting software psychology experiments need further examination, including: obtaining sufficient numbers of subjects with the proper knowledge, controlling for variations in experience, reducing the high variance in performance, isolating the crucial variables in programming performance and developing standard testing scales or methods.

Novice experimenters should restrict their work to one- or two-factor designs or correlational studies while applying basic statistical tools such as analysis of variance and regression analysis.

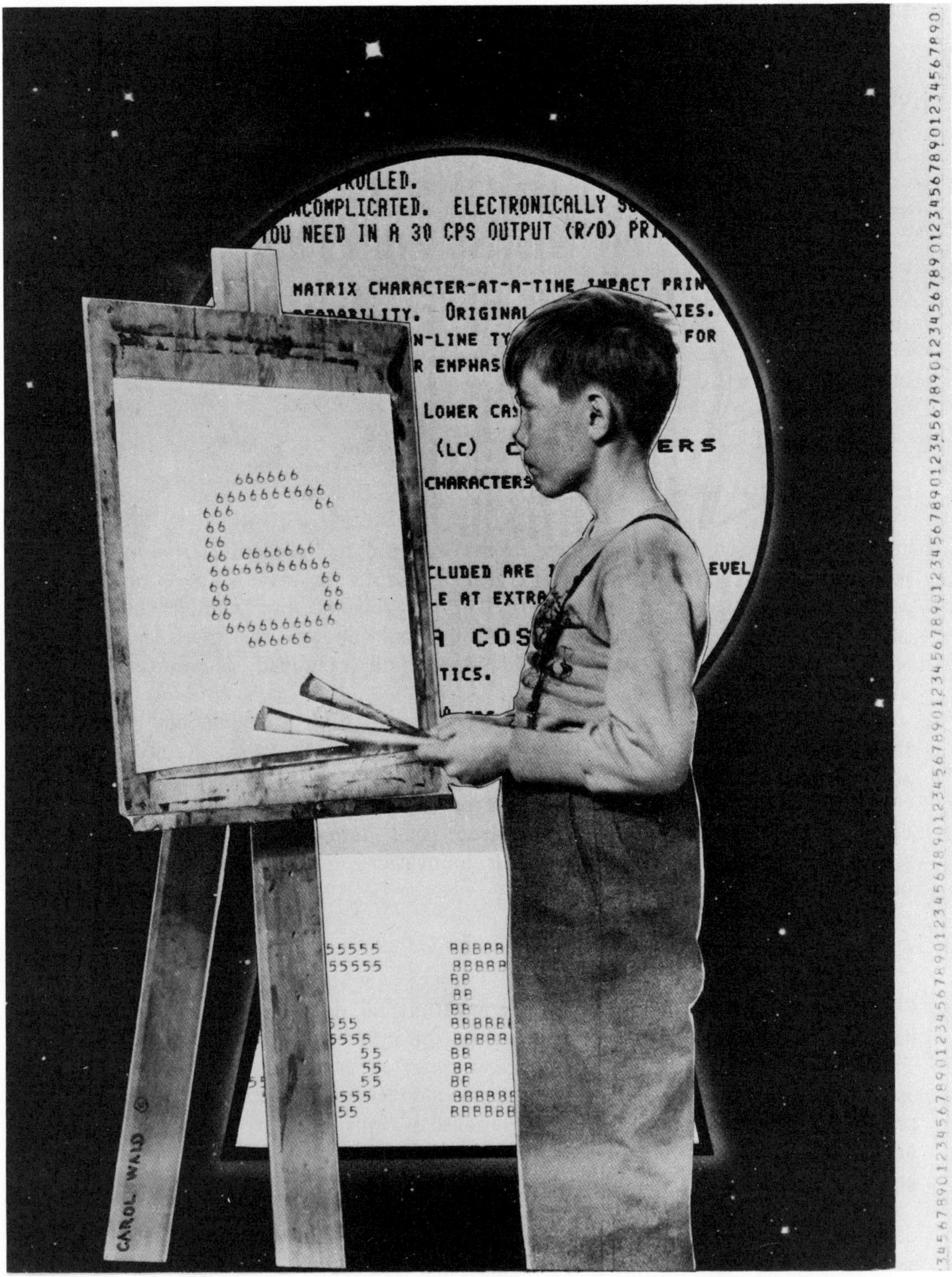

TROLLED.
UNCOMPLICATED. ELECTRONICALLY
YOU NEED IN A 30 CPS OUTPUT (R/O) PRI
MATRIX CHARACTER-AT-A-TIME IMPACT PRIN
ORIGINAL
N-LINE TY
FOR
R EMPHAS
LOWER CA
(LC)
ERS
CHARACTERS
CLUDED ARE
EVEL
LE AT EXTRA
A COS
TICS.

CAROL WALD ©

34567890123456789012345678901234567890123456789012345678901234567890123456789012345678901234567890123456789012345678901234567890:

3

PROGRAMMING AS HUMAN PERFORMANCE

Computer programming is an art, because it applies accumulated knowledge of the world, because it requires skill and ingenuity, and especially because it produces objects of beauty. A programmer who subconsciously views himself (or herself) as an artist will enjoy what he (or she) does and will do it better.

Donald Knuth, 'Computer Programming as an Art (1974)

Programming tasks – learning – design – composition – comprehension – testing – debugging – documentation – modification – physical, social, and managerial environment – syntactic/semantic model of programmer behavior – personality factors – personality testing

3.1 CLASSES OF COMPUTER USERS

The class of computer users is expanding and diversifying so rapidly that any list of user situations would soon be out of date. The bulk of professional programmers spend their time designing, composing, debugging, testing, documenting and modifying programs written in high-level or assembler languages. *System programmers* work on operating systems, compilers or utilities that are used by *application programmers*, who solve user problems. Application programs include banking, reservations, payroll, personnel management, accounts receivable, data collection, statistical analysis, inventory and management reporting systems.

For every professional programmer there are probably ten occasional programmers who write programs for scientific research, engineering development, marketing research, business applications, etc. And finally there are a rapidly growing number of programmer hobbyists working on small business, personal and home computing applications.

In addition to these classes of programmers using traditional procedural programming languages such as COBOL, BASIC, or FORTRAN, there is a fast-growing number of people who use specialized query and reporting languages such as MARK IV, System 2000 Immediate Access Language, EASYTRIEVE, QWIK-QUERY or the newer relational query languages such as Query-by-example and SQL.

Still simpler inquiry facilities such as parametric reservations and banking systems allow people to use computers with minimal training. Fill-in-the-blank or menu selection facilities make computer use possible without any training at all. Bank cash terminals are the best-known applications of computer systems requiring no training. Data entry stations are an important interactive terminal application whose high volume and low error requirements offer opportunities for improvement through human factors experimentation. Computer-assisted instruction facilities, decision support systems and command/control environments require complex learning and decision making skills.

Natural language users interact with the computer by stating their requests in English, or other natural languages, and conduct 'clarification dialogs' to resolve ambiguities. This mode, which requires no training, is still in the research stage, but developers are hopeful that useful systems can be produced. Critics argue that natural language systems will not be successful because they do not sufficiently structure computer usage.

Indirect users of computer systems require human intermediaries to achieve access. Library information retrieval systems or corporate information systems often operate by having the user pose requests informally to a human intermediary who formulates the query into the most appropriate form for computer processing.

A final group of computer users includes everyone who reads computer printouts such as utility bills, phone bills, and paychecks or uses computerized banking, word processing, and supermarket checkout counters. This group includes almost everyone living in technologically advanced countries.

3.2 PROGRAMMING TASKS

Programming is neither simple nor unidimensional; there is a rich and varied texture of tasks which fit under the term programming.

3.2.1 Learning

The first task for any programmer is to learn the programming language he or she works with. The more proficient a programmer is in the use of the programming language as a tool, the more valuable he or she will be. We adopt a crude and arbitrary scale for assessing programming experience:

1) Naive - nonprogrammer with no training
2) Novice - less than one year experience
3) Intermediate - one to three years experience
4) Expert - more than three years experience.

The rapid evolution of programming languages means that programmers must continue learning to maintain their skills. New programming features, styles of usage, languages, utilities, editors, control languages, and hardware require continuous training for the professional and occasional user. Programmers should have the capability and willingness to learn.

New languages and facilities should be designed to be easy to learn as well as easy to use.

3.2.2 Design

Programmers often become involved in the analysis and design phase. This phase has the least structure and poorest measures of success, but the greatest challenges. Design requires a detailed knowledge of the problem domain, experience in the application area, and creative insight. The programmer/designer must assess user needs, evaluate costs, and determine realistic schedules. Knowledge of programming language syntax is less important than an understanding of what programmers can accomplish.

Until we have more experience with formal program design languages, it will be difficult to evaluate the products of the design phase. Program design is a highly individualistic process which requires strengths in the problem area and experience; it is a specialty where quality can be measured only in subjective terms and where conflicting value judgments obscure measurement.

3.2.3 Composition

Coding, writing, or composing programs is usually the central task for programmers. This involves taking a problem or a design for a solution and representing it in programming language syntax which can be executed by a computer. Programs may consist of a few lines or of a few million lines of code. We create a crude and arbitrary classification of program size:

1) Small - less than 100 lines
2) Medium - 100 to 1000 lines
3) Large - 1000 to 10,000 lines
4) Very large - more than 10,000 lines.

Program composition may be an individual process, a team process, or a multiple team process. Coordination of programmers and programming teams is an essential component of the management of programming systems development.

3.2.4 Comprehension

Understanding or comprehending a program is a vital task in programming projects. Old programs or programs in current development are read to promote communication among workers, to prepare a modification, or to locate a bug.

There are multiple levels of comprehension. It is possible to follow each line of code without understanding the overall program function. It may also be possible to understand the program function but not understand each of the steps. There is also a middle level of understanding concerning control structures, module design, and data structures. Thorough comprehension involves the entire spectrum.

There may be differences in comprehension patterns for programs written by oneself and by others. The comprehension process may differ for short and long programs, for novices and professionals, for low-level and high-level languages, or for documented or undocumented programs.

3.2.5 Testing

Testing is verification that the program meets the design specifications. Testing may involve the construction of elaborate test data files to exercise the program or simple desk checking to assess adherence to specifications. Testing should be done by each program composer individually and by programmer teams who were not involved in the program composition.

3.2.6 Debugging

Removing errors from a program is a difficult task, which is best avoided. Unfortunately, human fallibility introduces errors during the program development process. These errors may be:

- syntactic: incorrect syntax in the use of the programming language
- semantic: errors in design or composition.

Syntactic errors are caught by the compiler and are not a serious problem. They may be annoying but are usually easily repaired. Semantic errors can be more troublesome since the program executes, but not according to our expectations. Bugs which reveal themselves by obvious flaws in the output may be easier to find than more subtle bugs which occur irregularly and do not have obvious impacts on the output. Design flaws may be difficult to uncover because the programmer has to accept his or her fallibility and then restructure thinking patterns. Composition bugs may be uncovered by attempting to recode or explain the code to a colleague. Once the bug is located, it must be repaired.

Dump, trace, check, and selective printing facilities can be helpful in revealing the execution sequence, which is usually not visible to the programmer.

3.2.7 Documentation

Documentation techniques and standards are hotly debated topics, but there is strong agreement about the importance of good documentation, especially in light of the high level of modification activity. Internal documentation, external writeups, system flowcharts, detailed flowcharts, pseudo-code and audio documentation are some of the approaches that have been used. Programming languages and their usage should facilitate 'self-documentation.' Recent research is beginning to focus on these topics, but we have only the haziest sense of what constitutes adequate documentation.

Automatic flowcharters and documenters are promoted by their developers, but their utility is questionable. Writing meaningful and appropriate documentation is a difficult skill which must be practiced. Some installations have found that documentation is improved by having documentation professionals who produce standardized formats, a uniform level of detail, lucid English paragraphs, and a product which reflects their skill and pride in a job well done.

3.2.8 Modification

Some estimates indicate that as much as 75 percent of the programming work involves modifying and enhancing old software. Modification requires competence in comprehension and composition and may be the most challenging task. Programmers must comprehend a large program in a short time and make modifications which do not interfere with the proper functioning of the entire program.

3.3 THE PROGRAMMING ENVIRONMENT

3.3.1 Physical and Social Environment

Environment is a key determinant of behavior. Environmental factors include such physical issues as the:

- room size
- room structure: windows, doors, ceilings, etc.
- brightness of the light
- air temperature and humidity
- arrangement of desk or workspace
- access to computer terminals or facilities
- noise: quality and intensity
- interference from others, including phone calls
- degree of privacy.

A pleasing physical work environment is helpful. A poor work environment is disruptive of quality work, demoralizing and a good motivation to work elsewhere.

McCue (1978) gives an intriguing description of the architectural considerations in constructing the IBM Santa Teresa Software Development Laboratory. Each programmer/designer has a private office with a terminal, adequate desk and file space for listings, and a large window. These offices surround a conference room for group meetings.

The social environment of an office also plays an important role. An atmosphere of friendliness, warmth, and cordiality makes going to work enjoyable and satisfying. People work for social interaction as well as for economic rewards.

Some programmers will work by themselves, others in teams. A good manager is sensitive to employee preferences and places them in the situation which best suits their style, while satisfying organizational restraints.

3.3.2 Managerial Environment

Beyond the physical environment and the social relationships with peers, the managerial structure plays a key role in employee satisfaction (Couger and Zawacki, 1978; Metzger, 1973). A good manager should be demanding enough to produce high motivation and morale, but sympathetic enough not to alienate and discourage employees. The ideal manager should be technically competent, but management acumen is probably the more vital and rare quality. A good leader will make the proper level of demands, provide sufficient feedback, express appreciation for a job well done, and be appropriately stern when employees falter.

Monetary bonuses and promotions should be used to reward consistent high performance. Other rewards may include improved office space, choice of tasks, support for education, or conference participation. In a volatile field like software development, continuing professional education is necessary to maintain proficiency. Interaction at seminars, workshops, and conferences provides for professional contacts which may be valuable in the future.

Management is a difficult skill to acquire. Good programmers may not make good managers. Training and careful supervision should be provided to programmers who are promoted to management positions.

Difficulties in managing may result from the organizational structure. A mature organization may not offer aggressive young employees sufficient room for promotion. A tightly structured organization may not provide sufficient diversity of experience. A highly bureaucratized organization may suppress the enthusiasm of creative employees with imaginative ideas. It is not easy to surmount these problems -- each manager and employee must learn to cope, change what they can, and accept the organizational limitations, or look elsewhere. Optimists believe that the grass is greener on the other side of the fence; pessimists believe the grass is brown everywhere.

3.4 THE SYNTACTIC/SEMANTIC MODEL

The purpose of theories is to explain empirical results and provide a basis for making predictions. The cognitive model of programmer behavior in this section is based on experimental results and has been useful in formulating hypotheses. It needs further verification and refinement, but it is a beginning.

Any model of programmer behavior must be able to account for at least those basic programming tasks described earlier:

- composition: writing a program
- comprehension: understanding a given problem
- debugging: finding errors in a given program
- testing: verifying that the program satisfies the design
- modification: altering a given program to fit a new task
- learning: acquiring new programming skills and knowledge.

In addition, a cognitive model must be able to describe these tasks in terms of:

- the *cognitive structures* that the programmer possesses or comes to possess in memory, and
- the *cognitive processes* involved in using this knowledge or in adding to it.

Recent developments in the information processing approach (Greeno, 1972) to the psychology of learning, memory and problem solving have suggested a framework for discussing the components of memory involved in programming tasks (Figure 3–1). Information from the outside world, to which the programmer pays attention, such as descriptions of the to-be-programmed problem, enter the cognitive system into *short-term memory*, a memory store with a relatively limited capacity (Miller, 1956, suggests about seven chunks), and which performs little analysis on the input information. The programmer's permanent knowledge is stored in *long-term memory*, with unlimited capacity for organized information. The component labeled *working memory* (Feigenbaum, 1974) represents a store that is more permanent than short-term but less permanent than long-term memory, and in which information from short-term and long-term memory may be integrated into new structures. During problem solving (e.g., generation of program) new information from short-term memory and existing relevant concepts from long-term memory are integrated in working memory, and the result is used to generate a solution, or in the case of learning, is stored in long-term memory for future use. Two main questions posed by the model summarized in Figure 3-1 are: what kind of knowledge (or *cognitive structures*) are available to the programmer in long-term memory, and what kind of processes (or *cognitive processes*) does the programmer use in building a problem solution in working memory.

3.4.1 Cognitive Structures are Multileveled

The experienced programmer has developed a complex multi-leveled body of knowledge, stored in long-term memory, about programming concepts and techniques. Part of that knowledge, which we will refer to as *semantic knowledge*, has to do with general concepts important for programming but which are independent of any specific programming language. Semantic knowledge includes low-level concepts, such as what an assignment statement does, what a subscripted array is, what data types are; intermediate notions such as interchanging the contents of two registers, summing up the contents of an array, a strategy for finding the larger of two values; and higher-level strategies such as binary searching, recursion by stack manipulation, sorting, and merging methods. A still higher level of semantic knowledge is required to develop general approaches to problems in such areas as statistical analysis of numerical data, stylistic analysis for textual data, or transaction handling for an airline reservation system. All of this semantic knowledge is abstracted

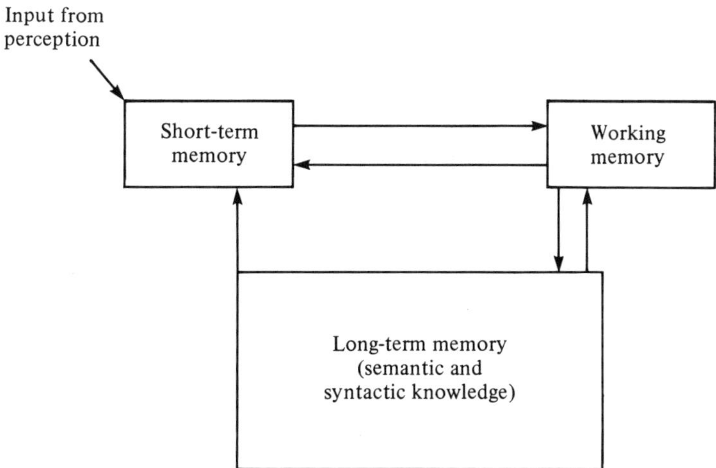

Figure 3-1: Components of memory in problem solving.

through experience and instruction in dealing with programming problems, but it is stored as general, meaningful sets of information that is more or less independent of the syntactic knowledge of particular programming languages or facilities, such as operating systems languages, utilities, and subroutine packages.

Syntactic knowledge is a second kind of information stored in long-term memory; it is more precise, detailed, and arbitrary (hence more easily forgotten) than semantic knowledge which is generalizable over many different syntactic representations. Syntactic knowledge includes the format of iteration, conditional or assignment statements, valid character sets, or the names of library functions. It is, apparently, easier for humans to learn a new syntactic representation for an existing semantic structure. This is reflected in the observation that it is generally difficult to learn the first programming language, like FORTRAN, PL/I, COBOL, BASIC, PASCAL, etc., but relatively easy to learn a second one of these languages. Learning a first language requires development of both semantic concepts and specific syntactic knowledge, while learning a second language involves learning only a new syntax, assuming the same semantic structures are retained. Learning a second language with radically different semantics (i.e., underlying basic concepts) such as LISP or MICROPLANNER may be as hard or harder than learning a first language.

The distinction between semantic and syntactic knowledge in the programmer's long-term memory is summarized in Figure 3-2. The semantic knowledge is acquired largely through intellectually demanding meaningful learning including problem solving and expository instruction which encourages the learner to 'anchor' or 'assimilate' new concepts within existing semantic knowledge or 'ideational structure' (Ausubel, 1968). Syntactic knowledge, which is arbitrary and instructional, is acquired by

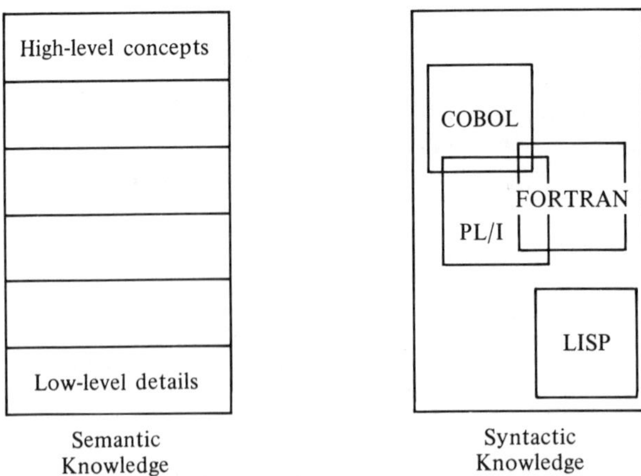

Figure 3-2: Syntactic and semantic knowledge in long-term memory.

rote, and is not well integrated within existing systems of semantic knowledge. The acquisition of new syntactic information may interfere with previously learned syntactic knowledge since it may involve 'adding' rather than 'integrating' new information. This kind of confusion is familiar to programmers who develop skills in several languages and find that they interchange syntactic structures among them. For example, PASCAL students, with previous training in FORTRAN, find assignment statements simple but often err while coding by omitting the colon in the assignment operator and semicolon to separate statements.

Our discussion of the two kinds of knowledge structures in computer programming shares characteristics with distinctions in mathematics learning. For example, the gestalt psychologists distinguished between 'structural understanding' and 'rote memory' (Wertheimer, 1959), between 'meaningful apprehension of relations' and 'senseless drill and arbitrary associations' (Katona, 1940), between knowledge which fostered 'productive reasoning' and 'reproductive reasoning' (Maier, 1933; Wertheimer, 1959). The flavor of the distinction is indicated by an example cited by Wertheimer (1959) suggesting two kinds of knowledge about how to find the area of a parallelogram; knowledge of the memorized formula $A = h * b$ and structural understanding of the fact that a parallelogram may be converted into a rectangle by cutting off a triangle from one end and placing it on the other end. Similarly, Brownell (1935) distinguished between 'rote' knowledge of arithmetic acquired through memorizing arithmetic facts (e.g., $2 + 2 = 4$) and 'meaningful' knowledge such as relating these facts to number theory by working with physical bundles of sticks. More recently, Polya (1968) has distinguished between 'know how' and 'know what.' Greeno (1972) has made a distinction between 'algorithmic' and 'propositional' knowledge used in problem solving, and Ausubel (1968) distinguished between 'rote' and 'meaningful' learning outcomes. Although these distinctions are vague and not fully understood, they do seem to reflect a basic distinction such as our concept of syntactic and semantic knowledge, that is relevant to computer programming. In his parody of the 'new math,' Tom Lehrer made a distinction between 'getting the right answer' and 'understanding what you are doing' (with new math emphasizing the latter). In both mathematics and computer science, a compromise is needed between syntactic knowledge and knowledge which provides direction for creating strategies of solution, that is, semantic knowledge.

3.4.2 Program Composition in the Model

To complete the model we must examine the processes involved in problem solving tasks, such as program composition. The mathematician, George Polya (1966) suggested that problem solving involves four stages:

1) Understanding the problem, in which the solver defines what is given (initial state) and what is the goal (goal state).
2) Devising a plan, in which a general strategy of solution is discovered.
3) Carrying out the plan in which the plan is translated into a specific course of action.
4) Checking the result, in which the solution is tested to make sure it works.

When a problem is presented to a programmer, we assume it enters the cognitive system and arrives in 'working memory' by way of short-term memory, and that in working memory the problem is analyzed and represented in terms of the 'given state' and 'goal state' (Wickelgren, 1974). Similarly, general information from the programmer's long-term memory (both syntactic and semantic) is called and transferred to working memory for further analysis. These two steps -- transferring, to working memory, a description of the problem from short-term memory and recalling general knowledge from long-term memory -- constitute the first phase in program composition.

The second phase, devising a general plan for writing the program, follows a pattern described by Wirth (1971) as stepwise refinement. At first the problem solution is conceived of in general terms such as general programming strategies and other relevant knowledge such as graph theory, business transaction processing, orbital mechanics, chessplaying, etc. We will refer to the programmer's general plans as 'internal semantics,' and suggest that this internal representation progresses from a very general outline, to a more specific plan, to a specific generation of code focusing on minute details. This 'funneling' view of problem solving from the general to the specific was first popularized by the gestalt psychologist Carl Duncker (1945) based on asking subjects to solve complex problems 'aloud.' General approaches occurred first, followed by 'functional solutions' (i.e., more specific plans), followed by specific solutions.

A top-down implementation of the internal semantics for a problem would demand that the highest (most general) levels be set first, followed by more detailed analysis. This process, described by Polya and Wickelgren as 'working backwards' or 'reformulating the goal' (from the general goal to the specifics), is one technique used by humans in problem solving. A bottom-up implementation would permit low-level code to be generated first, in an attempt to build up to the goal. Bottom-up is described as 'working forwards' or 'reformulating the givens' where the 'givens' include the permissible statements of the language, is another problem solving technique.

Structured programming, particularly the idea of modularization, is another technique to aid in the development of the internal semantics

(Dahl, Dijkstra and Hoare, 1973; Mills, 1974; and Parnas, 1972a, 1972b). Polya and Wickelgren refer to this technique as making 'subgoals.'

These design techniques lead to a 'funneling' of the internal semantics from a very general to a specific plan. Then code may be written, and the program tested. These steps are summarized in Figure 3-3 which shows program composition as the formulation of internal semantic structures followed by the application of syntactic knowledge to produce a program.

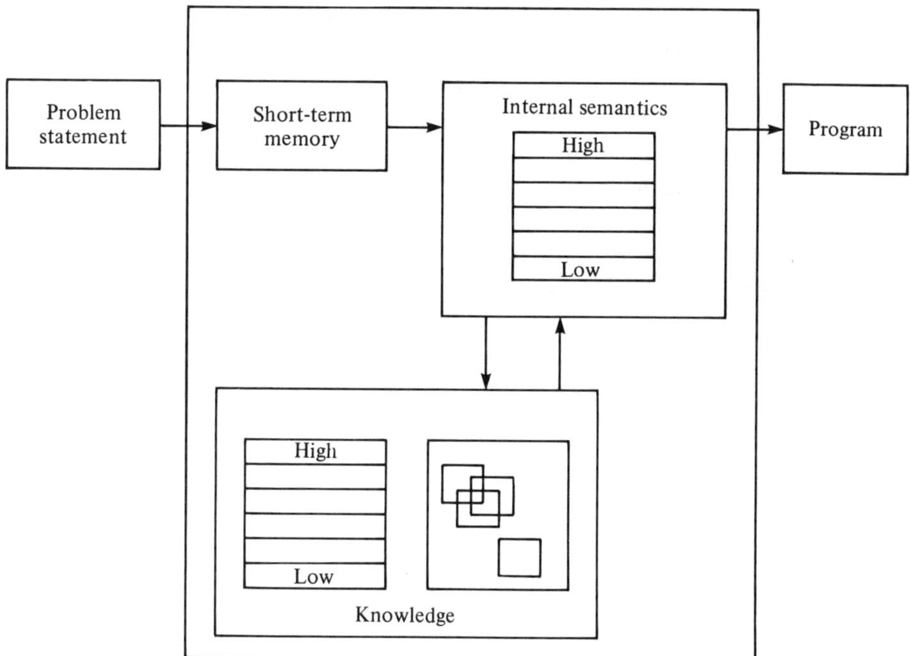

Figure 3-3: Program composition process: the formation of an internal semantic representation of a program to be written.

This model of program composition suggests that once the internal semantics have been worked out in the mind of the programmer, the construction of a program is a relatively straightforward task. The program may be composed in any familiar programming language which permits the necessary semantic constructs. An experienced programmer fluent in multiple languages will find it approximately equally easy to implement a table lookup algorithm in BASIC, FORTRAN, PL/I, or COBOL.

3.4.3 Program Comprehension in the Model

The program comprehension task is a critical one since it is a subtask of debugging, modification, and learning. The programmer is given a program and is asked to study it. We conjecture that the programmer, with the aid of his or her syntactic knowledge of the language, constructs a multileveled internal semantic structure to represent the program. At the highest level the programmer should develop an understanding of what the program does; for example, this program sorts an input tape containing fixed-length records, prints a word frequency dictionary or parses an arithmetic expression. This high-level comprehension may be accomplished even if low-level details are not fully understood. At lower semantic levels, the programmer may recognize familiar sequences of statements or algorithms. Similarly, the programmer may comprehend low-level details without recognizing the overall pattern of operation. The central contention is that programmers develop an internal semantic structure to represent the syntax of the program, but that they do not memorize or comprehend the program in a line-by-line form based on the syntax.

The recoding process by which programmers convert the program to internal semantics is based on the 'chunking' process first described by

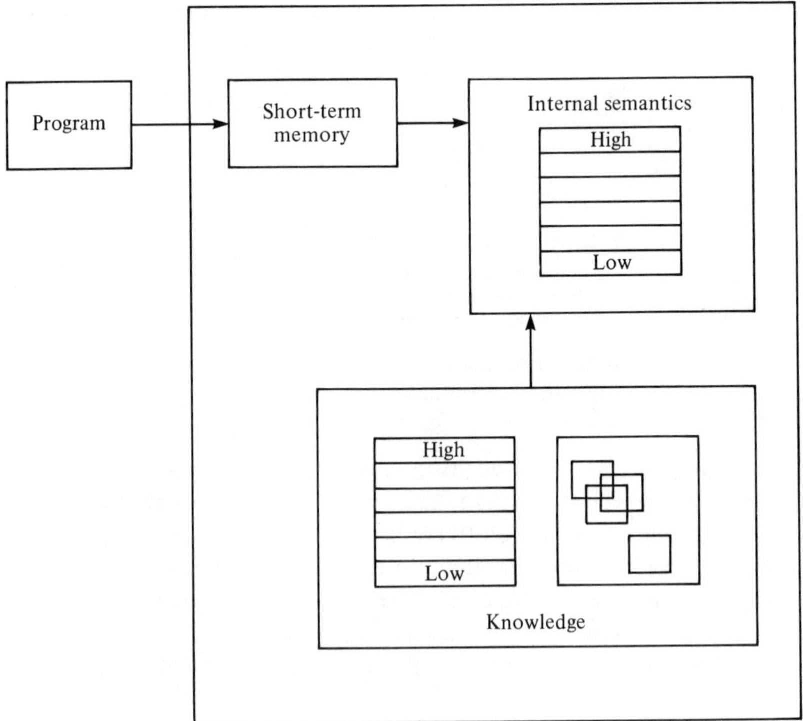

Figure 3-4: Program comprehension process: the formation of an internal semantic representation for a given program.

George Miller in his classic paper, 'The Magic Number Seven Plus or Minus Two' (Miller, 1956). Instead of absorbing the program on a character-by-character basis, programmers recognize the function of groups of statements and then piece together these chunks to form ever larger chunks until the entire program is comprehended. This chunking process is most effective in a structured programming environment where the absence of arbitrary GOTOs means that the function of a set of statements can be determined from local information only. Forward or backward jumps would inhibit chunking since it would be difficult to form separate chunks without shifting attention to various parts of the program.

Once the internal semantic structure of a program is developed by a programmer, this knowledge is resistant to forgetting and accessible to a variety of transformations. Programmers could convert the program to another programming language or develop new data representations or explain it to others with relative ease. Figure 3-4 represents the comprehension process.

3.4.4 Debugging and Modification in the Model

Debugging is a challenging task since it is an attempt to locate an error in composition. We exclude syntactic bugs which are recognizable by a compiler since these bugs are a result of a trivial error in program preparation or of erroneous syntactic knowledge which can be resolved by reference to programming manuals. We are left with two further types of bugs: those that result from an incorrect transformation from the internal semantics to the program statements and those that result from an incorrect transformation from the problem solution to the internal semantics.

Errors that result from erroneous conversion from the internal semantics to the program statements are detectable from debugging output which differ from the expected output. These errors can be caused by improper understanding of the function of certain syntactic constructs in the programming language or simply by mistakes in the coding of the program. In any case, sufficient debugging output will help to locate these errors and resolve them.

Errors that result from erroneous conversion from the problem solution to the internal semantics may require a complete reevaluation of the programming strategy. Examples include failure to handle out-of-range data values, inability to deal with special cases such as the average of a single value, failure to clear critical locations before use or attempts to merge unsorted lists.

In the modification task the first step is the development of internal semantics representing the current program. The statement of the modification must be reflected in an alteration to the internal semantics followed by an alteration of the programming statements. The modification task requires skills gained in composition, comprehension, and debugging.

3.4.5 Learning in the Model

Finally, we examine the learning task, the acquisition of new programming knowledge. We start with the training of nonprogrammers in their much debated 'first course in computing.' The classic approach focused on teaching the syntactic details of a language and used manufacturer distributed language reference manuals as a text. Much attention was paid to syntactic details with minimal time spent on motivational material or problem solving. Tests focused on the validity or invalidity of statements and the ability to determine the output of a tricky and useless program fragment.

By contrast, the problem-solving approach suggested that high-level, language-independent problem solving was the course goal and that coding was a trivial detail not worth the expense of valuable thinking time. Tests in these courses required students to cleverly decompose problems and produce insightful solutions to highly abstract and unrealistic problems.

Of course, both of these descriptions are caricatures of reality but they point up the differences in approaches. The classic approach concentrated on the development of syntactic knowledge and produced 'coders,' while the problem-solving approach concentrated on the development of semantic knowledge and produced high-level problem solvers who were unsuited to a production environment. Neither of these approaches is incorrect; they merely have different goals. A reasonable middle ground, the development of syntactic and semantic knowledge in parallel, is pursued by most educators.

Education for advanced programmers also has the syntactic/semantic dichotomy. Courses in algorithm design focus on semantic knowledge and attempt to isolate syntactic details in separate discussions or omit them completely. Courses which teach second or third programming languages can concentrate on the syntactic equivalents of already understood semantics. This makes it unwieldy to teach nonprogrammers and programmers a new language in the same course.

Learning a new language which has radically different semantic structures may be difficult for an experienced programmer since previous semantic knowledge can interfere with the acquisition of a new language. Learning a new language which has similar semantic structures, such as FORTRAN and BASIC, is relatively easy since most of the semantic knowledge can be applied directly. The confusion over syntactic forms is annoying but easily overcome.

In summary, we conjecture that semantic and syntactic knowledge are separate. The multilevel semantic knowledge, acquired largely through meaningful learning, is replicated in the multilevel approach to the development of internal semantic for a particular problem. The arbitrary syntactic knowledge, acquired largely by rote learning, is compartmentalized by language. Semantic knowledge is essential for problem analysis while syntactic knowledge is applied during the coding or implementation phase.

Machine related details, such as range of integer values or execution speed of certain instructions, and compiler specific information, such as experience with diagnostic messages, are more closely tied to the language specific syntactic information. This information is highly detailed, learned by repeated experience and easily subject to forgetting.

3.5 PERSONALITY FACTORS

Personality variables play a critical role in determining interaction among programmers and in the work style of individual programmers. Unfortunately too little is known about the impact of personality factors. The following list contains some personality issues and conjectures about their relationship to programming:

Assertive/passive. The assertive individual who is not afraid to ask pointed questions, is not intimidated easily, has initiative to get things done, is often seen as the superior programmer type.

Introverted/extroverted. The folklore about computer programmers includes both stereotypes: the introverted pencil chewer who sits quietly in a room writing weird programs and the extroverted pretentious boaster who proudly describes his or her latest superprogram. A friendly, warm cooperative style will be helpful in team programming and for interaction with users.

Internal/external locus of control. Individuals with strong internal locus of control feel able to and seek to dominate situations. They feel they have the capacity to influence their world and control events. Individuals with external locus of control feel that they are victims of events beyond their control and are perfectly content to allow others to dominate them.

High/low anxiety. Moderate levels of anxiety improve performance while extreme anxiety interferes, probably by reducing the size of the short-term memory available. When programmers become more anxious as deadlines approach, they tend to make even more errors, further raising anxiety and making the goal still harder to obtain.

High/low motivation. Highly motivated individuals can accomplish remarkable tasks. The manager who can improve morale and motivation can propel a staff to complete projects on time. No manager can ask for more than the enthusiasm of a dedicated staff.

High/low tolerance for ambiguity. The early stages of program design and composition may require a higher tolerance for ambiguity. Designers have to work in an environment in which only a small number of facts or components have been clearly established. Decisions must be made on limited data and there must be a willingness to take risks while proceeding to the next decision.

Compulsive precision. The later stages of program composition require a precise attention to details and the willingness to make sure that every detail has been accounted for.

Humility. Since most programs have bugs in them and programmers often make trivial errors, a successful programmer should probably not be too ego-involved in the perfection of the program. A more humble approach may leave the programmer open to suggestions and to the possibilities of errors.

Tolerance of stress. Some programming projects fall behind schedule and pressures may build up for rapid completion of a project. In these cases, an individual's tolerance for stress and capacity to work well in stressful situations may be an asset.

Interest in the more psychological aspects of human performance variation has led to research into cognitive style. Doktor (1976) defines cognitive style as a mode of information processing: the two poles are analytic and heuristic. Analytic implies sequential, linear, verbal symbolic processing, or left-brain oriented, and heuristic means intuitive, global, pictorial processing, or right-brain oriented. Difficulty in implementing management information systems can be the result of cognitive style mismatches between users and information design. In an experiment on the effects of think-time and cognitive style on Management Information System variations, it was suggested that information and report format appreciation may be associated with perception, whereas decision quality and computer interaction appreciation may be linked to assimilation (Zmud, 1977a). Subject perceptions of decision styles were examined by Zmud (1977b), who found that heuristic individuals possessed more favorable attitudes toward the simple styles (use of few rules, behavior anchored to external processes), while the analytics favored the more complex decision styles employing rules and utilizing internal decision processes.

Bariff and Lusk (1977, 1978) expanded the design for management information systems to include personality tests of the users. Their purpose was to translate behavioral profiles into design guidelines for the preparation of report formats and implementation procedures. The specific traits measured were tolerance for ambiguity, need-achievement, introversion/extroversion, and defensiveness. Within this area of user characteristics for decision support system design, Zmud (1977a) suggested research into user aspiration level, anxiety, risk-taking propensity, self-esteem, and individual attitudes and values.

Personality was a major factor in determining results on a simulated man-machine decision information system (Wynne and Dickson, 1976). Better performance was associated with modest levels of need-achievement relative to the group's mean, and lower defensiveness. Poorer performance was connected to relatively high need-achievement and to perceived high ratios of facilitating to debilitating anxiety in conjunction with greater defensiveness. The aggressive/humble dimension and introversion/extroversion did not significantly affect grade in an introductory programming course nor perceived ability in programming, according to another study (Newsted, 1975). However, the experimenter submitted that other dimensions, such as sense of humor, might have more significance.

The behavioral research in human use of computers, though limited and new, is making a place for itself. As awesome and complex as the computer may seem, many individuals learn to effectively use this tool. The difference between those who approach the computer and those who avoid it is poorly understood.

Weinberg (1971) best summarized the importance of personality in relation to programming tasks:

> Because of the complex nature of the programming task, the programmer's personality -- his individuality and identity -- are far more important factors in his success than is usually recognized ... there seems to be evidence that critical personality factors can be isolated and associated with particular programming tasks -- at least in the sense of their possession rendering one incapable of performing that task well. Consequently, attention to the subject of personality should make substantial contributions to increased programmer performance -- whether that attention is paid by a psychological researcher, a manager, or the programmer himself.

3.6 PSYCHOLOGICAL TESTING

The Myers-Briggs Type Indicator (MBTI) is an appealing psychological test which gives insight to programmers and their interaction (Myers, 1962). Based on the theories of the psychologist Carl Jung, it measures preferences in four personality dimensions:

- Extroversion/Introversion

- Sensing/Intuition
- Thinking/Feeling
- Judging/Perceptive

Detailed descriptions of each of these personality dimensions are in Figure 3-5. An individual's preference in each dimension is not as important as

Intuitives	Sensing Types
Like solving new problems	Dislike new problems unless there are standard ways to solve them.
Dislike doing the same thing over and over again.	Like an established routine.
Enjoy learning a new skill more than using it.	Enjoy using skills already learned more than learning new ones.
Work in bursts of energy powered by enthusiasm, with slack periods in between.	Work more steadily, with realistic idea of how long it will take.
Frequently jump to conclusions.	Must usually work all the way through to reach a conclusion.
Are patient with complicated situations.	Are impatient when the details get complicated.
Are impatient with routine details.	Are patient with routine details.
Follow their inspirations, good or bad.	Rarely trust inspirations, and don't usually get inspired.
Often tend to make errors of fact.	Seldom make errors of fact.
Dislike taking time for precision.	Tend to be good at precise work.

Perceptives	Judging Types
Tend to be good at adapting to changing situations.	Best when they can plan their work and follow the plan.
Don't mind leaving things open for alterations.	Like to get things settled and wrapped up.
May have trouble making decisions.	May decide things too quickly.
May start too many projects and have difficulty in finishing them.	May dislike to interrupt the project they are on for a more urgent one.
May postpone unpleasant jobs.	May not notice new things that need to be done.
Want to know all about a new job.	Want only the essentials needed to get on with it.
Tend to be curious and welcome new light on a thing, situation or person.	Tend to be satisfied once they reach a judgment on a thing, situation or person.

Figure 3-5: Effects of preference in work situations for Myers-Briggs Type Indicator.

Introverts	Extroverts
Like quiet for concentration.	Like variety and action.
Tend to be careful with details, dislike sweeping statements.	Tend to be faster, dislike complicated procedures.
Have trouble remembering names and faces.	Are often good at greeting people.
Tend not to mind working on one project for a long time uninterruptedly.	Are often impatient with long slow jobs.
Are interested in the idea behind their job.	Are interested in the results of their job, in getting it done and in how other people do it.
Dislike telephone intrusions and interruptions.	Often don't mind the interruption of answering the telephone.
Like to think a lot before they act, sometimes without acting.	Often act quickly, sometimes without thinking.
Work contentedly alone.	Like to have people around.
Have some problems communicating.	Usually communicate well.

Feeling Types	Thinking Types
Tend to be very aware of other people and their feelings.	Are relatively unemotional and uninterested in people's feelings.
Enjoy pleasing people, even in unimportant things.	May hurt people's feelings without knowing it.
Like harmony. Efficiency may be badly disturbed by office feuds.	Like analysis and putting things into logical order. Can get along without harmony.
Often let decisions be influenced by their own or other people's personal likes and wishes.	Tend to decide impersonally, sometimes ignoring people's wishes.
Need occasional praise.	Need to be treated fairly.
Dislike telling people unpleasant things.	Are able to reprimand people or fire them when necessary.
Relate well to most people.	Tend to relate well only to other thinking types.
Tend to be sympathetic.	May seem hard-hearted.

Figure 3-5: – *Cont.*

the interaction of preferences. Figure 3–6 shows how pairings of sensing/intuition and thinking/feeling influence personality and job preference. Going through the choices in Figure 3–5 and the preferences in Figure 3-6 can be a reassuring experience, confirming life choices and freeing us from the guilt of lack of success in some domains. The detailed descriptions that go with each of the 16 possible personality types

Combinations of Perception and Judgment, Compared

	ST	SF	NF	NT
People who prefer	Sensing + Thinking	Sensing + Feeling	Intuition + Feeling	Intuition + Thinking
focus their attention on	Facts	Facts	Possibilities	Possibilities
and handle these with	Impersonal analysis	Personal warmth	Personal warmth	Impersonal analysis
Thus they tend to be	Practical and matter-of-fact	Sociable and friendly	Enthusiastic and insightful	Intellectually ingenious
and find scope for their abilities in	Production Construction Accounting Business Economics Law Surgery etc.	Sales Service Customer relations Welfare work Nursing Gen. practices etc.	Research Teaching Preaching Counseling Writing Psychology Psychiatry etc.	Research Science Invention Securities analysis Management Cardiology etc.

Figure 3-6: Combinations of perception and judgment for Myers-Briggs Type Indicator.

are fascinating, for example the extrovert/intuitive/feeling/perceptive personality is:

> Warmly enthuiastic, high spirited, ingenious, imaginative, can do almost anything that interests him or her. Quick with a solution for any difficulty and very ready to help people with a problem on their hands. Often relies on spur of the moment ability to improvise instead of preparing work in advance. Can usually talk his or her way out of any jam with charm and ease.

An interesting part of the theory underlying the MBTI test is the insight it gives for programming team formation. Figure 3–7 shows the relationship of sensing types to intuitives and feeling types to thinkers. Good teams are not necessarily made up of similar personality types, but can benefit from pairing complementary personalities.

Other psychological tests and scales have been used with programmers and computer users. These include the Minnesota Multiphasic Personality Inventory (MMPI), which is used to determine psychological traits such as manic, schizophrenic, obsessive/compulsive, and hysterical behavior while providing information about a subject's desire to please, honesty, and candor. Another popular test is the Strong Vocational Interest Blank (SVIB), which matches subject likes and dislikes with professionals in a variety of professions. This test does not predict success

Intuitive needs a sensing type:

To bring up pertinent facts.

To apply experience to problems.

To read the fine print in a contract.

To notice what needs attention now.

To have patience.

To keep track of essential detail.

To face difficulties with realism.

To remind that the joys of the present are important.

Sensing type needs an intuitive:

To bring up new possibilities.

To supply ingenuity on problems.

To read the signs of coming change.

To see how to prepare for the future.

To have enthusiasm.

To watch for new essentials.

To tackle difficulties with zest.

To show that the joys of the future are worth working for.

Feeling type needs a thinker:

To analyze.

To organize.

To find the flaws in advance.

To reform what needs reforming.

To hold consistently to a policy.

To weigh "the law and the evidence."

To fire people when necessary.

To stand firm against opposition.

Thinker needs a feeling type:

To persuade.

To conciliate.

To forecast how others will feel.

To arouse enthusiasm.

To teach.

To sell.

To advertise.

To appreciate the thinker.

Figure 3-7: Mutual usefulness of opposite types in Myers-Briggs Type Indicator.

or measure aptitude; it merely suggests whether a subject is compatible with individuals currently in specific professions.

Programmer aptitude and ability tests are available, but their effectiveness is widely questioned. The Computer Programmer Aptitude Battery (CPAB) has five components: verbal meaning, mathematical reasoning, letter series, number ability, and diagramming (flowchart usage). The Berger Test of Programming Proficiency (BTOPP) was developed 'to measure an individual's knowledge and proficiency in the basic principles and techniques of programming.' It contains fifty questions covering flow diagrams and logic, input/output, disk file processing, tape file processing, programming-related operations, program design, data base, and cost awareness. The Wolfe Computer Aptitude Testing Company offers systems analysis, systems programming and three programming aptitude tests.

The Institute for Computers and Computer Programming offers tests for a Certificate in Data Processing and a Certificate in Computer Programming. Educational Testing Services has a College Level

Proficiency exam in FORTRAN and a Graduate Record Exam in computer science principles. The Association for Computing Machinery (ACM) periodically publishes Self Assessment Tests.

3.7 PRACTITIONER'S SUMMARY

Our understanding of the forces which motivate programmers and of the cognitive processes in programming is shallow. The tasks which programmers are expected to perform include program composition, comprehension, debugging, testing, modification, learning, documentation and design. The programmer's physical, social, and managerial environment is a key determinant of motivation and performance.

The syntactic/semantic model suggests that programming-related knowledge is split into two domains. Semantic knowledge, the first domain, is meaningfully acquired, language independent, resistant to forgetting and hierarchically organized from high-level problem domain related issues to lower level functions of programming. Syntactic knowledge, the second domain, is acquired by rote, language-dependent, easily forgotten if not used, and arbitrary.

Personality factors play an important role in motivation and performance. Personality traits may govern an individual's success at a task, in a managerial environment, or with a group of team members. Personality tests may be useful tools in understanding programmer behavior. Aptitude and ability tests are available to aid in hiring and training decisions.

3.8 RESEARCHER'S AGENDA

Refined definitions of programming tasks would aid the reductionist approach of experimental testing. The suggestion that some languages are easier to compose with than to comprehend or that some languages are difficult to debug should be explored to fathom the differential behavior for the tasks. The syntactic/semantic model needs refinement and validation to improve its predictive and descriptive capacity. The impact of personality differences should be investigated to see if different languages, programming environments, or interactive tools might aid specific personality types. Aptitude and ability tests need improvement and validation.

HALT
INTERSTATE
MISSOURI
70
STOP
一時
止まれ
STOP
SPEED
LIMIT
50
CAROL WALD ©

4

PROGRAMMING STYLE

I soon felt that the forms of ordinary language were far too diffuse ... I was not long in deciding that the most favorable path to pursue was to have recourse to the language of signs. It then became necessary to contrive a notation which ought, if possible, to be at once simple and expressive, easily understood at the commencement, and capable of being readily retained in the memory.

Charles Babbage, 'On a Method of Expressing by Signs the Action of Machinery' (1826)

Programming style issues – commenting styles – choice of variable names – indentation techniques – programming language features – conditional statements – iteration and recursion – syntactic choice – structured control structures – flowcharting – debugging studies

4.1 INTRODUCTION

An appealing domain for software psychology research is in developing guidelines for programming style. Stylistic guidelines for using available languages might quickly improve programming practice by applying effective standards. More complex design strategies, involving selective use of control or data structures, flowcharting or modular design could be taught and implemented in a relatively short time. Changes in programming language features or new data structures would take longer to implement and disseminate.

4.2 STYLISTIC GUIDELINES

A number of popular texts offer a set of style guidelines based on the author's introspection about how programs should be written. These are a point of departure, but conflicting and unsupported conjectures must be questioned until experimental evidence clarifies these issues.

4.2.1 Commenting

Commenting facilities exist in all programming languages, but there is controversy over their benefits and much discussion about the best kind of comments. Most introductory programming texts encourage students to comment (comments 'serve a valuable documentary purpose,' Cress et al, 1968) but some critics claim that they obscure the code, interfere with debugging by misleading the programmer, and are dangerous if not updated when the program is changed. In an early book Weinberg wrote 'the population of programmers seems hopelessly split on the desirability of using comments in programs. Some see them as a distraction which is likely to draw attention and energy from more fruitful documentation efforts. Others, equally skilled and conscientious, advocate the liberal use of comments, sometimes to the extent of explaining every statement in the program.'

An early unpublished study of commenting by Peter Newsted suggested that comments did not improve student comprehension of short FORTRAN programs. He speculated that comments might be helpful only in longer, more complex programs. Okimoto's pilot study (1970) tested the impact of incorrect or misleading comments and found they hindered comprehension when compared with correct comments, but non-commented programs could be interpreted even more quickly.

Weissman conducted a series of 10 experiments on University of Toronto Computer Science students using PL/I and ALGOL-W programs (Weissman, 1974a, 1974b). His measures included fill-in-the-blank questions, hand-simulations of program execution, and subjective self-evaluations ('Circle a number from 0 to 9 indicating how well you feel you understand the program'). Use of well-placed and meaningful comments was compared with only very brief initial comments in 50 to 150 line programs. Subjects with programs containing more extensive comments hand-simulated significantly faster (2.5 percent level), did modestly better on the fill-in-the-blanks questions, had significantly (10 percent level) higher scores in the self-evaluation, but made significantly more errors (5 percent level) in the hand simulation. These results, which generally favor use of comments, do not provide sufficient guidance about what kind of comments are helpful or define reasonable guidelines for the volume of comments.

In one of our early experiments, Ken Yasukawa constructed two versions of a 23 line FORTRAN program: one with a single comment ('This program counts the number of even, odd and zero input items') and the other with nine additional comment lines. The 31 subjects who received the single comment version had an average score of 9.2 out of 15 comprehension questions while the 28 subjects who received the heavily commented version had an average score of 10.0. This difference favoring heavier commenting was significant at the .07 level, as determined by a t-test. In a debugging task which followed, 10 out of 30 (33 percent) working on the single comment version and 12 out of 28 (43 percent) working on the heavily commented version found the bug and made an acceptable repair.

In a later experiment (Shneiderman, 1977a), 62 students, enrolled in an introductory FORTRAN programming course, were divided into two groups. Two test booklets were constructed using a 26 line FORTRAN program which operated on student grade information. The first form of the program (HI) used a single high-level comment block at the beginning of the program:

THIS PROGRAM READS AN INTEGER N WHICH TELLS HOW MANY DATA CARDS FOLLOW. THE N DATA CARDS CONTAINING STUDENT GRADES ARE READ INTO G ARRAY. THE CLASS AVERAGE IS FOUND AND THE NUMBER OF THE STUDENT WHOSE GRADE DEVIATES THE LEAST FROM THE AVERAGE IS FOUND AND PRINTED WITH HIS/HER GRADE

The second form (LO) did not have the high-level comment but contained 19 one line low-level comments such as:

RESERVE 500 LOCATIONS FOR THE G ARRAY
LOOP FROM 1 TO N
SET GJ TO THE FIRST VALUE OF G
COMPARE DEVGJ TO DEV
WRITE OUT J AND GJ

The test booklets contained a cover sheet of instructions:

You will be given a complete program written in FORTRAN and will be asked to make modifications to the program. Do not change any lines of the program, only make additions to the program. Show your additions on the printout sheet. Your additions should use as few new statements as possible.

(1) Modify the program to increase by 5 percent each of the values of the G array before any processing is done.
(2) Modify the program so that in addition to its present function it prints the average of the values in the G array.
(3) Modify the program to print the value of the smallest deviation of a G value from the value of A.

The test booklets were handed out so as to distribute the HI and LO forms randomly among the subjects. The subjects were given 30 minutes to respond to the three modification tasks. Then subjects were told to study the program statements for 8 minutes in preparation for a recall task. Subjects were told that the recall task would be graded on the number of lines perfectly recalled. Finally, 7 minutes were allowed for the recall task, during which time the programs were to be kept out of sight.

The three modification tasks were assigned a 10-point score and were graded by a teaching assistant who had extensive experience in grading student programs. The recall task was graded by two methods: the number of lines attempted and the number of lines perfectly recalled. Variant spellings of variable names or different statement labels were graded as incorrect. We attempted to make the grading as objective and replicable as possible.

A two-way analysis of variance was performed on the data. The main effect of comment (HI vs. LO) group was significant (3 percent level) as was the difference in modification task difficulty (0.1 percent level), but the interaction was not significant. One way analysis of variance showed significant difference for comment groups on both the number of lines attempted (5.2 percent level) and the lines perfectly recalled (5.1 percent level).

On both of these recall scores the HI comment group had higher mean scores (Table 4-1) revealing the advantage of using high-level meaningful comments which assist in the recoding process to higher-level semantic structures.

	Modification Scores			Recall Scores	
	1	2	3	Lines Attempted	Lines Perfectly Recalled
HI-level comments	6.5	8.6	4.2	18.6	15.9
LO-level comments	5.9	6.3	1.8	16.4	13.5

Table 4-1: Mean scores for performance measures in commenting experiment.

Comments are not stored in the internal semantic structure, but they facilitate the conversion by describing the function of a statement or group of statements. This notion conforms to programming practice, which urges functional descriptive comments but not low-level comments which reiterate the operation of a particular statement. For example a bad comment for the statement I = I + 1 would be 'ADD ONE TO THE VARIABLE I.' Useful comments are those which facilitate the construction of internal semantics by describing the meaning of statement groups such as 'SEARCH FOR THE LARGEST VALUE IN THE TABLE.' Comments should mediate between the program and the problem domain. An improvement on the previous comment example would be 'FIND THE STUDENT WITH THE HIGHEST TERM AVERAGE.'

The negative effects of comments appears to come from two sources: comments disrupt visual scanning of the program and lengthen the program requiring page turning to scan the entire program. These disruptive effects cause some programmers to add comments only when the program is debugged or to remove comments while studying a program.

4.2.2 Variable Names

Another factor influencing program comprehension is the choice of variable names used within a program. Newsted (1973) gave subjects an 'easy' or 'hard' program and measured comprehension with a multiple choice quiz. The program contained either mnemonic or nonmnemonic variable names. Newsted reported significant results for the difficulty of program, choice of variable name and their interaction. Surprisingly, the nonmnemonic groups performed as well on both the 'easy' and 'hard' programs. The mnemonic groups performed better on the 'hard' program than on the 'easy' program, but the nonmnemonic groups performed better than the mnemonic groups for both the 'easy' and 'hard' programs. The results of Newsted's experiment may have been biased since the programs contained a short paragraph defining the variables, thus possibly negating the initial advantage of the meaningful variable names.

Five of Weissman's ten experiments on PL/I and ALGOL-W programs studied variable name usage. Mnemonic names tended to be long (e.g. SPLIT—VALUE, MIDPOINT, STACK—LARGER—PIECE), while shortened mnemonics were created by merely deleting vowels (e.g. SPLT—VL, MDPNT, STCK—LRGR—PC) and meaningless variable names were long unrelated terms (e.g. RAISE—FINAL, BEQUEATH, LEECH—ENTOMB—CLOSE). The five experiments produced a complex and confusing set of results, but Weissman concludes that 'Both mnemonic and shortened mnemonic variable names were better than meaningless variable names, and mnemonic variables were slightly better than shortened mnemonics.' Significant differences appeared mostly on self-evaluations, suggesting that programmers think that long mnemonics are more helpful than they really are. It is far easier to scan programs with brief mnemonics and some programmers use Weissman's rule for shortened mnemonics as a standard. W.J. Hansen suggests long variable names are appropriate for global variables which are rarely used, while frequently referenced variables (such as loop indexes or subscripts) may be short.

One of our experiments, performed by Don McKay, was similar to Newsted's, but the programs did not contain comments. Four different FORTRAN programs were ranked by difficulty by experienced programmers. The programs were presented to novices in mnemonic (e.g. IDVSR, ISUM, COEF) or nonmnemonic (I1, I2, I3) forms with a comprehension quiz. The mnemonic groups performed significantly better

(5 percent level) than the nonmnemonic groups for all four programs (Figure 4-1).

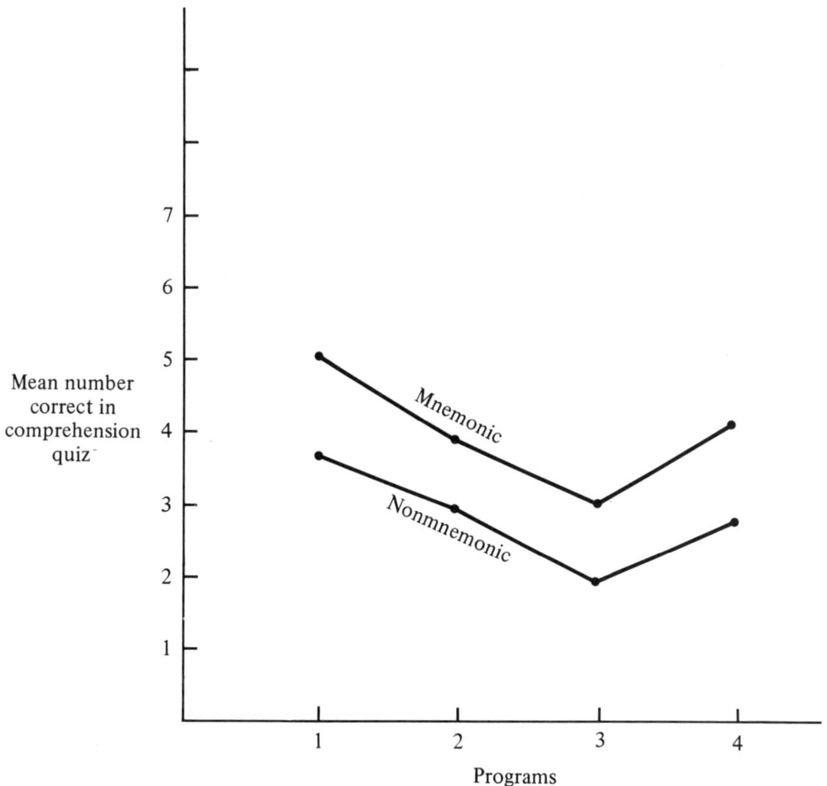

Figure 4-1: Mean comprehension scores in variable-name experiment.

In another experiment, intermediate-level student programmers were subjects in an investigation of variable names and debugging. The experiment was administered as part of a course quiz.

Two algorithms, sequential search and recursive binary search, were coded in PASCAL using either mnemonic or nonmnemonic variable names. Subjects were randomly assigned to one of two groups. One group received a mnemonic sequential search program followed by a nonmnemonic recursive binary search program. A second group was provided with a nonmnemonic version of the sequential search followed by a mnemonic recursive binary search program. Subjects were told each program contained one bug. Their task was to find the bug and correct it.

A method was devised to give partial credit. Full credit was given for locating and correcting the bug. Partial credit was awarded on the following basis: four-fifths credit for finding the bug but not correcting it, three-fifths credit for making two guesses as to which program statement was incorrect and one of them contained the bug, two-fifths credit for three guesses and locating the bug. No credit was given if the bug was not found.

The raw means appear in Table 4-2. None of the main effects nor interactions were significant by an analysis of variance.

		Program	
		Sequential Search	Recursive Binary Search
Type of Variable	Mnemonic	12.9	12.9
	Nonmnemonic	12.6	10.0

Table 4-2: Mean scores for finding bugs in variable-name experiment.

Since the subjects were familiar with the programs (both programs were previously discussed in class) the results are not surprising. Familiarity with the algorithms resulted in the programs being fairly easy to understand. The performance for the nonmnemonic recursive binary search appears to be much worse than the other groups. Since recursion was introduced shortly before the quiz, the recursive program may have been more difficult for the subjects. The more complex the program, the more mnemonic variable names aid comprehension.

In terms of the syntactic/semantic model, the mnemonic names simplify the conversion from program syntax to internal semantic structure. Meaningless variable names place an extra burden on the programmer to recode the variable's meaning and add complexity to the conversion process.

4.2.3 Indentation

When writing programs in a block-oriented structured language such as ALGOL, PL/I or PASCAL, programmers usually adopt an indenting scheme to present the code in a more readable form. Some programmers indent languages such as FORTRAN or COBOL, even when GOTOs are used.

Three of Weissman's experiments dealt with indentation for PL/I and ALGOL-W programs. Indentation did not improve performance on fill-in-the-blank or hand simulation tasks, but the self-evaluations generally favored indentation. A significant (2.5 percent level) interaction with commenting revealed that indented, commented programs were more difficult to hand-simulate and produced poorer self-evaluations. This surprising result goes against contemporary programming recommendations which urge commenting and indentation. However, scanning an indented program which has comments is apparently quite difficult: another case of 'too much of a good thing.'

Tom Love (1977) also studied indentation and found that it did not improve comprehension of short FORTRAN programs, as measured by program reconstruction.

We (Shneiderman and McKay, 1975) conducted an experiment on indentation by assigning intermediate programming students to two groups. One group received an indented form of an iterative binary search program followed by a nonindented merge program. The other group received a nonindented binary search program followed by an indented merge program. Each program was written in PASCAL and contained one bug. As in our debugging experiment on variable names, the task was to locate and repair the bug. The same grading scheme was used. Table 4-3 shows the mean scores, but no significant difference was found.

		Program	
		Binary Search	Merge
Form of program	Indented	13.6	9.2
	Nonindented	13.5	7.6

Table 4-3: Mean scores for finding bugs in indentation experiment.

The lack of significance for indentation in our experiment might not be disturbing except that Weissman, using PL/I and ALGOL programs, and Love using FORTRAN programs did not find significant differences with indentation either. This consistent pattern suggests that the advantage of indentation may not be as great as some believe. Indentation can disrupt program scanning even though it does help to organize the program. An incorrectly indented program would probably be a hindrance, but the value of indentation is not clear.

Indentation has the disadvantage that in deeply nested programs, the code is severely shifted to the right and lines may have to be split to accommodate margins. Neatly indented programs may increase a reader's confidence in the program, in fact subjective measures indicate programmers favor indentation. Assembly language programmers rarely indent and take advantage of the ease of scanning down the columns of statement labels, operators, operands, and comments.

As an alternative to indentation, blank lines might be inserted to guide program study. Delineation of functional units may be more precise with blank lines than with syntactically directed indentation. Indentations show where loops begin and end but fail to reveal functional units such as a program fragment that computes an average, maximum, or standard deviation.

4.3 PROGRAMMING LANGUAGE FEATURES

Early programming language researchers attempted to compare entire languages for all applications by any level of programmer, producing inconclusive results. Progress in programming languages and their usage comes when attention is focused on specific issues such as improving the conditional statement, recommending subroutine parameter passing rules, restricting use of control structures, or providing new data structures.

4.3.1 Conditional Statements

Conditional statements were the subject of provocative work of Sime, Green, and Guest (1973), which verified the advantage of nested IF-THEN-ELSE constructions (used in ALGOL, PL/I and PASCAL) over the IF-GOTO form (used in FORTRAN and BASIC). Their hypotheses were based on psycholinguistic considerations and not on the structured programming debate, which was only beginning at that time. Max Sime and his colleagues used nonprogrammers and created a curious 'mechanical hare' which acted as their computer. The programs that subjects composed dealt with cooking instructions for various foods and required use of IF statements only. Their results (Figure 4-2) showed that the nested structure was easier to use. In a later experiment they found a further improvement on the IF statement. All three forms are shown in Figure 4-3 with experimental results in Table 4-4. The third form which explicitly states the condition (IF A=B) and the negation of the condition (NOT A=B) and has a required end of conditional statement

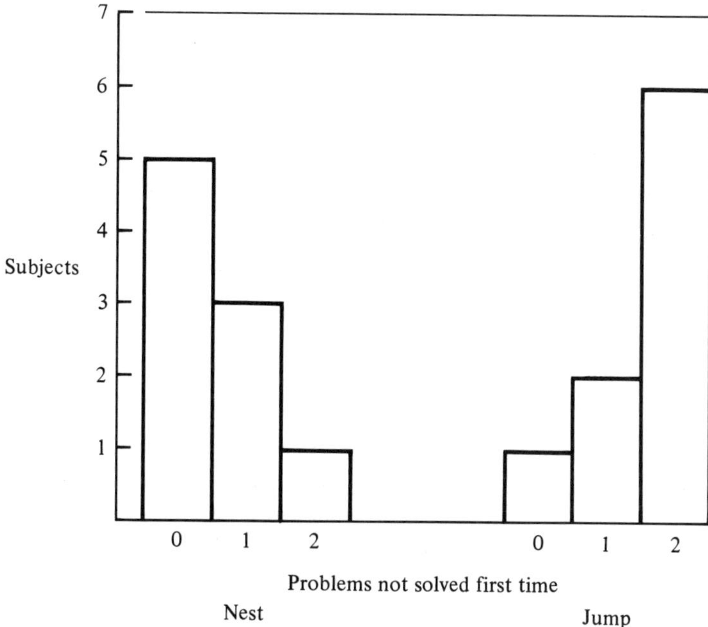

Figure 4-2: Histogram of number of subjects who made at least one semantic error in 0 problems, 1 problem, 2 problems (Sime, Green, and Guest, 1973).

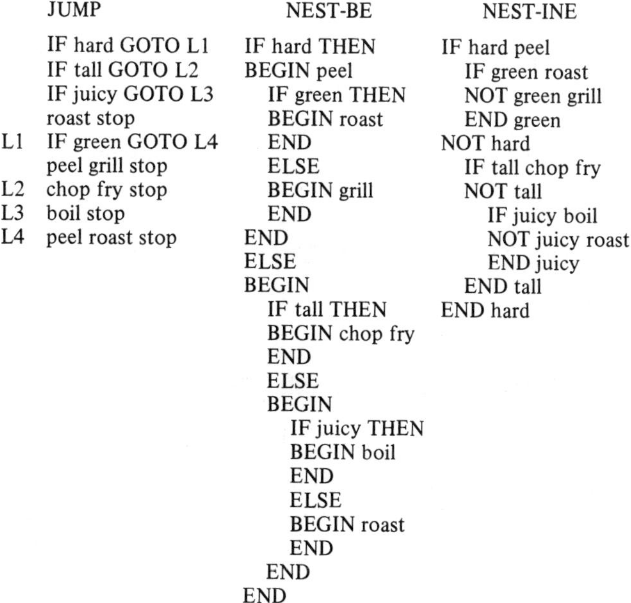

```
     JUMP                     NEST-BE              NEST-INE

     IF hard GOTO L1          IF hard THEN         IF hard peel
     IF tall GOTO L2          BEGIN peel             IF green roast
     IF juicy GOTO L3           IF green THEN        NOT green grill
     roast stop                 BEGIN roast          END green
L1   IF green GOTO L4           END                NOT hard
     peel grill stop            ELSE                 IF tall chop fry
L2   chop fry stop              BEGIN grill          NOT tall
L3   boil stop                  END                    IF juicy boil
L4   peel roast stop          END                      NOT juicy roast
                              ELSE                     END juicy
                              BEGIN                  END tall
                                IF tall THEN       END hard
                                BEGIN chop fry
                                END
                                ELSE
                                BEGIN
                                  IF juicy THEN
                                  BEGIN boil
                                  END
                                  ELSE
                                  BEGIN roast
                                  END
                                END
                              END
```

Figure 4-3: Three formats for IF statements in composition experiment (Sime, Green, and Guest, 1977).

	Group			
	NEST-INE	NEST-BE	JUMP	Significance
Semantic errors per problem	0.04 (0.08)	0.07 (0.27)	0.40 (0.22)	1%
Syntactic errors per problem	0.13 (0.17)	0.85 (0.75)	0.20 (0.25)	5%
Error-free problems per subject	2.33 (1.31)	1.15 (0.38)	2.60 (1.05)	5%
Error lifetimes	0.09 (0.50)	1.60 (0.78)	1.06 (0.87)	2%

Entries are medians, with semi-interquartile range in brackets.

Table 4-4: Comparison for error frequencies and lifetimes for conditional structures shown in Figure 4-3 (Sime, Green, and Guest, 1977).

(END A=B) might be a reasonable form for inclusion in future languages. It answers some of the problems raised in Weinberg, Geller and Plum's 'IF-THEN-ELSE considered harmful' (1975), by explicitly stating the negation, eliminating DO-END pairs, and taking advantage of the good features of the CASE statement. These narrowly focused experiments were carefully performed by competent psychologists with excellent resources. Further insights were obtained indicating the difference between forward (Given an input, what is the output?) and backward (Given an output, what must the input have been?) comprehension questions. A theory based on decision making 'taxons' was proposed.

Our work on FORTRAN IF statements (Shneiderman, 1976a) was motivated by controversy over the relative advantages of the logical IF:

```
IF(HOURS .GT. 40.0) GO TO 150
```

and the arithmetic IF:

```
IF(HOURS - 40.0) 100,100,150
```

The older arithmetic IF is felt to be more difficult to use even though it has the advantage of three-way branching when integer comparisons are performed. We tested comprehension performance for novice and intermediate subjects studying easy, medium and hard programs. The results, shown in Table 4-5 indicated no significant differences between the arithmetic and logical IF statements, but there was a significant interaction ef-

	FORTRAN Logical IF			FORTRAN Arithmetic IF		
	Hard	Moderate	Easy	Hard	Moderate	Easy
Experience level						
Novices	1.71	2.13	0.83	3.38	1.63	1.25
Intermediate-professional	1.05	1.45	0.62	1.50	1.15	1.65

Table 4-5: Mean number of errors on comprehension questions for FORTRAN logical and arithmetic IF statements (Shneiderman, 1976).

fect between IF statement form and experience. This implies that intermediate programmers had no more difficulty in using the arithmetic than logical IF, but novices did. We conjectured that the experts had learned to translate quickly the complex syntax of the arithmetic IF into an internal semantic form which represented the statement function, but that novices were struggling with the arithmetic IF syntax.

Deeply nested IF-THEN-ELSE statements are difficult to comprehend, but the alternative use of complex Boolean conditions is not necessarily more appealing (Figure 4-4). Nested IFs may be better when the tested items are unrelated and when forward comprehension questions are asked. The set of decisions to be made also plays an important role.

```
IF LEAFY
  CALL FRY
ELSE
  IF HARD
    IF GREEN
      IF ROUND
        CALL BAKE
      ELSE
        CALL CHOP
    ELSE
      CALL BOIL
  ELSE
    IF JUICY
      CALL SLICE
    ELSE
      CALL THROW AWAY.
```

```
IF LEAFY CALL FRY.
IF HARD AND GREEN AND ROUND CALL BAKE.
IF HARD AND GREEN CALL CHOP.
IF HARD CALL BOIL.
IF JUICY CALL SLICE.
CALL THROW AWAY.
```

Figure 4-4: Nesting vs. Boolean construction.

The CASE statement has received much attention in recent years, but the form available in most compilers restricts the test to integer variable names. The advantage of the CASE statement is that a multiway branch is accomplished in a single well-organized statement which has an explicit END statement. A convenient form might have a boolean expression prefixing each choice. Proper commenting can improve the readability of the syntax available in currently popular languages.

Embley (1978) proposes a control structure which combines the CASE statement and iteration in a simple manner. He demonstrates the effectiveness of his control structure through formal analysis and empirical testing. His four experimental groups, containing from 11 to 19 subjects, responded to ten comprehension questions for each of two programs. The subjects in the two groups working with Embley's proposed control structure did significantly better on the comprehension questions and had higher scores on self-evaluations, than the subjects in the two groups working with ALGOL68-like CASE and IF-THEN-ELSE statements.

4.3.2 Iteration and Recursion

The old-fashioned DO loop of FORTRAN has the disadvantage that terms can only be unsubscripted integer constants or variables, that increments have to be positive and that the body is executed at least once. The FOR loop in BASIC has none of these disadvantages, but doesn't have the freedom of PL/I or ALGOL to specify multiple ranges as in:

```
DO I = 1 TO 10 BY 1, 12, 14, 15 TO 100 BY 5;
```

The while statement in PL/I or PASCAL allows condition testing to terminate iteration. PASCAL arbitrarily limits FOR statement step sizes to plus or minus one. COBOL's PERFORM VARYING or PERFORM UNTIL gives great freedom, but the loop body must be in a separate paragraph. This approach avoids the necessity of a loop terminating statement such as CONTINUE, NEXT or END, but may disrupt program study.

An alternative way of expressing repetition in programs is through recursion. Recursion is the basis for LISP and its descendants, all of which have dedicated adherents who believe that recursion is a far superior way of expressing repetition. Commercial programmers see recursion, if at all, as an intriguing curiosity, while artificial intelligence researchers live and breathe recursively. What is remarkable is the strength of the attitudinal differences between these two cultures. What personality issue, experience factor, problem domain difference, or training makes this split so unbridgeable, with both sides so entrenched?

4.3.3 Syntactic Choice

Some programming languages, notably COBOL, permit programmers to use a wide variety of syntactic forms to express the same declaration or command. COBOL allows PIC, PICTURE, and PICTURE IS to be used interchangeably and allows at least the following equivalent forms:

```
IF A GREATER B ADD 1 TO A.
IF A GREATER THAN B ADD 1 TO A.
IF A IS GREATER THAN B ADD 1 TO A.
IF A IS GREATER B ADD 1 TO A.
IF A GREATER THAN B THEN ADD 1 TO A.
IF A GREATER B THEN ADD 1 TO A.
IF A GREATER B, ADD 1 TO A.
IF A > B ADD 1 TO A.
```

Although some applaud such flexibility, it can be confusing since it may be more difficult for a programmer to recognize an incorrect form. Comprehension or debugging experiments might reveal under which circumstances such freedom is helpful or harmful. Any one of the forms may be acceptable, but if several forms are used in a single program it may be more difficult to comprehend and debug.

4.3.4 Structured Control Structures

One component of structured programming is the use of higher-level control structures such as IF-THEN-ELSE or the DO-WHILE statement to replace lower-level GOTO statements. The higher-level control structures have the advantageous 'one-in, one-out' property which restricts entry and exit, facilitating composition and comprehension by limiting complexity. The study by Sime, Green and Guest (1973) supports the avoidance of GOTOs in IF statements, but does not consider other structures or real programming languages.

Lucas and Kaplan (1976) report on a PL/I experiment using graduate students at Stanford's Business School: 32 students were randomly separated into structured or unstructured groups and were required to compose one program and modify another. For the composition task the structured group was merely told not to use GOTOs although their training did not concentrate on techniques for avoiding GOTOs. For the modification task the structured group received a GOTO-less version. Performance was measured by number of runs, programming time, compile time, object code size, ease in composition, ease in debugging and enjoyment. The last three measures were subjective with higher scores indicating preference.

The results (Table 4-6) suggest that these students struggled to compose programs without GOTOs and may have had real difficulties in accommodating structured programming ideas. However, by the time they got to the modification task, they had become more familiar with using structured control structures. Structured control structures also appear to be easier to comprehend, and therefore easier to modify.

	Composition			Modification		
	Structured		Unstructured	Structured		Unstructured
Number of runs	14.63	*	8.87	10.06		10.25
Programming time	14.75		11.69	9.13	*	13.06
Compile time[2]	1.27		1.13	0.52	**	0.75
Bytes object code[2]	6690		5943	2462	**	4569
Easy to write[1]	4.00	*	5.19	5.13		4.63
Easy to debug[1]	4.00		4.69	4.75		4.63
Enjoyment[1]	4.63		4.88	3.44		4.31

* indicates significant differences at the 5% level.
** indicates significant differences at the 1% level.

Table 4-6: Mean scores for structured programming experiment (Lucas and Kaplan, 1976).

Weissman studied control structures in PL/I comprehension experiments at three levels:

1) structured constructs such as IF-THEN-ELSE
2) unstructured constructs with simple control flow
3) unstructured constructs with complex control flow, that is, many backward and forward GOTOs.

Using two programs, one approximately 50 lines and the other approximately 100 lines, Weissman required his 24 undergraduate and graduate subjects to take two quizzes, perform two modifications, and do three self-evaluations (Table 4-7). The self-evaluations yielded significant differences favoring the structured constructs, but none of the performance measures showed significant differences. For both quizzes and one modification, the structured control structures did have the highest mean scores. No pattern emerged for the differences between groups 2 and 3. In summary, Weissman's results mildly support the use of structured control structures, but there are unsatisfying aspects to the results.

Love (1977) studied control structures in 15–25 line FORTRAN programs by asking subjects to memorize structured or unstructured versions of the program. The structured versions used DO loops, logical IF statements, were well-organized programs and had a minimum of GOTO

	Control Flow Style		
	Structured	Unstructured Simple	Unstructured Complex
(5 minutes study of progam)			
1st self-evaluation	3.1	2.0	1.5
(15 minutes study)			
1st quiz	3.9	2.9	3.4
2nd self-evaulation	4.1	2.0	1.6
1st modification	1.4	2.0	1.3
2nd modification	3.1	2.8	2.9
3rd self-evaluation	4.5	2.6	2.0
2nd quiz	4.6	3.6	3.9

Table 4-7: Means for Weissman's control structures experiment.

statements. The unstructured forms used IF loops, arithmetic IF statements, numerous GOTOs and many statement labels. The structured versions were significantly easier to memorize and recall for both the undergraduate and graduate subject groups.

Sheppard et al (1979) report on two experiments with structured vs. unstructured control flow in 36 to 57 statement FORTRAN programs. Thirty-six professional programmers with an average of more than six years experience participated in each experiment. Using program memorization/reconstruction and modification tasks, the authors demonstrated improved performance when structured control flow was employed.

These controlled experiments and a variety of informal field studies indicate that the choice of control structures does make a significant difference in programmer performance. Evidence supports the anecdote that the number of bugs in a program is proportional to the square of the number of GOTOs, but absence of GOTOs does not automatically produce perfection. Control structures should have as high a semantic level as possible, avoiding machine related issues such as program step counters.

4.3.5 Flowcharting

The use of detailed and system flowcharts has been popular since the earliest days of programming. In recent years, critics have reflected the increasing anger that many programmers have when they are required to produce detailed flowcharts. Brooks (1975) called flowcharts 'a curse,' a 'space-hogging exercise in drafting,' and a 'most thoroughly oversold piece of program documentation.' Ledgard and Chmura (1976), using more moderate language, argue that 'program flowcharts can easily suppress much useful information in favor of highlighting sequential control flow, something which distracts the programmer from the important functional relationship in the overall design.'

Advocates of flowcharting, such as Marilyn Bohl in her 1971 book *Flowcharting Techniques*, claim that the flowchart is 'an essential tool in problem solving' and 'the person who cannot flowchart cannot anticipate a problem, analyze the problem, plan the solution or solve the problem.'

Early research on flowcharts emphasized its aid in presenting algorithms more clearly than prose. Kammann (1975) showed that housewives and Bell Telephone Laboratory professionals committed fewer errors when using a flowchart for a complex dialing procedure as opposed to written intructions. Wright and Reid (1973) showed similiar results, but found that the visually encoded flowchart became less distinct over time while the prose version could be more easily retained in memory. Mayer (1975) studied detailed flowcharts as an aid to learning computer programming. His experiment indicated that flowcharts may assist in program composition, but may hinder learning and comprehension performance.

During 1976 we conducted a series of five experiments to evaluate the utility of flowcharts in composition, comprehension, debugging, and modification tasks (Figure 4-5). Our attitude was modestly pro-flowcharting and we were interested in clarifying which tasks flowcharts aided most. As each experiment failed to reveal statistically significant differences for the group using flowcharts we tried to utilize problems with an increasing degree of branching and chose subjects who were flowchart users. The lack of significance in an experiment can be attributed to poor experimental design, but when five experiments all fail to show statistically significant differences we can no longer ignore the possibility that detailed flowcharts may not be as beneficial as supporters claim.

A possible explanation of our results is that programmers familiar with the syntax of FORTRAN prefer studying the code. In fact the flowchart is at a disadvantage because it is more spread out (the page flip and off-page connector problems) and it is incomplete (omitting declarations, statement labels and input/output formats). At best a detailed flowchart repeats the program syntax: a chef with English and French versions of a recipe should do no better than a chef with only one version.

Our experimental results can also be questioned since we used student programmers, short to medium sized programs, only FORTRAN, and a small number of problem situations. Flowchart critics cheered our results as the justification of their claims, while adherents found fault and pronounced confidence in the utility of flowcharts in their own work.

1. (Composition) 34 subjects wrote a flowchart and then the program receiving an average score on the program of 94. 28 subjects wrote only the program and got an average score of 95. No significant differences.
2. (Comprehension) Two tests forms were constructed: the first contained two programs (27 and 24 FORTRAN statements) with a flowchart for the first program only, while the second form contained a flowchart for the second program only. 25 subjects received the first form, 28 the second form. Table 4-8 shows the results. No significant differences for flowchart usage.
3. (Comprehension and debugging) 43 subjects (no-flowchart group) who had some instruction in the use of flowcharts and 27 subjects (flowchart group) who were required to turn in detailed flowcharts with their homework assignments were given comprehension and debugging tasks with a tic-tac-toe program (81 FORTRAN statement main program, 43 and 23 line subroutines). The no-flowchart and flowchart groups were broken into three groups each; one group received only the program code, the second received the program plus a one-page system flowchart and the third received the program plus a four-page detailed flowchart. The detailed results for this 2 by 3 experimental design are shown in Table 4-9 but none of the differences was statistically significant, even at the 0.10 level.
4. (Modification) Using the same experimental design as in experiment 3, 33 no-flowchart and 37 flowchart subjects were required to make two modifications to a heavily commented 48 statement FORTRAN program. Table 4-10 shows the results which were not significant for the flowchart factor.
5. (Comprehension) 58 subjects were split into three groups; the first received a 23-line FORTRAN array merging program, the second received the program plus a flowchart and the third the flowchart only. Execution questions required low-level comprehension of statement execution while interpretation questions required higher-level structural understanding. Table 4-11 shows the results which were, again, not statistically significant.

Figure 4-5: Flowchart experiment descriptions (Shneiderman et al., 1977).

One appealing explanation of the strong differences in reaction is the cognitive style differences produced by left or right brain emphasis. Right brained, visually oriented, pattern recognizing, intuitive types might prefer flowcharts while the left brained, verbally oriented, deductive types might prefer reading program code. It is also possible that managers are more right brained and prefer seeing flowcharts than the programmers who are left brained and emphasize language usage.

The syntactic/semantic model indicates that detailed flowcharts may not aid comprehension since they do not facilitate the recoding into higher level semantic structures. On the other hand system flowcharts (or

	Problem	
	1	2
Flowchart on 1	94.4	89.6
Flowchart on 2	97.0	94.4

Table 4.8: Mean percent correct for program composition.

Average % Correct (Comprehension)

	Flowchart used		
	None	Macro	Micro
Group NFC	52	34	46
FC	53	55	76

Average % Correct (Debugging)

	Flowchart used		
	None	Macro	Micro
Group NFC	12	11	4
FC	29	26	45

Average % Correct (Total Score)

	Flowchart used		
	None	Macro	Micro
Group NFC	34	23	27
FC	42	42	62

NFC: Flowcharts not required during training
FC: Flowcharts required during training

Table 4-9: Mean comprehension and debugging scores in tic-tac-toe experiments on flowchart use (Shneiderman et al., 1977).

	Flowchart Aid	Mean Percent Correct		Mean Time in Minutes	
		Mod I	Mod II	Mod I	Mod II
Training required flowcharts group	None	73	85	15.5	15.3
	Macro	88	77	16.1	14.2
	Micro	87	81	14.0	14.1
Training did not require flowcharts group	None	77	64	15.6	16.7
	Macro	77	71	15.4	13.9
	Micro	77	59	16.0	17.9

Table 4-10: Program modification scores using flowcharts (Shneiderman et al., 1977).

Materials Available for Study	Type of Comprehension Question	
	Execution	Interpretation
Flowchart	48.5	51.2
Program and flowchart	56.9	50.0
Program	57.8	62.4

Table 4-11: Mean percent correct for comprehension questions (Shneiderman et al., 1977).

macro flowcharts) should facilitate this recoding. System flowcharts will probably be most helpful with large programs where each box represents approximately one page of code. At this granularity, the system flowchart should facilitate comprehension of the relationship among modules, something which is difficult to perceive from the code. This assumption presupposes that the modules are functionally defined and related to the problem structure.

Other kinds of flowcharts may be useful. Macro or system flowcharts where each box represents 30–50 statements or a module may aid in showing the interaction pattern among modules. Intermediate flowcharting schemes such as HIPO charts or structured flowcharts (Nassi and Shneiderman, 1973) need experimental testing to ascertain their effectiveness.

4.4 DEBUGGING STUDIES

The debugging process and the distribution of bug types have been the subject of several studies. Programs submitted by 234 computer science students at the University of Wisconsin were studied while reviewing the impact of DITRAN, a diagnostic compiler for FORTRAN (Moulton and Muller, 1967). Of the 5158 programs submitted, 1859 (36 percent) had compilation errors and 1699 (33 percent) had execution errors which caused termination. Of the compilation errors, 26 percent involved arithmetic assignment, 22 percent statement format and sequence, 15 percent identifiers, and 7 percent DO statements. Of the execution errors 64 percent involved input/output operations, 31 percent reference and definition, and 4 percent arithmetic faults.

The number of syntactic errors was only half as large in a study of professional programmers at IBM's Yorktown Heights Research Center. Of 113 FORTRAN programs only 16 percent had syntactic errors, of 66 Assembler programs only 12 percent had syntactic errors, and of 139 PL/I programs only 17 percent had syntactic errors. A repetition of the study at a later date showed similar results (Boies and Gould, 1974).

Two similar experiments were conducted with thirty experienced FORTRAN programmers from Carnegie-Mellon University (Gould and Drongowski, 1974) and with ten professional FORTRAN programmers from IBM's T. J. Watson Research Center (Gould, 1975). Four statistical analysis programs were modified by adding three kinds of one-line bugs, thus producing twelve different listings with 29 to 59 executable FORTRAN statements. The bugs were classified as array bugs, involving an error in an array subscript, iteration bugs, involving incorrect loop control, and assignment bugs, involving changes to assignment statements. In the first experiment there were five groups with different debugging aids. The first group received only the program listing, the second group received the program listing plus input and output listings, the third group received the program listing with the correct output plus the input and output listings, the fourth group received the program listing plus information about which bug type was involved, and the fifth group was told the line number of the error. In the second experiment all subjects received only the program listings plus the input and output listings and were given access to an interactive debugging system. The median debug time was six minutes in the first experiment and seven minutes in the second experiment. The debugging aids had little effect on debug times, although those told the line number had a median debug time of less than three minutes. The interactive debugging system was rarely used in the second experiment even though the subjects were familiar with it. Bugs in assignment statements were substantially harder to identify than iteration or array bugs. Subjects generally reduced their debugging time the second time they viewed a program, suggesting that they maintain information about the program structure which is independent of the specific bug.

An intriguing study by Youngs compared the development and debugging processes for 30 novices and 12 professional programmers working in ALGOL, BASIC, COBOL, FORTRAN, and PL/I (Youngs, 1974). Both novices and professionals averaged 5.6 errors on the first run of a program, but novices averaged 19.4 and professionals 15.1 errors in the development sequence. Professionals apparently have higher competence in removing bugs. Tables 4-12 and 4-13 indicate proportions

	Proportion of Total Errors	
General Cause of Error	Beginners	Advanced
Syntax	0.12 (0.22) *	0.17 (0.31)
Semantic	0.41 (0.45)	0.21 (0.28)
Logic	0.35 (0.21)	0.51 (0.34)
Clerical	0.05 (0.08)	0.04 (0.06)
Other and Unknown	0.07 (0.05)	0.07 (0.01)
Total	1.00 (1.00)	1.00 (1.00)

* Parenthesized figures are for the first run only.

Table 4-12: Proportions of total errors tabulated by general cause for beginners and advanced programmers (Youngs, 1974).

	Proportion of Total Errors	
Specific Cause of Error	Beginners	Advanced
Statement sequencing	0.06 (0.03) *	0.12 (0.08)
Phrase omission	0.06 (0.08)	0.03 (0.05)
Statement omission	0.14 (0.14)	0.05 (0.06)
Statement insertion	0.04 (0.05)	0.01 (0.01)
Wrong variable/ literal/operator/ keyword/phrase	0.28 (0.20)	0.47 (0.35)

*Parenthesized figures are for the first run only.

Table 4-13: Proportions of total errors tabulated by selected specific causes for beginners and advanced programmers (Youngs, 1974).

of bug types but no clear cut difference between beginning and advanced programmers emerges.

Gannon (Gannon, 1975; Gannon and Horning, 1975) used detailed counts of errors, error occurrences, number of runs with errors, and *persistence* of each error (measured in number of runs) to compare the TOPPS and TOPPSII languages. Fifty-one undergraduate and graduate students, many of whom had professional experience, were assigned to one of the two languages so as to equalize experience. The sequence of 123 to 306 line listings for two problems were studied for the 10 of 26 TOPPS and 15 of 26 TOPPSII subjects who completed both programs. Gannon diligently traced 3937 occurrences of 1248 errors by hand and found that for each of the four measures TOPPSII subjects performed better but not to a statistically significant degree. The analysis for the nine programming language features (Figure 4-6) which differed between

TOPPS	TOPPS II
1. Expression evaluation right to left with equal precedence among operators.	* Expression evaluation left to right with "traditional" operator precedence.
2. Assignment operator.	* Assignment statement.
3. Logical operators ϵ and 1.	* Logical functions <u>all</u> and <u>any</u>.
4. Semicolon as separator.	* Semicolon as terminator.
5. Selection statements: <u>if</u>.	Selection statements: <u>if</u> and <u>case</u>.
6. Repetition statements: <u>repeat</u>.	Repetition statements: <u>repeat</u> and <u>for</u> <u>each</u> (element of an array).
7. Brackets used to close compound expressions: <u>end</u> and parentheses.	* Brackets used to close compound statements: <u>end</u>.
8. Automatic inheritance of environment.	Inheritance of environment only upon specific request.
9. Constants: literals.	* Constants: literals and named constants.

Figure 4-6: Differences in languages used in Gannon and Horning (1975); * indicates that the difference was significant at the 0.10 level.

TOPPS and TOPPSII, revealed that for at least one of the four measures there was at least a 5 percent level significant difference on six features. In every case the difference showed that the changes made to TOPPS and incorporated in TOPPSII reduced the errors.

Using similar experimental techniques Gannon (1977) studied the impact of statically-typed versus nontyped languages on error statistics. In statically-typed languages (e.g. COBOL, PL/I, FORTRAN), declaration statements associate a data type with an identifier to permit type checking and prevent mixed mode operations. In nontyped languages (e.g. BCPL, BLISS or Assemblers), each identifier refers to a group of bits and no restrictions on operations are imposed. Thirty-eight graduate and advanced undergraduate subjects were divided into two groups for this counterbalanced ordering experiment: 21 subjects worked with the statically-typed language first and then the nontyped language while the remaining 17 did the tasks in reverse order. The sequence of 48 to 297 line listings were collected and errors counted (Table 4-14). For those

	Typeless/Statically Typed Group		
Measure	Typeless	Statically Typed	Level
Errors	18.40 (6.80)	7.87 (2.73)	<.5%
Total errors	28.87 (11.53)	8.93 (3.27)	<2.5%
Occurrences	90.80 (57.20)	29.20 (15.33)	<.5%
Total occurrences	125.80 (84.73)	31.40 (16.87)	<.5%
Error runs	21.20 (19.47)	10.07 (7.27)	<2.5%
	Statically Typed/Typeless Group		
Measure	Typeless	Statically Typed	Level
Errors	13.17 (6.39)	12.44 (3.33)	
Total errors	24.00 (14.22)	22.39 (5.89)	
Occurrences	59.83 (40.94)	38.17 (14.78)	<.5%
Total occurrences	99.61 (76.78)	51.72 (18.83)	<1%
Error runs	14.83 (14.50)	10.83 (7.44)	<1%

Table 4-14: Error statistics from data typing experiment (Gannon, 1977).

completing both programs, 18 out of 21 who began with the statically-typed language and 15 out of 17 who began with the nontyped language completed both programs.

The results favoring the statically-typed language are statistically significant by most measures. The order effect suggests that those who begin with static typing carry their learned data abstractions to the non-typed language.

Gannon's conclusion to this well executed experiment suggests that 'at least in our environment, the features of a statically-typed language increase programming reliability' and that 'subjects who are less able and experienced are helped most by a statically-typed language.'

4.5 PRACTITIONER'S SUMMARY

Numerous low-level comments can clutter a listing and interfere with comprehension, but occasional high-level comments relating operations to high-level semantic knowledge in the problem domain can be helpful. Mnemonic variable names can be helpful when they add semantic information not available elsewhere in the program and certainly when there are numerous variable names in a program. Indentation is frequently advocated but its efficacy has not been demonstrated experimentally.

Higher-level control structures such as the IF-THEN-ELSE and DO-WHILE appear to improve programming task performance, especially during modification. Professional programmers can cope with unpleasant syntactic forms more successfully than novices. More powerful semantic structures can improve programming performance. Detailed standard flowcharts do not seem to improve programming performance.

Designers of languages should recognize that specific features may have a statistically significant effect on performance and should thoroughly test alternative proposals.

4.6 RESEARCHER'S AGENDA

The stylistic features, language constructs, and design techniques described in this chapter need to be studied further and the results validated and refined. Beyond the issues presented in this chapter, related issues such as page formatting of programs (Do blank lines improve comprehension? Does splitting a loop across pages harm comprehension?), default options (When are defaults helpful? harmful?), data sharing techniques (Is parameter passing better than global variable sharing?), top-down design (Is it really better in all cases?), modular design (How big is a module?), or flowcharts (What kind of flowcharts do help?) can be studied experimentally.

Experiments should provide validation and suggest refinements to the syntactic/semantic model or offer clues to the formation of an alternative model of programmer behavior.

© CAROL WALD

5

SOFTWARE QUALITY EVALUATION

What I mean by the word *quality* cannot be broken down into subjects and predicates. This is not because quality is so mysterious, but because quality is so simple, immediate and direct.

Robert Pirsig, *Zen and the Art of Motorcycle Maintenance* (1974)

Review of proposals for measuring computer program quality - Boehm, Brown and Lipow's quality characteristic tree - Gilb's software metrics - Halstead's software science - productivity measures - reliability - maintainability - McCabe's graph metric - performance studies

5.1 INTRODUCTION

Software quality measurement is an infant discipline. As this specialty matures, the ability to measure will develop, but in its youthful phase, there are conflicting opinions as to what and how software characteristics should be measured. With time, reliable and useful standard measuring concepts will emerge.

Boehm, Brown and Lipow (1977) identify key issues such as the definition of criteria for software quality which are measurable, sufficiently nonoverlapping, and which allow automatic evaluation. They conclude that an automated tool for software quality evaluation should not merely produce a variety of metrics but should identify where and how a product is deficient. This is an ambitious goal since we do not even agree on which metrics are useful or on satisfactory values for metrics. The simple quantitative formulas for quality have counterexamples in which programs having high ratings are of low quality. Software design methodology is evolving so rapidly that it is difficult to establish useful metrics and to 'write metrics in stone' could reinforce practices which might later prove to be undesirable.

Boehm, Brown and Lipow confront the question of computing a single overall metric for quality and conclude that this is not feasible due to the conflict among the individual quality characteristics. Managers must decide on the relative importance of:

1) on-time delivery
2) efficient use of resources such as:
   a) processing units
   b) memory
   c) peripheral devices
3) maintainable code issues such as:
   a) comprehensibility
   b) modifiability
   c) portability.

The desirability of the component characteristics varies with the organization in which the software product is utilized. For example, a government agency whose software is highly classified, used solely on one machine, and not shared with other agencies, may put a lower value on portability. Developers of software libraries may value portability over efficiency while creators of personnel systems may focus on modifiability.

5.2 BOEHM, BROWN AND LIPOW'S METRICS

To measure quality, one must determine what characteristics to measure. Boehm, Brown and Lipow define a hierarchical software quality characteristic tree (Figure 5-1) in which the arrow direction indicates logical implication. For example, a program that is maintainable must also be testable, understandable, and modifiable. The structure's higher level reflects the uses of the software quality evaluation. Boehm, Brown and Lipow emphasize software package acquisition and feel that the major concerns are:

1) How well (easily, reliably, and efficiently) can I use the package as it is?
2) How easy is it to maintain (understand, modify, retest)?
3) Can I use it if I change my environment (portability)?

The lowest level characteristics (rightmost on Figure 5-1) are 'primitives' which may be combined into the medium level characteristics. These primitives (that is, device independence, self-containedness, accuracy, completeness, robustness/integrity, consistency, accountability, device efficiency, accessibility, communicativeness, self-descriptiveness, structuredness, conciseness, legibility, and augmentability) are recommended as quantitative metrics of both the primitives and the higher level characteristics. Definitions for characteristics are found in Figure 5-2.

Boehm, Brown and Lipow developed 51 candidate metrics for the primitive characteristics and then evaluated these metrics by their correlation with program quality; potential benefits in terms of insights and decision inputs for the developer and user; quantifiability; and feasibility of automating evaluation. Examples of the types of metrics considered are:

Device Independence Are computations dependent on word size? Are hardware dependent statements flagged?

Self Containedness Does the program initialize core storage prior to use? Are program input/output devices positioned prior to use?

Accuracy Are the numerical methods used by the program consistent with applications requirements for accuracy?

Completeness Are any 'dummy' subprograms referenced?
Robustness Are input data ranges checked?
Consistency Is the type of a variable consistent for all uses?

Their detailed and complex scheme, based on practical experience, is appealing to programmers but Boehm, Brown and Lipow offer no clear-cut demonstration of its effectiveness, reliability, or applicability in other environments. The lengthy list of issues acts as a checklist for reviewing a program rather than offering guidance in construction. Such checklists can be useful, but they tend to grow long and cumbersome, match the needs of a specific organization, and become language/system specific.

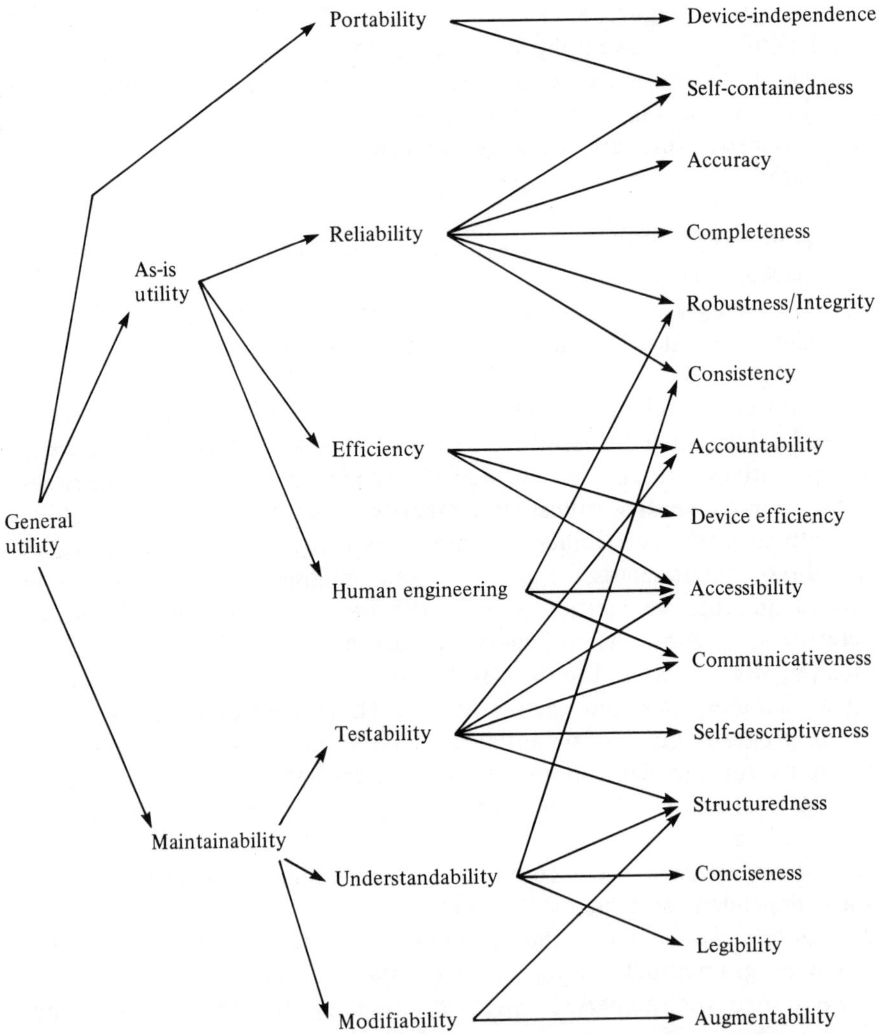

Figure 5-1: Software quality characteristic tree (Boehm et al., 1976).

Glossary

Accessibility. Extent to which code facilitates use of its parts.

Accountability. Extent to which code can be measured.

Accuracy. Extent to which the output produced by code are sufficiently precise to satisfy their intended use.

Augmentability. Extent to which code a can be expanded in computations functions, or data storage requirements.

Availability. Degree to which a system of resource is ready to process data. Availability. MTBF/(MTBF + MTTR).

Communicativeness. Extent to which code facilitates the specifications of inputs and provides outputs whose form and content are easy to assimilate.

Completeness. Extent to which all parts of code are present and developed.

Conciseness. Extent to which excessive information is not present.

Consistency. Extent to which code contains uniform notation, terminology, and symbology within itself, and external consistency to the extent that the content is traceable to the requirements.

Device independence. Extent to which code can be executed on computer hardware configurations other than its current one.

Efficiency. Extent to which code fulfills its purpose without wasting resources.

Human engineering. Extent to which code fulfills its purpose without wasting users' time and energy or degrading their morale.

Legibility. Extent to which function is easily discerned by reading code.

Maintainability. Extent to which code facilitates updating.

Modifiability. Extent to which code facilitates the incorporation of changes.

Portability. Extent to which code can be operated easily and well on computer configurations other than its current one.

Reliability. Probability that an item (device or program, system) will function without failure over a specified time period or amount of usage.

Robustness. Extent to which code can continue to perform despite a violation of the assumptions in its specifications.

Self-containedness. Extent to which code performs its explicit and implicit functions within itself.

Self-descriptiveness. Extent to which reader of code can determine its objectives, assumptions, constraints, inputs, outputs, components, and revision status.

Testability. Extent to which code facilitates establishment of verification criteria and supports evaluation of its performance.

Understandability. Extent to which purpose of code is understandable to reader.

Usability. Extent to which code is reliable, efficient, and human-engineered.

Figure 5-2: Glossary of terms for Figure 5-1 (Boehm et al., 1976).

5.3 GILB'S SOFTWARE METRICS

Gilb (1977) presents a set of basic software metrics, making no claim as to their completeness. He emphasizes that each application requires its own concepts or tools and that his text is intended to provide basic concepts on which the user can build. Gilb builds a strong convincing case for precise measurement based on the history of the physical sciences.

Among the metrics Gilb mentions is program *reliability*, which he defines as the probability that a given program operates for a certain period of time without a logical error. The pragmatic measure for program reliability is one minus the ratio of inputs causing execution failures and the total number of inputs.

Maintainability (the probability that a failed system will be restored to operable condition within a specified time) is described as a function of system design (diagnostic aids, documentation, recovery procedures), personnel, and support facilities such as diagnostic test tools.

Repairability is distinguished from maintainability in that all resources (tools, people, parts) are assumed to be immediately available. It depends more on the nature of the object being repaired.

The characteristic of *serviceability* (the ease or difficulty with which a system can be repaired) is described by Gilb, but it is not considered quantifiable at present. It is related to repairability.

Availability of a system is computed by dividing the time actually available by the time that the system should have been available. Gilb defines intrinsic availability, operational availability, and use availability.

The *attack probability* is an expression of the frequency with which latent problems occur. Examples of attacks are sabotage, invalid data values, program logic errors, or even a breakdown of a computer's air conditioning.

Gilb illustrates a scale for generating a risk measure for a database in his discussion of the *sensitivity* characteristic. Related characteristics include: *security probability* (the probability of rejecting an attack); *integrity probability* (probability of system survival); and the *accessibility* (ease of access to a system) or security measure.

The ratio of correct data to all data is given by Gilb as a measure of the *Accuracy* (freedom from error). As did Boehm, Brown and Lipow, Gilb states that accuracy is necessary for reliability. *Precision* is defined as the degree to which the errors tend to have the same sort of cause. Gilb measures it by the ratio of the number of actual bugs at the source to the number of corresponding root bugs observed in total which are caused by source bugs. For example, if one error (bug) causes 100 error messages during a specific time, the precision equals 0.01.

Gilb's second larger category is *flexibility* which includes: *logical complexity, built-in complexity, open-ended flexibility (adaptability), tolerance (of system input variance), generality, portability*, and *compatability*.

For the logical complexity, Gilb proposes a measure of 'binary decisions' in the logic. Such a measurement may be made manually or automatically. The number of nonnormal exits from a decision statement gives the absolute logical complexity. Gilb suggests that logical complexity has been found to be of significance in predicting the cost of computer programs.

Built-in flexibility (the ability of a system to handle different logical situations) is the ratio of usable complexity to total complexity. A built-in flexibility of one indicates that all complexity is desired. This measure is applicable in judging the suitability of software packages against alternatives.

Open ended flexibility (or the measure of the ease with which new functions can be added to a system) may be grossly measured by counting the linkages between modules. Whether or not this indicator is meaningful has yet to be demonstrated.

Tolerance (the ability of a system to withstand a degree of variation in input without malfunction or rejection) is the number of permissible variations which a system will handle 'sensibly.' Tolerance may be designed into a system. There is, however, a tradeoff between the cost of tolerance and the cost of failure due to lack of tolerance.

Gilb's metric of generality (degree to which a system is applicable to a different environment) varies between 0.0 and 1 (for 100 percent). For portability (ease with which a system can be moved from one environment to another) Gilb gives the following measure:

$$P(G) = 1 - E(T)/E(R)$$

where: E(T) = resources needed to move a system to a target environment; E(R) = resources needed to create the system for the resident environment. The portability concept is useful in evaluating the effectiveness of a system that is expected to be moved.

Compatability (the measure of portability that can be expected of systems when they are moved from one given environment to another) must be measured by average, maximum, and minimum portability measures because only portability (not compatability) is measurable in practice.

Gilb's *structure metrics* include: *redundancy ratio, hierarchy, structural complexity (modularity)* and *simplicity*, and *distinctness*.

The redundancy characteristic is a relative one which is measured by the ratio of a quantity for the system being measured to the quantity for some reference system. A redundancy of 1.0 indicates minimum redundancy. An example of the redundancy ratio follows. If a code for a series of 1000 objects is 6 digits 000000–999999 then the digit redundancy is 6/3 or 2.0.

Basic measures of a hierarchy are: depth (number of levels); total number of elements or nodes in the hierarchy; and breadth (number of elements at one level). These measures are related to those of structural complexity which is measured by the number of subsystems or modules and structural simplicity which is the ratio of the number of module linkages to the number of modules. The usefulness of these concepts has not been demonstrated with quantitative data. Rather, 'intuitive' reasoning has been used in the literature when describing these concepts. Hierarchical functional design for programs was also discussed by Stay (1976), the IBM HIPO manual, Walston and Felix (1977), and Rehling (1977).

Gilb defines distinctness as a measure of the failure-point independence of one piece of software with that of another piece performing the same function. The measuring tool is the ratio of the number of bugs in the first module alone to the number of bugs in the first module which simultaneously occur in the second. The following classes of errors are purportedly detectable and correctable using distinct software: design errors leading to system errors, resource problems, numeric errors, order code error, timing errors, data transmission and software errors.

The *performance metrics* described by Gilb are: *efficiency*, *effectiveness*, and *transformation*.

Efficiency is defined as the ratio of useful work performed to the total energy expended, while effectiveness is a group measure comparing: operational reliability, system readiness and design adequacy. Efficiency and effectiveness are tradeoffs against each other. For example, it might be very effective to do triple verification of data registration by operators, but it would be very inefficient.

A transformation measure is the energy or resources needed to convert data from one state to another. The measurement may be in such terms as money, time, personnel, electricity, or logical cycles. The measure is important to measure the effect (in performance) of changes to algorithms, modules, etc.

Gilb's *resource metrics* are: *financial datametrics*, *time resource datametrics*, and *space metrics*. Financial datametrics include: total system cost, incremental costs, capital investments, operational costs, and return on investment. Time resource datametrics include measures of computer time and personnel time. Space metrics involve the amount of space (bits, words, characters, etc.) for storing data.

Finally, Gilb includes *diverse metrics* of *information*, *data*, *evolution*, and *stability*. Information is the interpretation of data, and is not directly measurable. Data has many possible forms which should be taken into account when measuring. Bits are useful measures of data when relating to machine cost. Evolution (the designed characteristic of a system development which involves stepwise change) may be measured by such indicators as: number of program instructions changed; percentage of instruction manuals changed; number of new data elements in a database, etc.

Stability (the measure of lack of perceivable change in spite of an occurrence which would normally cause change) is given as a percentage of change in a system due to a change in environment. An example would be the percentage of the original number of payroll programs changed due to a change in tax laws.

This lengthy enumeration of metrics is more provocative than productive. Gilb's work does open up your mind to fresh possibilities, but the reality of applying these ideas is disheartening. Many of the metrics are difficult to obtain, and even if we can compute a value, we have no sense of the range of good values. The lack of independence of the metrics adds to the confusing complexity and makes it difficult for programmers to predict the effect of a program change on a group of metrics. Still, Gilb's pioneering effort is significant because he puts us solidly on the yellow brick road to the Emerald City of software quality measurement.

5.4 HALSTEAD'S SOFTWARE SCIENCE

Halstead's software science (Halstead, 1977; Fitzsimmons and Love, 1978) approaches the human preparation of computer programs using 'methods and principles of classical experimental science.' Halstead's method is based upon the ability to count, for any program, the number of unique operators (such as IF, =, DO, PRINT) ($n1$), the number of unique operands (such as variables or constants) ($n2$) the total usage of the operators ($N1$), the total usage of the operands ($N2$) the number of occurrences ($F1j$) of the jth most frequently occuring operator where $j=1,2,...,n1$ and the number of occurrences ($F2j$) of the jth most frequently used operand where $j=1,2,...,n2$.

From these basics, Halstead defines the vocabulary n as:

$$n = n1 + n2$$

and the implementation length as:

$$N = N1 + N2$$

For example, Figure 5-3 shows a 13-line FORTRAN subroutine and tables giving operator and operand counts. $n1$ the number of unique operators is 10, and $n2$ the number of unique operands is 7 giving a vocabulary, n, of 17. $N1$ the usage of operators is 28 and $N2$ the usage of operands is 22, giving an implementation length, N ,of 50. An equation for implementation length (Figure 5-4) was tested on 14 algorithms published in *Communications of the Association For Computing Machinery* (*CACM*) in 1961. The observed length N and the predicted length N' for the 14 algorithms were surprisingly close. Verification of these equations using larger samples was accomplished at the Computing

```
      SUBROUTINE SORT (X, N)
      DIMENSION X(N)
      IF (N .LT. 2) RETURN
      DO 20 I = 2,N
         DO 10 J = 1,I
            IF (X(I) .GE. X(J))GO TO 10
            SAVE = X(I)
            X(I) = X(J)
            X(J) = SAVE
   10 CONTINUE
   20 CONTINUE
      RETURN
      END
```

	Operator	Count
1	End of statement	7
2	Array subscript	6
3	=	5
4	IF ( )	2
5	DO	2
6	,	2
7	End of program	1
8	.LT.	1
9	.GE.	1
$n_1 = 10$	GO TO 10	1
		$28 = N_1$

	Operand	Count
1	X	6
2	I	5
3	J	4
4	N	2
5	2	2
6	SAVE	2
$n_2 = 7$	1	1
		$22 = N_2$

Figure 5-3: Sort program and Halstead frequency counts for operators and operands (Fitzsimmons and Love, 1978).

Center of Purdue University, by James Elshoff of General Motors Research Laboratories (1976c, 1978), Love and Bowman of General Electric (1976), and others.

A second metric, called volume, was developed by Halstead to measure program size. Size must be measurable in order to quantitatively

Halstead's Metrics

Length Equation

a. $N' = n_1 \log_2 n_1 + n_2 \log_2 n_2$

Volume Metric

b. $V = N \log_2 n$

Potential Volume

c. $V^* = (2 + n_2^*) \log_2 (2 + n_2^*)$

Boundary Volume

d. $V^{**} = (2 + n_2^* \log_2 n_2^*) \log_2 (2 + n_2^*)$

Relations between Operators and Operands

e1. $A = (V^{**} - V^*)/V^*$

e2. $B = n_2^* - 2(V^{**} - V^*)/V$

e3. $n_2 = A n_1 + B$

e4. $A = ((n_2^*)/(n_2^* + 2)) \log_2 (n_2^*/2)$

$B = n_2^* - 2A$

Program Level

f1. $L = V^*/V$

f2. $L^{-} = ((n_1^*/n_1))(n_2/N_2)$

f3. $L^{-} = n_1^*/n_1$

f4. $L^{-} = n_2/N_2$

Intelligence Count

g1. $I = L^{-} \times V$

g2. $I = ((2/n_1)(n_2/N_2))(N_1 + N_2) \log_2 (N_1 + n_2)$

Programming Effort

h1. $E = V/L$

Time Equation

i1. $T^{-} = (n_1 N_2 (n_1 \log_2 n_1 + n_2 \log_2 n_2) \log_2 n)/2 n_2 S$

Language Level

j1. $\lambda = LV^*$

j2. $\lambda = L(L \times V) = L$ squared times V

Time Equation

$T = E/S$

Error Equation

$E = (V^*)$ squared times λ squared

$B = E/E(0)$

where $E(0)$ = mean no. of elementary discriminations between partial errors in programming and B = no. delivered errors.

Figure 5-4: Halstead's software science equations.

measure the size changes which occur when an algorithm is converted from one language to another. Halstead's volume metric,

$$V = N(log2\ n),$$

gives program volume in dimensions of bits, making it independent of the character set of the language used to express the algorithm. For the sort program of Figure 5-3 the volume is 205. Halstead derives the equation for potential volume, V^*, or minimal volume to take into account the possibility of defining an algorithm in a more powerful language (thus reducing volume). The potential volume, V^*, does not change as an algorithm is translated from one language to another but actual volume, V, does.

Halstead considers the question of how the number of unique operators, $n1$, varies with the number of unique operands, $n2$. Equation e3 is used to calculate an estimated value of $n2$ using values of $n2^*$ and $n1$ (where $n2^*$ is the minimal value of the number of unique operands). A comparison of observed and calculated values for $n2$ has regularly produced correlation coefficients above .95.

The metric of program level was developed by Halstead to compare implementations of an algorithm in alternative languages. Without a quantitative measure for program level, alternative implementations can be ranked only on an intuitive basis. Halstead defines program level as potential volume divided by program volume. He derives the equation in terms of operators and operands (Figure 5-4, equation f4). As with other metrics, Halstead 'validates' this metric by comparing observed and measured values getting a correlation coefficient of 0.90.

The intelligence count metric is a measure of 'how much a program says' and is defined as the program level times the volume. The equation derived is language independent. This was demonstrated by calculating the intelligence count, I, for Euclid's algorithm in ALGOL, PL/I, FORTRAN, ASSEMBLY, POTENTIAL Language, and TABLE-LOOK-UP. The I value for PL/I was 13, for FORTRAN, 11, for the others, 12. This metric can also be used to give the content count for English passages.

Halstead defines a 'pure' algorithm as one without those constructs (impurities) that would prevent an algorithm from conforming to the relationships observed in deriving his metrics. He defines six impurities:

1) Complementary operations (i.e. the successive application of two complementary operations to the same operand).
2) Ambiguous operands (i.e. the use of a given operand name to refer to different things in different parts of the program).
3) Synonymous operands (use of two different names for the same thing).

4) Common subexpressions (failure to assign and use a name for a specific combination of terms).
5) Unwarranted assignment (assignment of a unique name to a combination of terms with one use of the name).
6) Unfactored terms.

Removal of these impurities from a program improves agreement between V^* and VL. Novice programmers often write programs with many impurities while writers of programs published in the literature use almost none. The unwarranted assignment seems to be a questionable impurity. Simplification of a large complicated mathematical formula by assignment of a unique name to a part of it, then using the unique name once, can make modification easier. Also, if part of the equation is a recognizable mathematical formula, use of such a name can enhance clarity.

Halstead derives a metric of programming effort (i.e. the total number of elementary mental discriminations required to generate a program, E) as:

$$E = V/L.$$

He includes the time element by introducing the concept of 'moment' (the time required for the human brain to perform the most elementary discrimination) estimating that 5 to 20 moments (denoted by S) occur per second. A time equation (Figure 5-4, equation i1) is expressed using S. Experiments using the *CACM* algorithms in PL/I, FORTRAN, and APL; programs from textbooks; and machine language programs indicate that the time equation gives a good (a difference of 12.2 percent for the machine language experiments) estimate of the implementation time actually observed (Gordon and Halstead, 1976).

The language level metric (Figure 5-4, equation j1) provides a measurement which may be used to determine whether a 'higher level' language offers improvement over a previous language.

The applications of Halstead's theory include: estimation of programming time (based on the relationships of programming time to $n2^*$ and language level, using an S of 18 discriminations per second); estimation of program size; estimation of the initial number of errors to be expected in a given program; and estimating the number of delivered bugs in a program. Halstead approaches the question of optimum modularization from the following viewpoints: (1) equalization of length, (2) minimization of modular potential volume, (3) limiting length of error free programs, and (4) psychological concepts of 'chunks.' From these four approaches Halstead derives a single relationship:

$$M = n2^*/6,$$

Where M = the number of modules; $n2^*$ = the conceptually unique input and output parameters in an algorithm. He says that programs modularized according to his scheme, will be easy to write, debug, comprehend, and maintain.

IBM demonstrated another possible application of Halstead's theory by applying the software relationships to hardware circuitry which was expressed as a computer program. A final application was demonstrated by Elci who used the software science relationships to yield reasonably accurate estimates of the numbers of instructions required for 40 different operating systems.

Halstead's software science is appealing, the experimental evidence convincing, and the psychological foundations reasonably sturdy. It might be useful to have compilers compute and print Halstead's metrics for each compilation to provide direct feedback to programmers. But, even if experience proves Halstead's approach valuable, it is not complete since it ignores specific issues, such as choice of mnemonic variable names, comments, control flow complexity and choice of algorithms or data structures; and general issues, such as portability, flexibility and efficiency.

5.5 PROGRAMMING PRODUCTIVITY MEASURES

The measurement and evaluation of programming productivity are addressed by Zak (1977) and Walston and Felix (1977). Zak lists the following five productivity attributes: correctness, ability to achieve schedules (related to development cost and time), adaptability, efficiency and freedom from bugs. He concedes that there is controversy concerning what variables should be measured and what effect they have on productivity. Zak gives the following metric for programming rate:

$$R = L/(ST)$$

where R is the programming rate in lines of source code per person-month; L is the lines of code in the finished product; S is the staffing level; and T is the calendar time (scheduled) in months. Zak includes survey results from 43 managers and technicians regarding the variables that effect programmer productivity. The consensus was that the following are the most relevant: quality of the external documentation; programming language; availability of tools; programmer experience in data processing; programmer experience in the functional area; effect of project communication; independent modules for individual assignment; and well-defined programming practices. Zak presents experimental results (Weinberg and Schulman, 1974) from a study in which five experienced programming teams worked on the same program. Each team was given a different objective (minimum core, output clarity, program clarity, minimum source statements, minimum hours). When productivity was evaluated in terms of the primary objectives, each team ranked first in its primary objective. This demonstrates that programmer productivity can be influenced by indicating to programmers what the goals are.

Walston and Felix (1977) emphasize a search for a method of estimating programmer productivity. The method described in their work involves measuring productivity by the lines of code by project (not for individual programmers). Walston and Felix used questionnaires submitted by line project managers at regular reporting periods. Sixty projects ranging from 4000 to 467,000 lines of code with an expenditure of from 12 to 11,758 person-months are in the database. A wide variety of programs written in 28 high-level languages and using 66 different computers was included. The database contains individual project information such as: number of delivered lines of source code, pages of documentation delivered, source languages used, total effort to produce source code, duration of the project in months, and use of improved programming techniques (that is, structured programming, top-down development, chief programmer team, and design and code inspections) expressed as a percentage of code using each technique. From the database one may derive the productivity, which is defined as the ratio of the delivered source lines of code and the average number of people required to work on the project (computed by dividing the total effort in person-months by the duration of the project in calendar months).

Walston and Felix plot the data relating the delivered lines of code, L, and the total effort in person-months, E, in the log-log domain so that they become approximately linear. When the linear coefficients are transformed back to the original domain of the data, they become power relationships. A least squares fit for the plotted data yields

$$E = 5.2L$$

where L = thousands of lines of delivered source code. Critics argue that the high variance and the use of log-log plots makes this result ineffective for prediction or planning.

Walston and Felix identify 29 variables (Figure 5-5) which show a high correlation with productivity. These variables are combined into a productivity index, I, which is computed as follows:

$$I = \text{SUM}(W(i)X(i)) \qquad i = 1...29\text{(number of variables)},$$

where $W(i)$ = question weight calculated as 1/2 log (base 10) of the ratio of total productivity change indicated for a given question. $X(i)$ = question response (+, 0, -), depending on whether the response indicates increased, nominal, or decreased productivity. An index was computed for 51 projects and a plot of actual productivity for each project versus the computed I and the least squares relationship was made.

1. Customer interface complexity.
2. User participation in definition of requirements.
3. Customer-originated program design changes.
4. Customer experience with the application area of the project.
5. Overall personnel experience and qualifications.
6. Percentage of programmers doing development who participated in the design of functional specifications.
7. Previous experience with operational computers.
8. Previous experience with programming languages.
9. Previous experience with applications of similar or greater size and complexity.
10. Ratio of average staff size to duration (people/mo.).
11. Hardware under concurrent development.
12. Development computer access, open under special request.
13. Development computer access, closed.
14. Classified security environment for computer and 25% of programs and data.
15. Structured programming.
16. Design and code inspections.
17. Top-down development.
18. Chief programmer team usage.
19. Overall complexity of code developed.
20. Complexity of application processing.
21. Complexity of program flow.
22. Overall constraints of program design.
23. Program design constraints on main storage.
24. Program design constraints on timing.
25. Code for real time or interactive operation or executing under severe timing constraint.
26. Percentage of code for delivery.
27. Code classified as nonmathematical application and I/0 formatting programs.
28. Number of classes of items in the data base per 1000 lines.
29. Number of pages of delivered documentation per 1000 lines of delivered code.

Figure 5-5: Variables that correlate with programming productivity (Walston and Felix, 1977).

Other conclusions drawn by Walston and Felix are that productivity is highest when there is no 'original' or reused source code for a project and that productivity decreases when the development effort is spread over more than one location. They discovered, by plotting the relationship between documentation and delivered code, that the number of pages of delivered documentation varies directly as the number of lines of source code. They illustrate, via graphs, the relationships: project duration and delivered code; average staff size and total effort; computer cost and total effort.

Walston and Felix's efforts are based on measuring programmer productivity by lines of code. When using lines of code as a productivity measure, care must be taken to ensure that programmers do not deliberately lengthen code, biasing the measurement. The use of lines of code as a productivity measure assumes that programmers adhere to programming standards, ensuring that they do not produce 'poorer' code in an effort to produce more lines.

5.6 RELIABILITY

Reliability of a data processing system involves not only hardware reliability but also the operating staff and software reliability. Hardware reliability can be quantitatively evaluated rather easily in terms of the period of time that elapses between hardware failures (that is, the mean time between failures, MTBF). By sampling the time until failure of many copies of the same part, a vendor can determine the distribution and describe the lifetime of parts probabilistically. The 'bug counting' methods proposed for quantitatively evaluating software are analogous to the methods for predicting hardware reliability. One of the earliest of the software reliability models was developed by Jelinski and Moranda (Gilb, 1977; Musa, 1977; Brooks and Weiler, 1977). Their hypothesis is that the error detection rate is proportional to the number of errors remaining in a program. The model assumes that the time between error occurrences is exponential and that each error is immediately corrected. Jelinski and Moranda obtained failure rate data from NASA and the Navy Tactical Data System. Shooman (Schick, Wolverton, 1977; Brooks and Weiler, 1977) derives a software reliability model for predicting the mean time between failures (MTBF). His exponential model (1977) assumes:

1) The total number of errors in a program is fixed.
2) If we record the cumulative number of errors corrected during debugging, then the difference represents the remaining bugs.
3) We will never find all errors.
4) Most programs reach a reasonably debugged state.

He also evaluated the ratio of software errors to program size, saying that a designer can estimate the number of errors by program size. Like the Jelinski-Moranda model, Shooman's model assumes that the failure rate is proportional to the number of software errors remaining in a program. It also assumes that introduction of errors when correcting others is negligible.

Brooks and Weiler (1977) contend that the Jelinski-Moranda model is merely a special case of the Shooman model (a case where one error is discovered and removed at a time) and that the Shooman model is the 'general' one. G. Hansen (1977) is another proponent of the 'bug counting' method and views software reliability in terms of MTBF. He contends that when a software package is first released, there are only a few users so that there are few failures (giving a fictitiously high MTBF). During the next two or three years the MTBF rises slightly as obvious errors are eliminated. Later, when there are more users and more testing, the MTBF drops significantly. Then the software matures and the MTBF sharply increases. Hansen gives the following formula for MTBF:

$$MTBF = ((N) + (N\text{-}1) + \ldots + (N\text{-}I))C \; / \; M$$

where N = number of copies of a product in use for a given year; M = number of bugs encountered in a given year; C = estimate of number hours the product is used in one year; I = number of years the product has been used. Like Shooman, Hansen concludes that size and complexity greatly affect MTBF.

Musa (1975, 1977) is another of the 'bug counters' who states that the mean time to failure 'offers promise of a good monitoring metric.' Musa says that a model superior to the Jelinski-Moranda and Shooman models could be constructed if one (when predicting a measure of MTBF) first thought in terms of execution time (rather than elapsed time) then tried to relate execution time to calendar time. Parr (1977), in his critique of bug counting methods, says that Musa's statement amounts to the observation that the intensity of testing and the observed failure rate of a software system can be adjusted directly by testing at a different rate. Musa's theory is being applied to projects ranging from 3 to 300 people and 5000 to 20,000 lines of code and which include such applications as real time control systems, business systems, and systems including large data bases.

The bug or error counting models, particularly those of Jelinski-Moranda and Shooman, are criticized by Parr and Littlewood (1977). Parr feels that the bug counting methods, which assume that future failure rates are predicted on the basis of past bug history, fail to consider internal program structure. He states that the false analogy between hardware and software reliability is the root of most of the problems with the bug counting models. He emphasizes that, unlike a hardware system, there is no degradation of parts with time and that repair is not made by replacing parts. Parr claims that there is no probabilistic model describing failure behavior of software parts and that errors are design problems. Parr complains that the observed failure rate can be altered by the choice of input cases that are likely or unlikely to create software problems. He states that MTBF can be biased by removal of easy errors first, by desk debugging, or rerunning tests.

Parr points out that for large-scale systems which are maintained for long periods, functional requirements change causing additional problems in failure interval analysis. The error counting methods, according to Parr, are best suited to very short term forecasting where the main effort is in removal of errors because the method does not provide for building information about development planned for software.

Littlewood is also critical of bug counting methods, saying that Shooman's assumptions are naive and that he has never seen a program where the assumption that software failure rate is proportional to the remaining number of errors is valid. Littlewood writes that operational reliability should be measured, repairs should be assumed to be instantaneous and that only execution time should be considered. He emphasizes that software has no natural degradation and that once it is perfect, it will not fail and the MTBF is infinite.

Littlewood took the failure rate as the critical measurement and modeled reliability improvement in a Bayesian fashion. He contends that his own model is flexible and that it allows exact distribution of time to failure to be computed, but recognizes that there should be many rather than one reliability metric. His reasoning for preferring a Bayesian method is that subjective interpretation of probability seems more appropriate for software than the 'frequential approach' and that Bayes theorem allows continuous updating of previous reliability measures as new data is used. Littlewood also believes that a program may become progressively worse if failures are frequent enough. He agrees with Mill's conjecture that never finding the first bug gives more confidence in program reliability than finding the 'last.'

Gilb (1977) references a TRW (TRW-SS-74-14) report summarizing an experiment in reliability measurement. In the experiment, two programs based on the same specifications but written by two different programmers were evaluated. The first version was written in a simple and straightforward way by an engineering oriented programmer while the second was written by a 'superprogrammer' who used 'clever loops and tricks.' Based on TRW's criteria for complexity and documentation, version 1 was estimated as being 95.8 percent reliable while version 2 was rated as 89.3 percent reliable. Results of 1000 tests gave ratings of 99.7 and 96.3 respectively for versions 1 and 2. The pretesting metric, based on the intuitive assumption that reliability and complexity are related, predicted the more reliable program. This simple study with only two subjects is interesting, but verification with more subjects is necessary.

There is a plethora of literature dealing with reliability and reliability models, but there does not seem to be a uniform, accurate, and practical approach to predicting and measuring reliability. More research is needed to collect software error data and to analyze it in order to improve methods of reliability prediction and measurement. We need better models which are based on performance data and discriminate among different programs or programming environments.

5.7 MAINTAINABILITY

Software maintenance, which is the major programming cost in most installations, is affected by design decisions such as: data structures, logical structure, documentation, diagnostic tools; and human considerations such as specialization, experience, training, intelligence, motivation. In addition, organizational considerations such as: geographical access to the problem, alternative plans, organizational communication, responsibility, and measuring procedures influence software maintenance efforts. Design techniques such as inspections, automated audits of comments, test path analysis programs, use of pseudocode documentation, dual maintenance of source code, modularity and structured program logic flow are generally accepted means for improving the maintainability of software.

Gilb (1977) discusses the use of historical data in a real system to construct a hypothetical maintainability curve. Job repair statistics noting the number of program repairs and the time needed to do them are used to construct a curve indicating the different probabilities of repair within certain time limits. This method might be accurate for monitoring a program to insure that it still meets design specifications. For example, suppose that the original specifications stated that 95 percent of all bugs causing serious problems should be repaired within an hour. If for 100 bugs repaired, the maximum time for the repair of 95 was 50 minutes and the average time was 30 minutes, and the worst single repair time was 10 hours, the program maintainability satisfies the design specifications. Similar methods may be written into contracts with software vendors. In the event that software fails to perform as specified in the contract, the vendor would be held financially responsible.

Another maintainability measurement is 'bebugging' (also called seeding or capture/recapture by Schick and Wolverton (1978) and 'inspection statistics' by Mills). It is based on intentional and random insertion of errors into a source program to calibrate the error finding process. Gilb describes a bebugging experiment in which five groups of programmers were timed as they searched for a seeded bug. Group one was given a commented listing; group two was told the class of error; group three was given input data and the resulting output; group four was given the same input with 'correct' output; and group five was told exactly which line number should be corrected. Results of this experiment indicate that simple source program reading is more effective than use of test data; it was more difficult than anticipated for experienced programmers to find bugs; and variations between individuals in homogeneously selected groups of programmers are at least 2 to 1 and up to 10 to 1.

Gilb recommends the use of an adapted 'bebugging' method as a maintainability measurement. He compares bebugging to the zoologist's method of estimating the number of fish in a lake. A large sample (say 1000) of fish are marked and allowed to mix with the total lake population. If a new sample of 1000 are then removed and 50 are marked, we can estimate a population of 20000. This assumes that the original sample was random and representative and that the remainder of fish (or errors) is homogeneous.

Assume that a program has 100 seeded bugs. During debugging, of 550 bugs located, 50 are 'seeded.' We can assume that since 50 are 'real bugs,' 500 real bugs of the type corresponding to the seeded bugs remain. A major issue in bebugging is insuring that the seeded bugs represent the 'native' bugs. Gilb suggests collecting statistics by error type from real programs. Another method is to assume that any source statement type can cause a bug and to insert bugs proportional to the frequency of statement types. However, this method seems counterintuitive -- certain source statement types are more prone to contain bugs than others.

Gilb reports that Lipow of TRW has used bebugging to estimate the probability distribution of remaining software errors. Lipow assumes that the probability of finding an error is constant; it does not depend on the number of errors already found, and only one error can be found during one test. Using Lipow's method, one can make observations regarding the maximum number of bugs that might remain, the least number, and the percentage of certainty that there are no more than 'x' number of bugs left. Historical data about the cost of finding and repairing bugs would serve as a basis for estimating the probable completion date, amount of computer testing required, and human resources needed to meet the schedule.

5.8 COMPLEXITY/COMPREHENSION

5.8.1 Logical, Structural, and Psychological Complexity

Program complexity can be logical, structural or psychological. Logical complexity involves program characteristics which make proofs of correctness difficult, long, or not possible. For example, the increase in the number of distinct program paths increases logical complexity. Psychological complexity refers to characteristics which make it difficult for humans to understand software. For this section, the term complexity will be used to mean logical complexity and comprehensibility will be used for psychological complexity. Such quantitative measures as the number of 'IF' statements is a useful complexity measure because it is easily automated. Other rough measures of program module complexity are the module size (number of lines) and the number of nonnormal exits from a decision statement (IF, ON, AT END, etc.). Logical complexity has been found to be a good predictor of program cost. It also has potential for predicting and explaining relationships with other system properties such as effort, reliability, flexibility, and performance (Gilb, 1977).

5.8.2 McCabe's Complexity Measure

McCabe (1976) describes a graph–theoretic complexity measure and illustrates its use in managing, testing and controlling program complexity. The theory assumes that complexity is not dependent on size (that adding or subtracting functional statements does not change complexity) and that complexity depends only on the decision structure of a program.

McCabe provides a mathematical technique which offers a quantitative basis for modularization and allows identification of modules that will be difficult to test or maintain. McCabe says that merely restricting module size does not ensure 'good' modularization and points out that a 50 line module with 25 'IF–THEN' constructs can have 33.5 million distinct control paths.

His approach is to measure and control the number of paths through a program. Mathematical preliminaries include the definition of the *cyclomatic number* $V(G)$ of a graph with n vertices, e edges and p connected components as:

$$V(G) = e - n + p$$

McCabe utilizes the following theorem: In a strongly connected graph, G, the cyclomatic number is equal to the maximum number of linearly independent circuits.

In applying the theorem, McCabe associates a one exit digraph with a program. Each node in the graph corresponds to a block of code where flow is sequential and each arc corresponds to a program branch. Each node can be reached from the entry node and each node can reach the exit node. Figure 5–6 shows an application of the theorem to a program control graph. This graph is *strongly connected* because there is a path joining any pair of arbitrary distinct vertices Thus the maximum number of linearly independent circuits in the graph is $9 - 6 + 2$.

The general strategy is to measure program complexity by computing the number of linearly independent paths, the cyclomatic complexity, $V(G)$, controlling the 'size' of programs by limiting $V(G)$ and using $V(G)$ as the basis for a testing methodology.

McCabe's experience with the complexity measure includes the use of a tool called FLOW (written in APL) which accepts FORTRAN source code and breaks a job into subroutines, analyzing the control structures of each subroutine. McCabe remarks that one can often recognize an individual programmer's 'style' by noting similar patterns in the graphs generated by the tool. McCabe found that an upper bound of 10 was reasonable for the cyclomatic complexity. When programmers in his organization exceed this, they either must recode or modularize. In one instance where 24 FORTRAN programs ranged in complexity from 16 to 64, the programmers revealed that these routines were chosen for analysis because they were 'problem' routines.

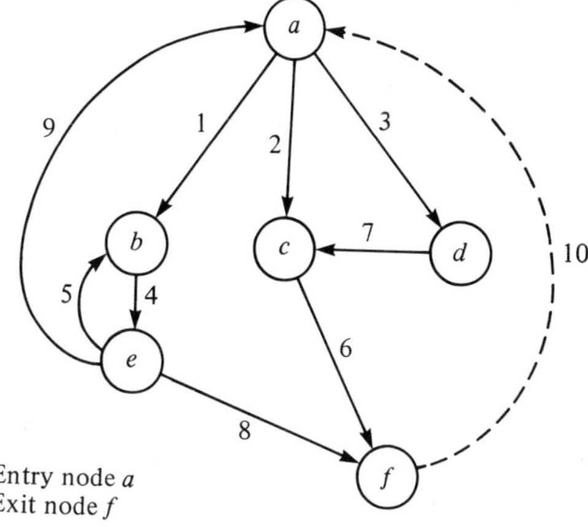

Figure 5-6: Example of graph theoretic complexity measurement (McCabe, 1976).

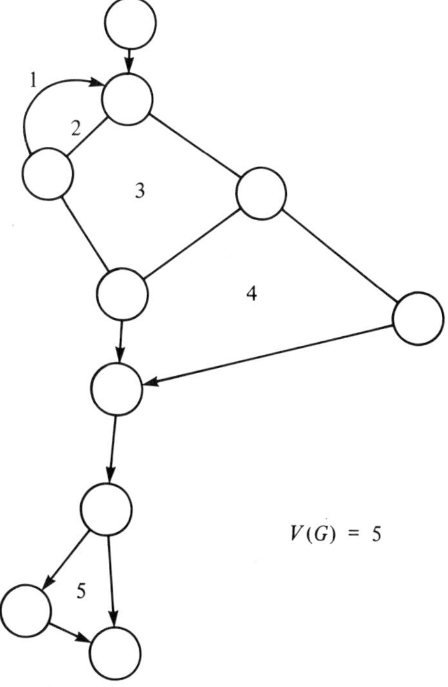

Figure 5-7: Region counting gives cyclomatic complexity (McCabe, 1976).

McCabe presents two simplified calculation methods. The first involves adding one to the number of predicates. Compound predicates such as IF A AND B are counted as two predicates. The second method requires use of Euler's theorem: If G is a connected planar graph with n vertices, e edges, and r regions, then:

$$n - e + r = 2.$$

By rearranging the terms we get the cyclomatic complexity equal to the number of regions (Figure 5-7).

McCabe comments on structured versus nonstructured constructs and describes a measure for 'structuredness.' He feels that there are instances where an unstructured construct is best but that a definition of the unstructured components of a program and a measure of program structuredness are needed to distinguish between those programmers who wisely use unstructured constructs and those who do not. He illustrates four control structures (Figure 5-8) which give all unstructured programs and states a number of theorems and results. Graphs 5-8(a-d) are described as follows:

a) branching out of a loop
b) branching into a loop
c) branching into a decision
d) branching out of a decision.

A nonstructured program contains at least two of the graphs and has a cyclomatic complexity of at least three. Essential complexity, ev, is defined to reflect lack of structure as follows:

$$ev = v - n$$

McCabe addresses the relationship between testing and cyclomatic complexity. He states that if a program has a calculated complexity of v and the number of paths tested is ac (actual complexity) and $ac < v$, then:

1) there are more paths to be tested, or
2) v - ac decisions can be removed, or
3) portions of the program can be reduced to inline code (that is, complexity has been increased to conserve space).

McCabe's cyclomatic complexity approach is a helpful tool in preparing test data and may provide useful information related to program complexity. However, his metric ignores choice of data structures, algorithms, mnemonic variable names, or comments; and it avoids important considerations such as portability, flexibility, and efficiency. Additional work is necessary to clarify the conditions under which cyclomatic complexity can be useful.

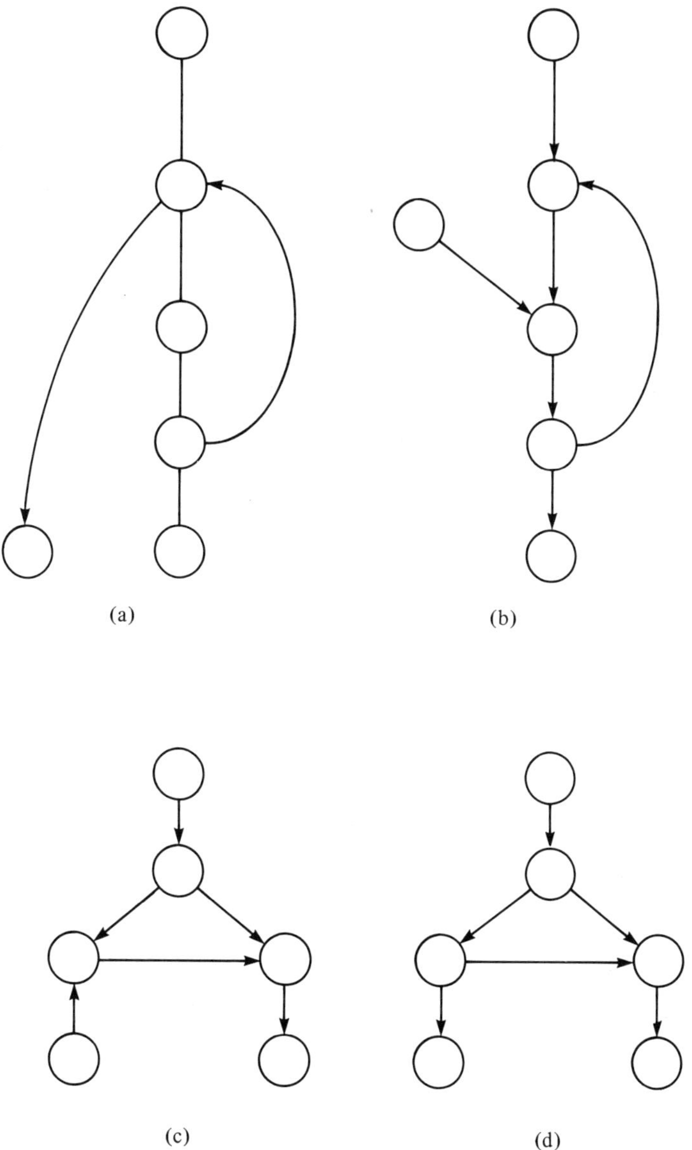

Figure 5-8: Four unstructured program graphs (McCabe, 1976).

5.8.3 Structural Complexity

Stevens, Constantine and Meyers (1974) describe structural complexity, which may be measured in terms of absolute or relative. *Absolute structural complexity* is a measure of the number of modules while *relative structural complexity* is the ratio of the number of module linkages to the number of modules. Stevens et al. identify and examine types of connections between modules which could be considered as measures of structural complexity. No experimental evidence is given to support the measures. Connections are defined as being references to labels or addresses defined outside a module. The goal is to minimize the connections between modules, eliminating paths over which changes and errors could propagate. System complexity is also affected by the degree to which each connection couples two modules (that is, makes them interdependent). *Coupling* measures the strength of association between two modules. So, measuring coupling is a way of measuring complexity. Since coupling depends on other factors (how complicated the connection is; whether the connection refers to the module itself or something inside it; what is being sent or received), it is difficult to have one measure of coupling.

A quantifiable measure of system complexity is that of 'common environments,' which refer to the interfacing with the same area of storage, data region, or device by two or more modules. Since among n objects there are $n(n-1)$ ordered pairs, a common environment of N elements shared by M modules results in $NM(M-1)$ paths. A FORTRAN program of three modules sharing a COMMON area with 25 variables has 150 paths.

Interface complexity is the amount of information needed to state or understand the connection. The more syntactic units in the statement of a connection, the higher the coupling. For example, the greater the number of parameters in a call line, the higher the coupling.

The type of connection also affects coupling. A connection referencing an entire module by its name gives lower coupling than a connection referencing internal elements of the module. Coupling is also increased by passing a 'switch' from one module to tell the other module what to do.

Cohesiveness refers to the relationships among pieces of a module. *Binding* is a measure of the cohesiveness. The goal is 'high' binding. The scale of cohesiveness from lowest to highest is: coincidental, logical, temporal, communicative, sequential, and functional. Coincidental binding results when there is no meaningful relationship among elements in a module. Logical binding means there is some logical relationship between data elements; temporal binding implies that elements in a module are time related; communicational binding means that the module has elements that are related by a reference to the same input or output; in sequential binding, the output data from one element is input to the next element; and in functional binding, all the elements in the module are related to the performance of a single function. These characteristics described by Stevens et al. can be used as an indicator of software complexity.

5.8.4 Comprehensibility

Shneiderman (1977) has investigated: the facilitating effect of high-level and low-level comments for program modification; the correlation between recall and modification performances; and the relationship between comprehension and memory. Sheppard, Borst and Love (1978) conducted an experiment (as part of a research project designed to identify those software characteristics which are related to psychological complexity) to evaluate the effect of the following three independent variables: mnemonic variable names, complexity of control flow, and general program type on a programmer's understanding of a computer program. They also evaluated the contribution of Halstead's metric, E (the amount of effort required to generate a program) and McCabe's $V(G)$ (complexity measure) to the prediction of program understanding.

Sheppard et al. had 36 professional programmers (in five locations) as experimental subjects. The first exercise was a ten minute study of a short FORTRAN program and a five minute recall period in which a functionally equivalent program was to be reconstructed. This provided a basis for comparing the participants' skills and controlling for initial learning experience. Next, participants were presented with three programs which were studied for 25 minutes each and which were then to be recalled in 20 minutes. Three classes of programs (engineering, statistical, and nonnumeric) were used. Three levels of structure were also defined. One level adhered to the tenets of structured programming; the second was partially structured; the third was unstructured with backward transfers and arithmetic IF statements. There were also three levels of mnemonicity for variable names. Halstead's E and McCabe's $V(G)$ were computed for each of the 81 programs.

The experimental results indicate that the least structured program was the most difficult to reconstruct and the partially structured program was the easiest. No significant differences in performance were observed for mnemonic variable name level, nor did performance vary as a function of the order in which programs were presented to the participants. McCabe's $V(G)$ was found to be strongly correlated with program length (number of statements), while Halstead's E displayed only moderate relationships with length or $V(G)$. Length and $V(G)$ were moderately related to performance while E was not.

The experiment demonstrates that ability to correctly recall programs is influenced by individual differences in participants, program characteristics, and level of program structure.

A final suggestion for evaluating comprehensibility, and therefore program quality, is to use memorization/reconstruction. I propose (Shneiderman, 1978b) that every module should meet a 90–10 rule -- a competent programmer should be able to reconstruct functionally 90 percent of the program after 10 minutes of study. The competent programmer theory of software psychology is akin to the 'reasonable man (or woman) theory of justice.' This suggestion is based on the assumption that a competent programmer (that is, someone who is potentially responsible for maintenance) should be able to grasp the module's meaning and operation in approximately 10 minutes. A more casual approach would be the 80-20 rule and more rigorous standards would imply a 95–5 rule. This concept, based on several memorization/reconstruction experiments (see Section 2.5.6 and Chapter 4), needs testing and validation.

5.9 PRACTITIONER'S SUMMARY

Quality can be controlled and improved. The first step is to make explicit to all project participants what quality characteristics are critical. A manager can guide team members by indicating whether on-time delivery, efficient use of resources, or maintainability is the dominant goal. This crude guidance can be refined by selecting specific metrics for performance and defining goals using these metrics. Detailed tabulation of time spent by each programmer, time spent on each module, and error patterns can provide helpful guidance in predicting project completion, forecasting performance, evaluating personnel, and improving procedures on future projects. Unfortunately, no acceptable set of metrics has emerged. Project managers may wish to try several to determine which work best for their environment.

5.10 RESEARCHER'S AGENDA

Gilb's metrics, Halstead's software science, reliabilty models based on bug counting, bebugging, performance based strategies, McCabe's metrics and memorization are possibilities which merit further testing. The erratic performance of these metrics suggests that researchers have not yet been able to account for a sufficient portion of the variance in performance. A commercially acceptable approach would have to be more reliable than these approaches have been. A sound theoretical understanding of human performance in programming could lead to the design of improved metrics, but verification must be carried out experimentally.

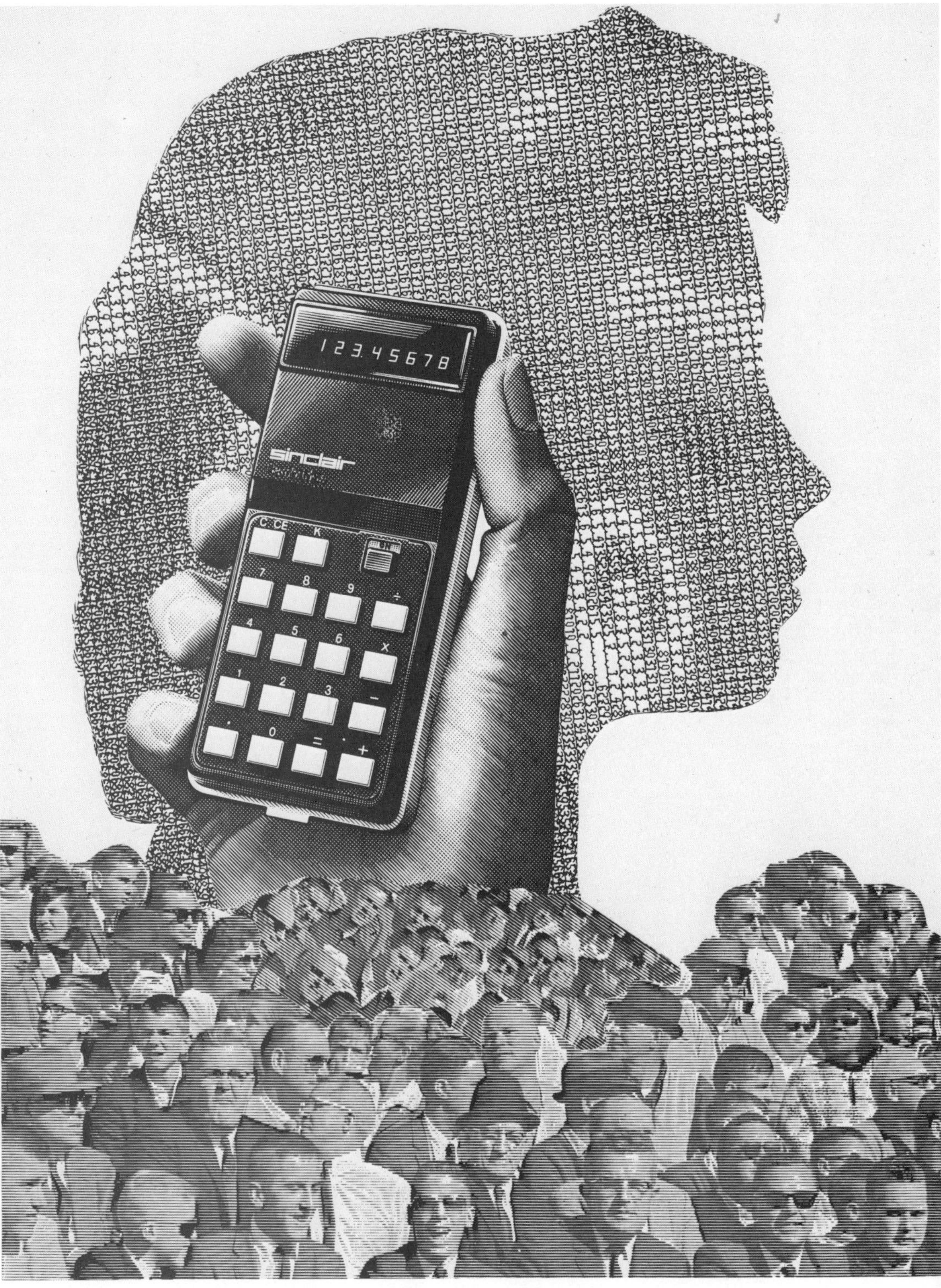
123.45678
sinclair
C CE
K
7
8
9
÷
4
5
6
x
1
2
3
−
·
0
=
+

6

TEAM ORGANIZATIONS AND GROUP PROCESSES

This is a Man Age. The machines are simply tools which man has devised to help him do a better job.

Thomas J. Watson

Team organizations for developing reliable computer programs on schedule – conventional team – egoless team – chief programmer team – group processes for detecting errors, improving communication and training novices – inspections – walkthroughs – formal technical reviews – MECCA method – peer review – group testing

6.1 INTRODUCTION

The first two decades of programming history produced the image of the introverted, isolated programmer surrounded by stacks of output. Other workers have left the office but our intense programmer, ignoring the absence of colleagues, scribbles rapidly, with a felt tip pen, in hopes of eliminating the last annoying bug before a 9 AM deadline. Fortunately this image is becoming only a wild caricature of reality. The lonely days of the programming frontier are giving way to community, interdependency and stability. This passage is happening gradually –– the pioneers still resent the settler groups and seek to preserve their freedom and independence. Personality studies of programmers (Couger and Zawacki, 1978) still show their social need for interaction is significantly lower than for many other professionals. The image of the programmer as a 'loner' appears to have some validity, but it is hopefully changing. Table 6–1 shows the extremely low social need of programmers compared to other workers. The high growth needs and the high potential for motivation of data processing professionals is also apparent.

Although some mourn the passage of the days of explorers and pioneers, the benefits of stable civilization, which depends on social interaction, are attractive. Pioneering individuals are necessary, but their productivity and reliability are erratic. As organizations become more dependent on computerized systems, production schedules cannot be violated, maintenance must be fast, and error rates must be low. To satisfy these needs, managers are turning to novel team organization strategies such as egoless programming teams or chief programmer teams; and to group review processes such as structured walkthroughs and code inspections. Although individual accomplishments will always be critical, the importance of group processes is increasing.

6.2 TEAM ORGANIZATIONS

Most professional programming projects require individuals to be organized into teams or even groups of teams. The best structure for a team will depend on the number of people, their experience, their personality, the project, and the organizational environment (Metzger, 1973).

6.2.1 The Conventional Team

The conventional approach to team structure is to have a senior programmer direct the work of several junior programmers. With experience the senior programmer may become a project leader, directing several teams, and the junior programmers may become senior programmers. This traditional hierarchical approach is appealing because competence is rewarded by promotion, responsibility/authority lines are clear, and it is simple to understand. The project leader may direct 3 to 10 teams and the senior programmer may direct 3 to 10 junior programmers. Assignments are made by superiors, work is done individually, and progress is evaluated by superiors. Competition among team members is seen as a healthy stimulus to high performance levels.

Critics of the conventional approach argue that programming is different from other fields, such as marketing where each salesperson has similar tasks and interaction is low. These critics claim that programmers are working on specialized portions of a highly interrelated project, that programming is a complex task with a variety of phases, each demanding different skills, and that the errors of one individual can interfere with another's performance. A further complaint about the conventional team

	Social Need	Growth Need	Motivating Potential
DP professionals	4.19	6.02	157.5
Sales	5.41	5.70	146.0
Other professionals	5.48	5.59	153.7
Service	5.45	5.38	151.7
Managerial	5.65	5.30	155.9
Clerical	5.21	4.95	105.9
Structural work	5.14	4.54	140.6

Table 6-1: Survey results on personality issues (Couger and Zawacki, 1978).

is that the most competent programmers are promoted to managerial positions where they may be incompetent and where their skills as a programmer are lost to the project.

In spite of these complaints the conventional team and its variants are widely employed with positive results. The chance of success is improved if the manager is technically competent, makes reasonable demands of the team members, rewards good work, and encourages a balance between competition and cooperation.

6.2.2 The Egoless Team

The excessive involvement of programmers in their products led Weinberg (1971) to propose 'egoless programming,' a state of mind in which programmers separate themselves from their products. This separation allows them to ask for advice without fear of showing incompetence, accept comments about their programs without being defensive, and laugh about errors in their programs. A natural corollary of egoless programming is egoless teams where an egalitarian community atmosphere replaces the harsh authoritarian lines of the conventional team. Egoless teams encourage cooperation rather than competition, and the success or failure of an individual is seen as the result of communal effort. Project definition, goals, and assignments are made by the entire team. If one team member experiences difficulty in his or her task, others willingly contribute their efforts.

This quaint 19th-century utopian vision of programming communities is appealing, but it depends on the good will, competence, and productivity of the team members. It is not clear how long egoless approaches can endure if one of the programmers is incompetent or consistently fails to deliver on promises. Without an authority figure to reward and punish and without a clear direction for promotion, egoless teams may have a difficult time maintaining the intense level of cooperation necessary for stability. Egoless teams probably succeed best when the members are approximately equally competent and have had experience working together. Giving the team the power to hire and fire may increase stability but can encourage competitiveness and defensiveness among members.

An egoless atmosphere is healthy and many teams attain this state for a time, but it may be difficult to maintain in the long run. Egoless approaches may work exceptionally well for a specific group of individuals on a specific project, but traditional approaches seem more stable across the spectrum of environments. If high-level managers can produce stable egoless teams, they will be rewarded with quality work, low turnover, high morale, and loyal employees.

6.2.3 Chief Programmer Teams

The loss of programming competence through promotion to management positions and the excessive isolation of programmers prompted the idea of chief programmer teams (Baker, 1972b). By building a team structure with defined roles, rather than assigning portions of a program to each programmer, advocates claim higher productivity, fewer errors, better adherence to schedules, and increased job satisfaction. The chief programmer team resembles a surgical team in which the chief surgeon plans the operation and carries out the critical surgical procedures, the assisting surgeon prepares the patient while the anesthesiologist, chief nurse, and other assistants perform their specialized functions. The chief programmer is the main designer and writes the most important code sections. The backup programmer carries out vital operations and is ready to assume the chief programmer role if necessary. Programmers are added when the design specifications are ready for implementation. The programming librarian prepares jobs for execution, retrieves outputs, and maintains copies of the current versions of programs in a publicly accessible workroom. A manager and secretary perform administrative services such as budgeting, allowing the technical staff to concentrate on the project. Since the chief programmer, backup programmer, and programming librarian work on all portions of the project, they can maintain standards and respond to delays. The publicly accessible listings are designed to obtain the goals of egoless programming and promote team cooperation.

The chief programmer team concept is an outgrowth of the increasing appreciation of the complex skills required in programming. Some large organizations have had rules that managers above a certain salary level should not program, but this restriction meant that senior programmers whose experience was necessary could not participate in programming projects. The chief programmer title, like the chief surgeon, was meant to provide senior programmers with high respect and salary while enabling them to continue programming.

The chief programmer team approach also encourages cooperation among team members and apprenticeship training of junior programmers. Watching a chief programmer at work provides junior programmers the same opportunity that medical residents have in making rounds with the chief surgeon. The surgical training aphorism of 'See one, do one, teach one' might apply to programming as well.

While the motivations behind the chief programmer team are appealing, there are problems in application. Too much of the success of a project depends on the chief programmer -- a competent one can work miracles, a poor one can produce disasters. Programming projects take months or years and no two are alike; but surgical procedures take only hours, and there is a strong similarity between the operations that a cardiac surgeon might be required to perform. Role specialization may be a problem too -- there may be periods when the programming librarian has little to do and some programmers may prefer to take care of job preparation. Since the chief programmer makes assignments and gets to do the most difficult parts, he or she may get most of the credit while the backup programmer and assisting programmers feel that their work is valued less. They do not have the satisfaction of having a portion of the project that is wholly their own. In spite of these problems, the idea of keeping senior programmers involved in programming, rather than moving them into management, is a good one. Programming is too important and complex to be left to the control of junior personnel.

Experimental testing of the chief programmer team concept is difficult since controlling all the variables is nearly impossible. Baker (1972a, 1972b) reports on the application of chief programmer teams in the now famous New York Times Information Bank project. He lists impressively low error rates and claims that the high quality of the system was due to the use of structured programming, top-down design, and the chief programmer team approach. Baker recites the advantages of the chief programmer team as:

> First, the use of senior personnel directly in the design and programming process led to a cleaner, more rapidly implemented design. Second, use of a programming librarian to do many of the clerical tasks associated with creating, updating, and maintaining programs reduced interruptions and diversion which tend to cause programming errors. Finally, the higher degree of specialization and smaller number of programmers led to a reduction in the number of misunderstandings and inconsistencies.

These are subjective statements which need to be verified experimentally. In the uncontrolled environment of that project it is hard to know how much the outcome was influenced by the capability and high motivation of Baker and Harlan Mills, who was an active participant.

The participants in this study were also the designers of the study and were interested in demonstrating the effectiveness of their new programming techniques. Researchers should always be careful of their own biases and the 'Hawthorne effect,' the increased motivation produced by the participant's knowledge that he or she is participating in an experiment. The name comes from a researcher in the 1920's who found that light bulb assemblers increased their performance no matter what experimental condition (decreased or increased heat, noise, light, etc.) they were put into.

6.3 GROUP PROCESSES

Team organizations are long-term strategies for encouraging cooperation during major projects. Short-term team or group processes are designed to bring individuals together for specific tasks such as evaluating program designs or code. Group processes may be used in conjunction with or independently of team organizations. Like group therapy they are designed to encourage cooperation, build interdependence, and help individuals overcome their anxieties.

Some social psychological research suggests that small groups encourage individuals to perform at higher levels since they feel that group members will recognize good work and criticize poor performance. On the other hand, learning is hindered by small groups since anxiety and fear of failure is heightened.

6.3.1 Inspection Techniques

The goal of Fagan's (1974, 1976) design and code inspections is to eliminate errors as early as possible during the program development process. Error rework is more economical in the early stages; so level 0, level 1, and level 2 inspections were developed to be completed at the statement of objectives, design (architecture, specifications), and code phases respectively. Productivity is increased by detecting errors earlier in the process because rework diverts productive effort and customer installation is less time consuming when there are fewer errors in the final product. Fagan, on the basis of experiments performed at IBM, estimates that use of level 1 and level 2 inspections saves about one programming month per 1000 noncomment source statements.

The inspections themselves are a formal method of finding design and code errors. The inspection team consists of a moderator with special training who serves as 'coach', the programmer who produced the design, the coder/implementer, and the tester.

In a level 1 inspection there is an overview for the entire team in which design documentation is distributed. The designer gives the 'big picture' and then describes the details. The overview is followed by individual study of the design. During the inspection, the coder describes how the design will be implemented. All logic is covered and, if possible, every branch is taken. The last phase is follow-up during which every issue, concern, or error is resolved.

Fagan emphasizes that people must be taught to find errors effectively and need to be trained to focus on high cost errors. Errors found in the inspection are analyzed by type, origin, cost, and indicative clues. Fagan shows a form for collecting inspection data which has a list describing errors (such as logic errors, tests and branches, interface calls etc.) and has space for indicating categories such as 'missing,' 'wrong,' or 'extra,' and a column for tabulating subtotal and total errors. The level 1 and level 2 inspections indicate which modules have the greatest error density and might need to be redesigned or recoded or at least very carefully tested. The distribution of error types for a group of error prone modules can be compared with a 'normal/usual percentage distribution.' If large disparities are noted between the sample and the 'standard,' designers should discover why and remedy the problem for the remainder of the project.

6.3.2 Structured Walkthroughs

The term *structured walkthrough* was applied by IBM (1973) authors to describe a design review process involving four to six participants for one to two hours. The characteristics of a structured walkthrough were listed as:

1) It is arranged and scheduled by the developer (reviewee) of the work product being reviewed.
2) Management does not attend the walkthrough and it is not used as a basis for employee evaluation.
3) The participants (reviewers) are given the review materials prior to the walkthrough and are expected to be familiar with them.
4) The walkthrough is structured in the sense that all attendees know what is to be accomplished and what role they are to play.
5) The emphasis is on error detection rather than error correction.
6) All technical members of the project team, from most senior to most junior, have their work product reviewed.

These characteristics leave much room for interpretation, and most installations make local variations. More formal reviews, which have longer lead times and involve senior personnel or user representatives, increase the importance and tension. The materials are carefully prepared and written critiques are returned several days after the walkthrough.

More informal reviews can be scheduled quickly among close and trusted associates to get quick feedback even on hastily prepared materials (Yourdon, 1978).

6.3.3 Formal Technical Reviews

Freedman and Weinberg (1977) propose formal technical reviews for improving a broad range of technical products of programming: functional specifications, designs, code, documentation, test plans, software tools or packages, training material and plans, procedures and standards, and operations and maintenance policies. They claim that the three to seven participants in a review should:

1) point out needed improvements
2) confirm the acceptability of portions of the entire work
3) improve the uniformity, predictability, quality and manageability.

To achieve these goals, Freedman and Weinberg require formal technical reviews to have:

1) a written report that is available to everyone including management
2) active and open participation of all participants under the direction of an experienced group leader who is not the developer of the product being reviewed
3) responsibility for the quality of the written review shared among all participants.

These broad rules are refined into a list of helpful rules and advice:

1) Be prepared, by reading materials before the review
2) Be willing to associate with other participants and the developers of the product being reviewed
3) Watch your language -- be humble, avoid critical negative phrasing
4) At least one positive and one negative statement should be made by each participant
5) Raise issues, do not resolve them
6) Avoid discussions of stylistic issues
7) Stick to programming standards
8) Only technically competent people should attend reviews
9) Record all issues in public
10) Stick to technical issues

11) Remember education of junior members is a goal of the review process
12) Do not evaluate the producers, only the product
13) Distribute the report as soon as possible.

These rules offer participants and the leader some guidance about proper behavior. Still the success of the formal technical review depends on the skill of the leader whose sound technical background must be complemented by a sensitivity for group dynamics.

Formal technical reviews, structured walkthroughs, and inspections have much in common even though the advocates of these approaches emphasize differences. The written reports describing these team approaches may focus on specific issues such as the enumeration of error types in code inspections, the developer being the leader in structured walkthroughs and the higher involvement of participants in producing a written report in formal technical reviews. In spite of these attempts to create differences, most people recognize the powerful advantages to group reviewing and adopt a flexible approach which allows for local variation and novelty. Even though as much as ten percent of a programmer's time may be spent on group review processes, managers are increasingly aware of the benefits. Group reviewing increases product reliability, maintainability, adherence to standards, adherence to schedule; while encouraging social interaction, supporting training and improving morale.

6.3.4 MECCA Method

The MECCA (Multi-Element Component Comparison and Analysis) method, developed by Gilb (1977), is a formal method of comparing alternatives such as among software designs. Applications of the method include hardware and software selection or comparison of alternative operating systems. In comparing alternative software designs, presumably the one receiving the 'higher rating' via the MECCA method would produce higher quality code, so the MECCA method may be considered an indirect measure of software quality. Using other software metrics in conjunction with the MECCA method could improve validity.

The steps in the method include: formulation of objectives, breaking of objectives into hierarchical structure; weighting of elements; collection of facts on all detailed elements; awarding points to elements for 'relative' good; calculation of weighted average points; and finally, evaluation, criticism, analysis, and adjustment. This iterative process is continued until an acceptable result is obtained and the result is reported.

Applying the method requires completion of the MECCA Element

Data-Collection Form on which characteristics of alternatives are written. The entries could include such things as contract guarantees and user experiences with software.

The MECCA Point Calculation Form is used to note the structure of the multilevel module. Elementary points are noted and weight times point calculations are made and pushed to the next level. Total points and weighted points are calculated. This is repeated until the top level is reached. The alternative receiving the highest number of points is considered the best. The MECCA method relies on human effort and judgment, but it is partially automatable in that programs have been written to compute weights and present results.

6.3.5 Peer Review and Peer Rating

The concept of peer review or rating, while relatively new to the data processing industry, has proved to be useful in predicting performance and in evaluating products (such as technical articles and books) of an individual's performance in other areas. Peer reviews are global predictions of performance by peers and peer ratings are evaluations of specific product performance.

Studies performed in 1946 (Doll and Longo, 1956; Lewin, 1976; Hollander, 1957) concluded that peer evaluations were more valid in predicting how individuals would fare in Officer Candidate School or in combat situations than objective tests. The same study found that peer evaluations were better predictors of future performance than supervisory ratings. Possible reasons for the superiority of peer review over supervisory review include: the closer daily contact of peers; individuals show their best side to superiors; peer review provides a larger number of judgments than one evaluator's opinion (Roadman, 1964). Studies done in 1970 with 4000 men in the Israeli army concluded that peer review was a better predictor than I.Q. tests, educational levels, or interview scores. Peer ratings have also been shown to indicate success or failure in other areas (Doll and Longo, 1956; Lewin, 1976; Kane, 1978), such as Naval Air Training, Officer efficiency, and managers in life insurance companies. Peer ratings are 'good predictors' even when the evaluators are untrained (Doll and Longo, 1956). Also, in the case of the Naval Air Trainee experiment, the ratings were done early (during the 8th week) in the association. Experiments have shown that friendships (Lewin, 1976) appear to play a minor role in peer review and that results using subjects with no prior acquaintanceships were similar to those with close association. However, some experiments (Lewin, 1976; Kane, 1978) indicate that rivalry and racial prejudice tend to affect peer review. That is, younger, less senior, more highly educated managers tended to be rated

Difference Between Highest and Lowest of Four Ratings per Program, Averaged over 15 Programs	Number of Cases	Percentage	Cumulative Percentage
0	2	4.6	4.6
1	12	11.3	15.9
2	19	27.2	43.1
3	12	24.6	67.7
4	7	15.4	83.1
5	6	10.8	93.9
6	7	6.2	100.0

Table 6-2: Combined results from three peer review field studies with professional programmers.

lower by peers than by superiors, and both blacks and whites rated same race peers higher. However, these biases can be eliminated by the introduction of anonymity into the peer review process. Confidential reviews will eliminate personality clashes and the refusal of individuals to critique those who might adversely effect their careers (Symington, 1975). Peer evaluation has been shown (Lewin, 1976) to be stable across groups and does not seem to be affected when group composition changes. It should be emphasized that 'peer review' should be exactly that; for example, in a 'peer review' of a member of a secretarial pool, only members of the pool, and not managers, should participate.

Research in the use of peer rating to evaluate computer programs has been proposed (Anderson and Shneiderman, 1977). The peer review process serves as a tool for programmer education, programming team communication, and programmer self-evaluation. Such a 'feedback' technique is necessary because we have poor software quality metrics.

After a pilot study in 1977, three peer reviews were conducted during 1978 at the Defense Mapping Agency (DMAAC) in St. Louis, General Electric (GE) in Arlington, Virginia, and the Bureau of the Census in Suitland, Maryland. In each field study, five professional programmers, with similar background and experience, participated in the review. Participants provided one program representing their 'best' work. Notes indicating authorship were removed and copies were made for distribution to each participant. Each person reviewed four programs (one for each of the others). GE programmers provided FORTRAN IV and FORTRAN 77 samples, DMAAC programmers provided FORTRAN V samples, and Census programmers provided ASCII COBOL samples. GE and DMAAC samples ranged from 50 to 275 lines in length while Census samples ranged from 100 to 650 lines.

Each study was conducted in a well lighted, comfortable conference or class room in an 'informal' atmosphere. Distractions and interruptions were not allowed. Participants worked on one program during each of four timed periods (35 or 45 minutes). Raters completing a program before the time elapsed were not permitted to go forward or backward but were encouraged to take a break. Participants were asked to work individually and not to discuss the programs during the study. Thirteen subjective questions (Figure 6-1) were answered for each program, and com-

Evaluation Form Program Number______ Evaluator Number______

Please make any written comments you wish after each question or on a separate sheet.

	No		Neutral or Don't Know				Yes
1. Were reasonable variable names used?	1	2	3	4	5	6	7
2. Were sufficient and useful comments provided?	1	2	3	4	5	6	7
3. Were spaces and blank lines used properly to produce a program with a pleasing format?	1	2	3	4	5	6	7
4. Was the low-level logic of the program comprehensible?	1	2	3	4	5	6	7
5. Was the high-level design (for example, top-down or modular) apparent and reasonable?	1	2	3	4	5	6	7
6. Was the algorithm a good choice?	1	2	3	4	5	6	7
7. Was this program easy to comprehend overall?	1	2	3	4	5	6	7
8. Would it be easy for you to modify this program?	1	2	3	4	5	6	7
9. Is this program compiler-independent?	1	2	3	4	5	6	7
10. Is this program machine-independent?	1	2	3	4	5	6	7
11. Would you have been proud to have written this program?	1	2	3	4	5	6	7
12. Are the data structures used in a sensible way?	1	2	3	4	5	6	7
13. Would you find it hard to improve this program?	1	2	3	4	5	6	7

Figure 6-1: Evaluation questions for peer review.

ments were written on plain sheets of paper. At the end of the fourth period, participants completed the Summary Evaluation (Figure 6-2). To preserve anonymity, the administrator copied program comments to separate sheets prior to distributing them to the author/programmers (approximately one hour after the review for Census and GE subjects). Two reports, one indicating how his or her program was rated by others and the other comparing how each participant rated in relation to others,

Evaluator Number _____

Summary Evaluation

Which program was of the highest quality? _____

Which program was of the lowest quality? _____

Which program was second highest in quality? _____

Final Evaluation

	No						Yes
Did you learn anything useful about programming style during the peer review process?	1	2	3	4	5	6	7
Do you think you would modify your programming behavior to produce good sample programs if you were told to expect a peer review every 6 months?	1	2	3	4	5	6	7
Do you think the peer review process may be effective in improving programming in your organization?	1	2	3	4	5	6	7
Do you think the administrators of the peer review have done their best to preserve your anonymity?	1	2	3	4	5	6	7

GENERAL COMMENTS ABOUT THE PEER REVIEW PROCESS AND SUGGESTIONS FOR IMPROVEMENT.

Figure 6-2: Summary evaluation for peer review.

were distributed to each participant (Figures 6-3 and 6-4).

Comparison of results of all participants for all questions and programs indicate that in over half the cases, at least three of four raters for a question gave the same rating or ratings that differed only by one. In all other cases, at least two raters showed similar agreement. These encouraging results indicate that raters are fairly consistent in rating subjective questions. Ratings would probably be more consistent if raters discussed the meaning/intent of each question prior to the review in order to decrease the chance of different interpretation of the questions and the rating scale.

The ratings for subjective questions for all programs (Table 6-2) shows that in only 43.1 percent of the cases is the difference between the high and low rating for questions two or less. However, these figures are greatly affected by cases where three raters give the same high rating and one rater gives a low rating (possibly as a result of misunderstanding the question or rating scale), which produces a large difference. Analysis of the difference in the highest and lowest ranking (lowest minus highest) for a program by the four raters shows that in 55.4 percent of the cases there was a difference of no more than one.

Of the fifteen participants in the three field studies, ten indicated (by a rating of five or more on a scale of 1 to 7, where 7 was the 'yes' rating) that they learned something during the peer review process. Twelve indicated that they thought they would modify their programming behavior to produce good samples if they expected a peer rating semiannually. Eleven indicated that the peer rating process might be effective in improving programming in their organization. Verbal comments made by GE programmers regarding the merits/capablities of FORTRAN 77 and FORTRAN IV, suggest that the process was educational.

Response to the question about preserving anonymity (nine participants gave ratings of three or less) indicate, that, despite precautions, anonymity is a problem. Programmers who work together, who are familiar with the type of work done in a particular shop, or who assist peers with programs, are able to identify the authors of code. Solutions include composing peer rating teams of larger numbers of people who do not work together.

PEER REVIEW FOR DEFENSE MAPPING AGENCY AEROSPACE CENTER (DMAAC)

REPORT FOR PROGRAMMER 1

MISSING DATA INDICATED BY 0

	Rater 1	Rater 2	Rater 3	Rater 4	Average	Group Average
Subjective question 1	7	5	5	1	4.5	5.1
Subjective question 2	6	3	3	6	4.5	4.9
Subjective question 3	6	2	5	1	3.5	3.6
Subjective question 4	6	4	4	6	5.0	4.9
Subjective question 5	6	4	6	2	4.5	4.4
Subjective question 6	4	4	2	4	3.5	3.8
Subjective question 7	6	3	4	6	4.7	4.9
Subjective question 8	6	5	3	6	5.0	5.2
Subjective question 9	6	6	1	1	3.5	3.9
Subjective question 10	4	6	1	1	3.0	3.2
Subjective question 11	7	3	4	2	4.0	4.1
Subjective question 12	5	4	2	6	4.2	4.6
Subjective question 13	7	4	4	4	4.7	4.4

This program was ranked 3 3 2 2

1 is the highest ranking

Figure 6-3: Participants report for peer review.

Report for Evaluator 1

Comparison of Evaluators

Subjective Question	Program 1				Program 2				Program 3				Program 4				Program 5			
1	7	5	5	1	6	3	6	3	2	7	6	6	5	6	5	5	7	7	5	6
2	6	3	3	6	7	5	6	6	7	7	6	6	1	5	2	2	6	6	6	3
3	6	2	5	1	6	6	2	5	1	5	1	1	1	5	2	1	6	7	4	5
4	6	4	4	6	5	6	2	6	6	6	6	6	2	5	4	1	7	6	5	6
5	6	4	6	2	7	4	4	2	7	7	5	2	2	5	3	1	6	7	4	5
6	4	4	2	4	4	4	4	4	5	4	2	4	4	4	3	4	4	4	4	4
7	6	3	4	6	6	4	5	5	7	7	7	6	2	3	2	1	6	6	5	6
8	6	5	3	6	7	5	6	6	7	7	7	6	2	2	3	3	6	7	5	5
9	6	6	1	1	2	6	1	7	7	6	1	1	1	2	4	7	6	6	6	1
10	4	6	1	1	4	6	1	1	4	4	1	1	4	3	4	1	4	7	6	1
11	7	3	4	2	6	4	1	4	6	7	4	4	3	2	4	1	6	6	4	5
12	5	4	2	6	6	4	5	6	6	6	4	5	4	5	4	4	6	5	4	2
13	7	4	4	4	6	4	1	4	6	7	3	3	3	3	3	3	7	7	5	4
					*				*				*				*			

Program 1 was ranked	3	3	2	2
Program 2 was ranked	3	2	4	1
Program 3 was ranked	2	1	3	3
Program 4 was ranked	4	4	4	4
Program 5 was ranked	1	2	1	1

Final Evaluation Response

Question	Ratings				
1	5	1	4	5	2
2	5	1	6	4	5
3	5	1	5	3	7
4	7	7	7	2	6
	*				

An asterisk indicates your ratings.

Figure 6-4: Overall report for peer review participant.

These field trials suggest that peer ratings of programs are productive, enjoyable, nonthreatening experiences. Such reviews can serve as educational tools and as incentives for programmers to produce higher quality code to submit for semi-annual peer reviews. The evaluation questions need refinement to increase consistency of scoring and long term studies are necessary to verify if programmers change behavior when they anticipate peer ratings.

6.3.6 Group Testing and Debugging

Anyone familiar with computer center operations recognizes the importance of the commons room where programmers gather as they debug their programs, take a break to chat or wait for fresh output. Informal encounters are an opportunity to learn about system features or idiosyncrasies, ask for help from knowledgeable colleagues, or try out new ideas among friends. One form of assistance that is often asked for is help in testing or debugging a program. Programmers realize that by explaining the operation of their program, they discover flaws that had previously eluded them. The idea of group testing and debugging surely came from an attempt to formalize these coffee break encounters.

Myers (1978) conducted an intriguing experiment to validate the effectiveness of individual testing and group testing patterned after code inspections. Category A subjects tested a 63 statement PL/I string manipulation program individually by using a terminal to execute programs against test cases generated after examining the program specifications. They did not have access to the program listing but could execute it against data files. Category B subjects were given the same environment plus the program listing. Category C subjects were organized into three person teams and were asked to test the programs manually with the code inspection process. A questionnaire on PL/I and code inspection experience was used to assign subjects to groups.

Table 6-3 shows the results which suggest that group testing is only modestly more effective than individual testing, although group testing does consume more time per error found. This is not to be taken as an indictment of group processes, since the claimed benefits of groups include facilitation of cooperation, education, and increased reliability. I believe that managers would accept the increased cost of group testing even for the modest improvement. A surprising result of the experiment was that there was a wide variation in which of the 15 known errors the programmers found. Only three errors were found by more than 75 percent of the subjects. Of the remaining errors, no pattern was found

	Individual + specs + terminal	Individual + specs + terminal + listing	Group Walkthrough + specs + listing
Mean number of errors found	4.5	5.4	5.7
Variance	4.8	5.5	3.0
Range	1-7	2-9	3-9
Man-minutes per error	37	29	75

Table 6-3: Results of experiment on program testing methods (Myers, 1978).

which would indicate that some were easy and others were difficult to find. This suggests that individuals have radically differing debugging styles.

Myers carries out a hypothetical experiment based on his data and suggests that the best approach is to have two individuals test a program by studying the listing. After working separately to find errors, the two individuals pool their results. Program testing requires unorthodox thinking patterns, a willingness to explore unusual circumstances, and the capacity to break away from mainline behavior. Weinberg (1971) even suggests that social deviance and paranoid tendencies may be prerequisites for successful program testers. Group processes may act to suppress deviant behavior, encourage conformity, and repress bold ideas.

Group processes may be less productive in program testing than in evaluating designs -- certainly different behavior is required for these different phases of program development. Defenders of group processes argue that the benefits include supportive feedback, increased desire to demonstrate competence before colleagues, development of trusting relationships and educational opportunities.

The effectiveness of group processes as an educational experience was demonstrated in a controlled experiment by Lemos (1978, 1979) on 215 undergraduate programming students. Students who were required to meet with colleagues during class time and make written critiques of each others work did better on the final exam than students who had no group debugging experience.

6.4 PRACTITIONER'S SUMMARY

Team organization strategies which increase cooperation are probably a good idea, but care must be exercised so as not to give up the advantages of conventional team organization, that is, clear lines of authority, reward for superior performance and the stimulation of a competitive environment. New team organization strategies have the positive goals of increasing cooperation, preventing loss of technical skills through promotion, and reducing compartmentalization of function.

Group processes such as inspections, structured walkthroughs, and technical reviews encourage cooperation, increase communication, support education, and reduce variation in performance. Group processes may consume a great deal of time, but they are worthwhile investments since they improve the product and develop a more appealing work environment.

6.5 RESEARCHER'S AGENDA

Studying team organization and group processes experimentally is a difficult task due to the difficulty of obtaining sufficient numbers of subjects and of establishing experimental controls. Carefully designed hypothesis testing experiments are preferred, but case studies are a more realistic alternative. Different team organizations or group processes could be applied in the same project and a comparison of the product conducted.

An intriguing study would be to examine team formation and behavior changes as the team members become more familiar with each other. Teams with extreme reputations, good or bad, might be studied in detail to understand what makes a team succeed or fail.

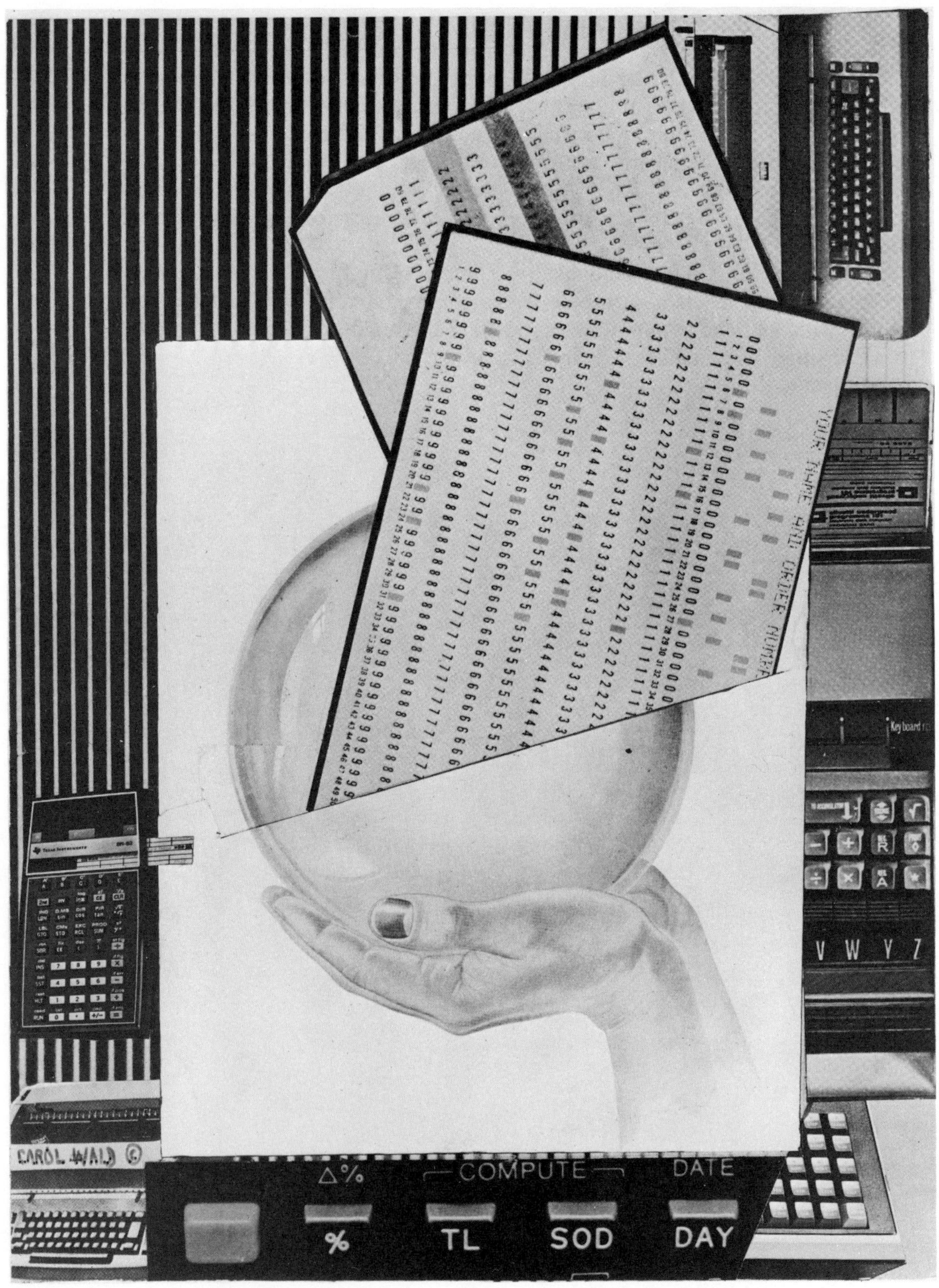
CAROL WALD ©
Δ%
COMPUTE
DATE
%
TL
SOD
DAY
V W Y Z

7

DATABASE SYSTEMS AND DATA MODELS

Centuries of specialist stress in pedagogy and in the arrangement of data now end with the instantaneous retrieval of information made possible by electricity. Automation is information and it not only ends jobs in the world of work, it ends subjects in the world of learning.

Marshall McLuhan, *Understanding Media: The Extensions of Man* (1964)

Introduction to database systems and data models - human factors issues in database design - data models - hierarchical, network and relational models - subschemas and views - data model selection - subschema design

7.1 INTRODUCTION TO DATABASE SYSTEMS

This section provides a brief description of database systems and data models for those who are not familiar with these subjects. The terminology introduced will be used in later discussion of database query and manipulation languages. Database systems are an important area for experimental studies since the class of users may be an order of magnitude larger than the class of programmers. The experience of programming language designers may not be suitable for database languages because the problems and users are different.

Database systems are complex software packages designed to facilitate the management of large databases (Figure 7-1). A *data definition language* enables the database administrator to write a *schema* which describes data items, logical relationships among data items, some parameters of physical file organization, privacy/security control, and integrity checks. A *data manipulation language* enables application programmers to develop user oriented systems by invoking high-level operations, such as FIND, STORE or DELETE, with little concern for disk manipulation or storage structure details. Some database systems provide easy-to-use *self-contained query languages* in addition to the more complex *host-embedded data manipulation languages* which require knowledge of a host language such as COBOL, PL/I, FORTRAN or Assembler.

The database system includes processors for data description and data manipulation languages as well as a run-time package to carry out the operations. Most database systems provide utilities which are tools for the database administrator, whose role is to coordinate user requests, ensure security, protect integrity, and create a system which runs effectively for the entire user community.

A critical database design issue is the selection of the *data model* employed by the database administrator, applications programmers, and end users. The data model consists of the structures which can be de-

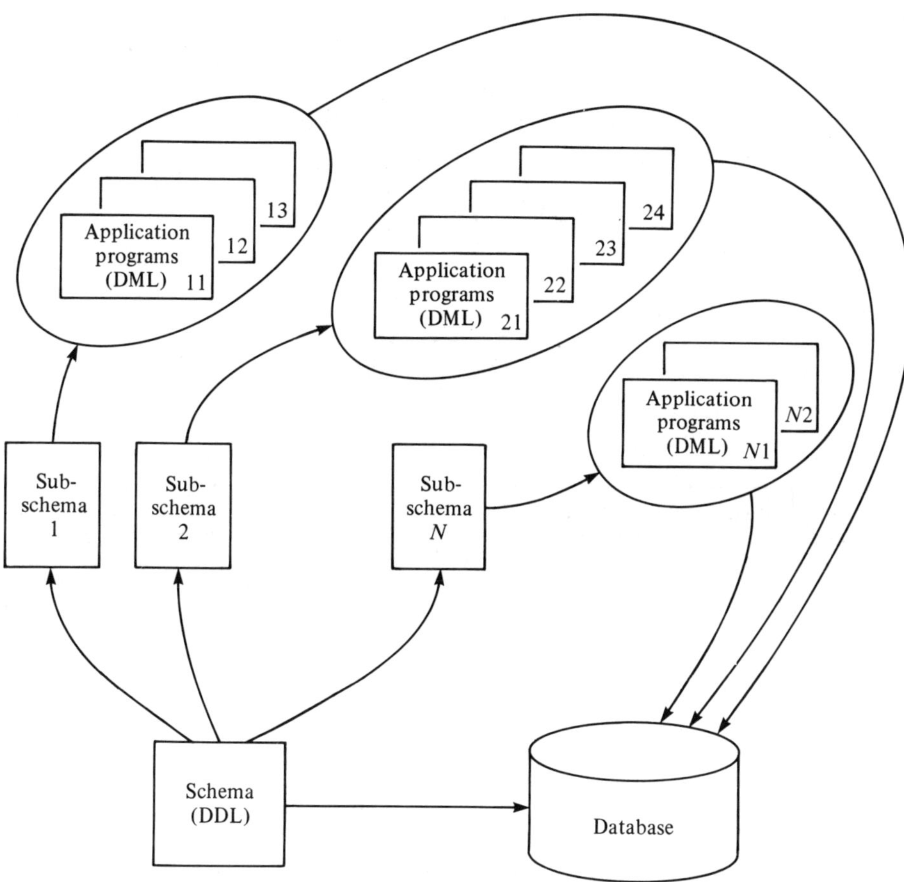

Figure 7-1: Database system.

scribed in the data definition language and the operations provided by the data manipulation language. A variety of data models has been proposed, but three have become popular: the hierarchical, network, and relational data models.

The hierarchical data model, often called the tree structure model, limits the complexity of the logical data relationships to simple tree-like patterns. The network model, based on the CODASYL Data Base Task Group Report (1971), allows more complex linkages which may be in the form of networks. The elegant relational model, based on the ideas of E. F. Codd (1970), requires data and relationships to be shown as tabular structures. Other data models have been proposed, but lively controversy and industry attention has been focused on these three.

7.1.1 The Hierarchical Data Model

In the hierarchical data model individual data items, such as EMPLOYEE-NAME, AGE, SALARY or WEIGHT, are grouped into *segments*, and the segments are organized into tree structures. Figure 7-2 shows a simple tree structured database representing information about ski resorts. The SKI-RESORT segment contains data items describing

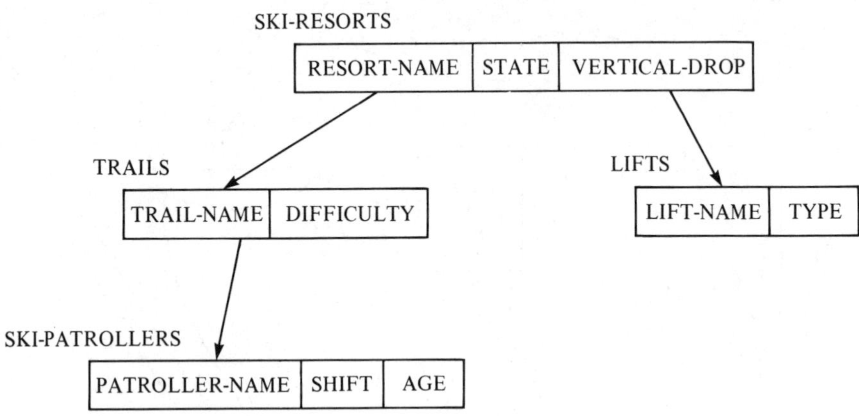

Figure 7-2: Schema diagram for tree-structures ski information database.

each resort. Each SKI-RESORT has several TRAILS and several LIFTS. Each of the TRAILS is patrolled by several SKI-PATROLLERS. Figure 7-2 is a *schema diagram* showing the pattern of relationships among segments. Figure 7-3 shows the *instance diagram* which indicates actual database values. For each instance segment at the tail of an arrow in the actual database there are several instance segments at the head of the arrow: this is a one-to-many relationship. The database administrator uses a data definition language to describe the schema which is used by the database system as a guide to storing the data instances. Figure 7-4 gives a simplified version of data definition language statements for the ski resort example.

The hierarchical model is easy to understand but limits the complexity of data relationships. In this example we have no convenient way of showing which lifts serve which trails. If a ski patroller works on more than one trail, redundant segments will have to be included. While the hierarchical model makes downward relationships obvious (for example, the trail names at a given resort), upward relationships are more obscure (for example, the states which have ski resorts with expert trails). By using elaborate pointer features, redundant data entries and additional indexes, the disadvantages can be overcome, but the cost is in lost effi-

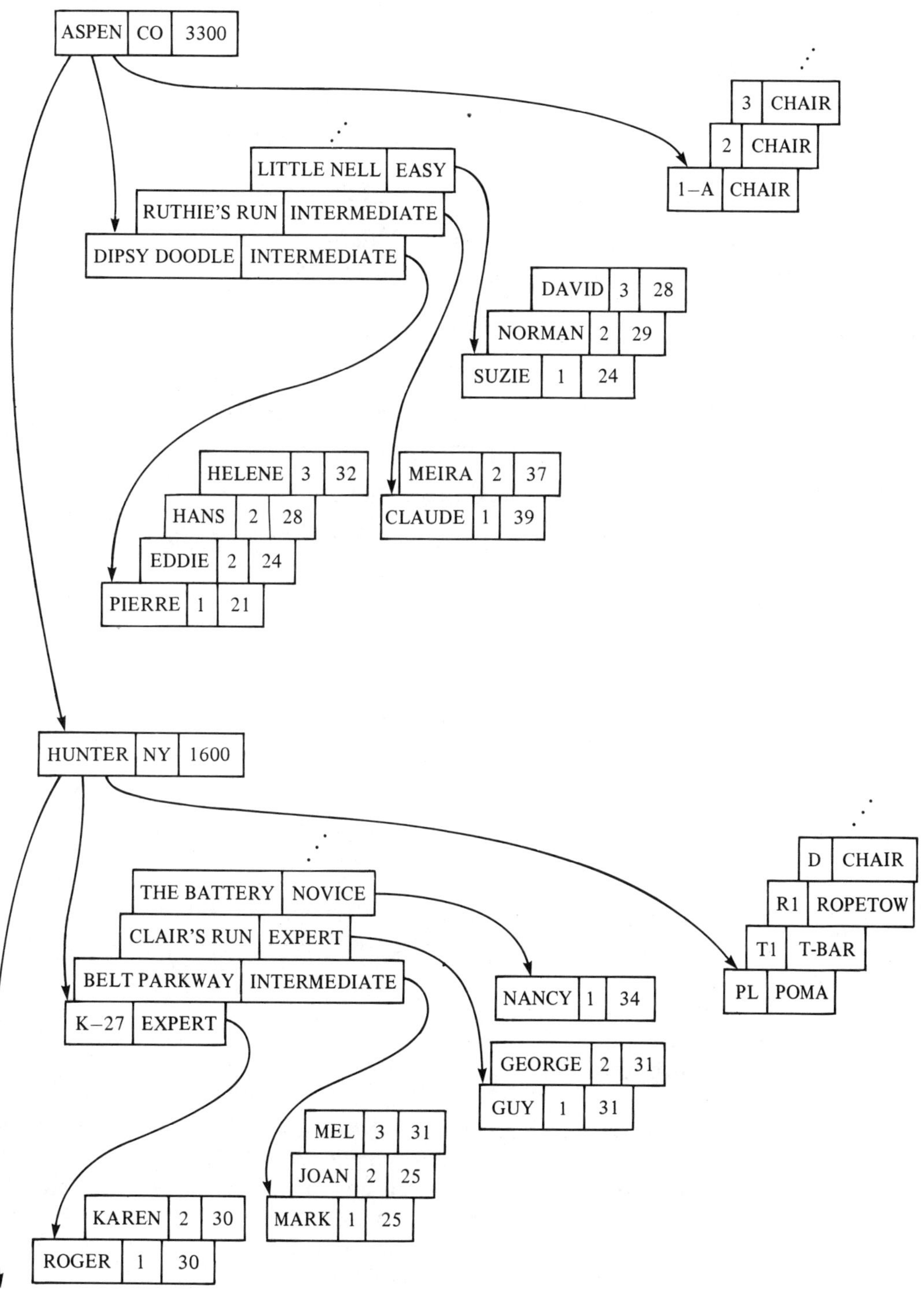

Figure 7-3: Instance diagram for tree-structure ski information database.

```
DATABASE        NAME = SKI-INFORMATION
SEGMENT         NAME = SKI-RESORTS
FIELD           NAME = RESORT-NAME, LENGTH = 30
FIELD           NAME = STATE, LENGTH = 2
FIELD           NAME = VERTICAL-DROP, LENGTH = 4
SEGMENT         NAME = TRAILS, PARENT = SKI-RESORTS
FIELD           NAME = TRAIL-NAME, LENGTH = 35
FIELD           NAME = DIFFICULTY, LENGTH = 10
SEGMENT         NAME = SKI-PATROLLERS, PARENT = TRAILS
FIELD           NAME = PATROLLER-NAME, LENGTH = 25
FIELD           NAME = SHIFT, LENGTH = 1
FIELD           NAME = AGE, LENGTH = 2
SEGMENT         NAME = LIFTS, PARENT = SKI-RESORTS
FIELD           NAME = LIFT-NAME, LENGTH = 5
FIELD           NAME = TYPE, LENGTH = 10
END
```

Figure 7-4: Schema definition for tree-structure ski information database.

ciency and increased complexity. In short, the hierarchical model is excellent for simple tree-structured data relationships, but it loses its appeal when elaborate relationships among data items must be maintained. IBM's Information Management System (IMS) and MRI's System 2000 are two popular commercial database systems based on the hierarchical model.

7.1.2 The Network Model

In the network model, individual data items are grouped into *records* which may be organized into *data-structure-sets* by the use of pointers. Each data-structure-set has an *owner* and a group of *member* records. The schema describes *record types* and *data-structure-set types* while the actual database contains *record instances* and *data-structure-set instances*.

In our ski information system each SKI-RESORTS record owns a group of TRAILS records and a group of LIFTS records. Each TRAILS record is owned by only one SKI-RESORTS record and in turn owns a group of SKI-PATROLLERS records. The owner-member relationships are assigned names, usually made up of the owner and member record names. Figure 7-5 shows a schema diagram, called a *Bachman diagram*, which shows the record types and data-structure-set

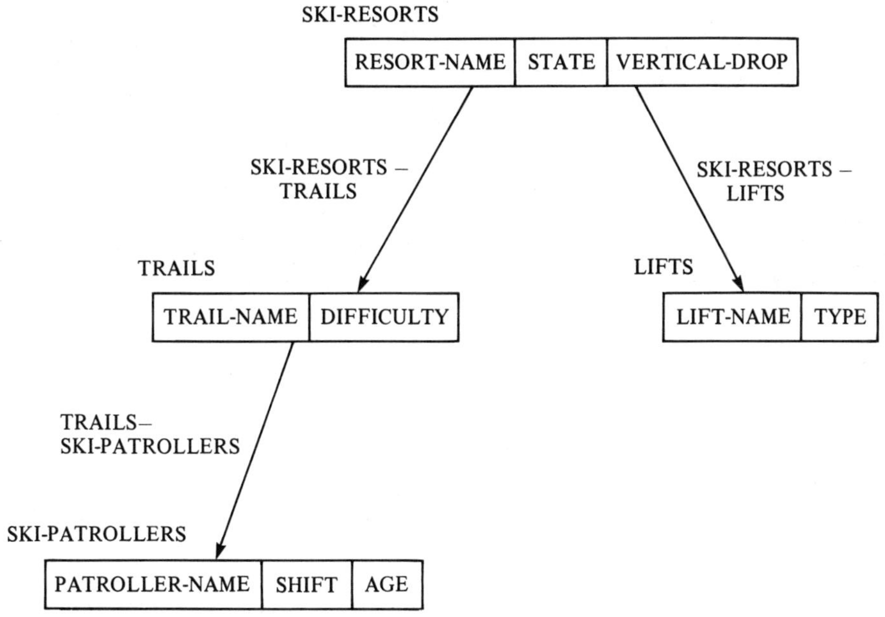

Figure 7-5: Schema diagram for network-model ski information database.

types. Figure 7-6 shows an instance diagram demonstrating how a portion of this database might appear. Figure 7-7 is a schema for this database written in a simplified data definition language based on the ideas in the CODASYL Data Base Task Group Report (1971).

The one-to-many relationships which were available in the hierarchical model are also available in the network model. The network model permits additional linkages which can easily show *many-to-many relationships*. For example, each lift may service several trails and each trail may be accessible from several lifts. By adding a LINK record,

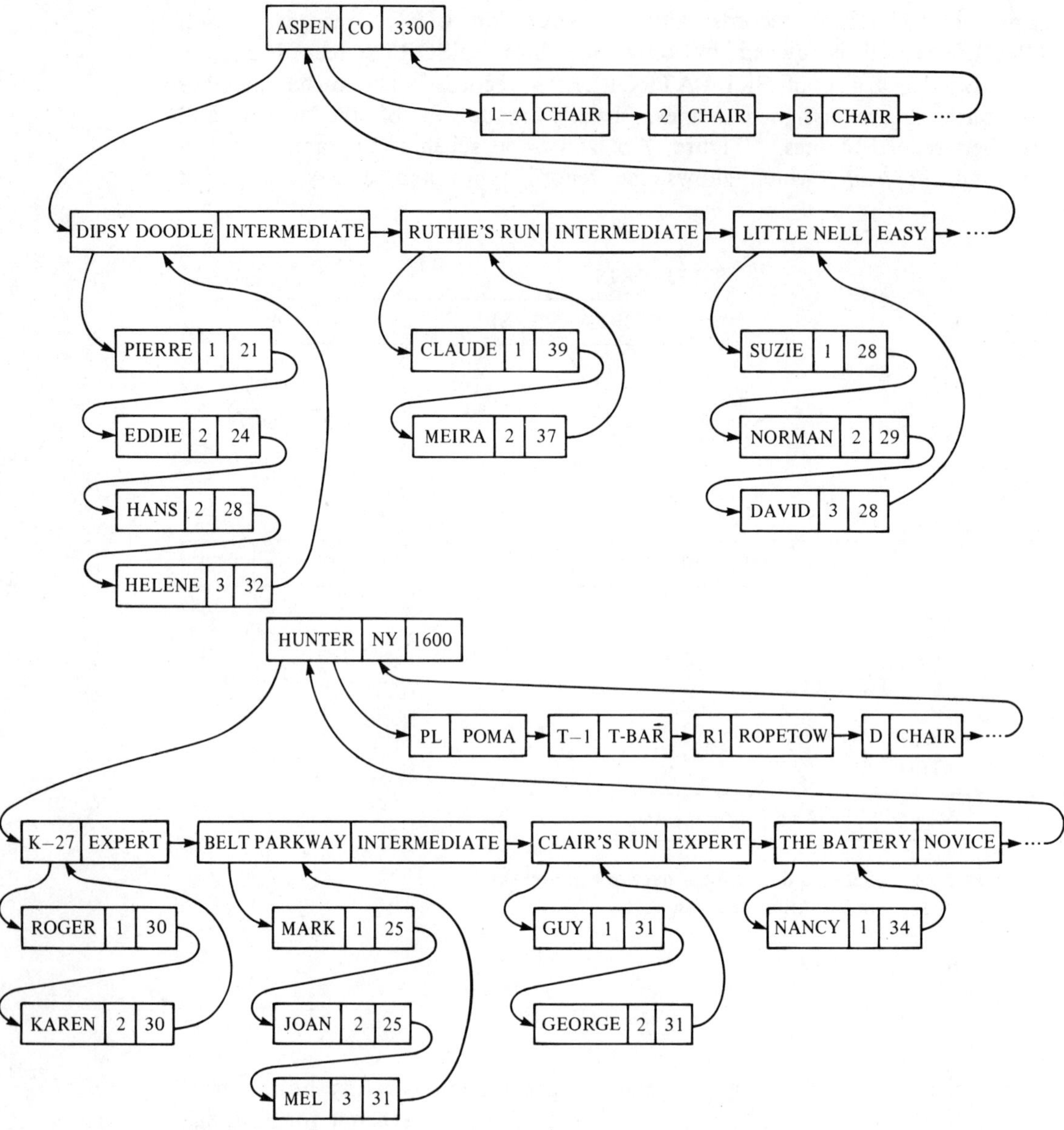

Figure 7-6: Instance diagram for network-model ski information database.

```
SCHEMA NAME IS SKI-INFORMATION.
RECORD NAME IS SKI-RESORTS.
    02 RESORT-NAME;      TYPE IS CHAR 30.
    02 STATE;            TYPE IS CHAR 2.
    02 VERTICAL DROP;    TYPE IS CHAR 4.
RECORD NAME IS TRAILS.
    02 TRAIL-NAME;       TYPE IS CHAR 35.
    02 DIFFICULTY;       TYPE IS CHAR 10.
RECORD NAME IS SKI-PATROLLERS.
    02 PATROLLER-NAME;   TYPE IS CHAR 25.
    02 SHIFT;            TYPE IS CHAR 1.
    02 AGE;              TYPE IS CHAR 2.
RECORD NAME IS LIFTS.
    02 LIFT-NAME;        TYPE IS CHAR 5.
    02 TYPE;             TYPE IS CHAR 10.
SET NAME IS SKI-RESORTS-TRAILS.
    OWNER IS SKI-RESORTS.
    MEMBER IS TRAILS.
SET NAME IS TRAILS-SKI-PATROLLERS.
    OWNER IS TRAILS.
    MEMBER IS SKI-PATROLLERS.
SET NAME IS SKI-RESORTS-LIFTS.
    OWNER IS SKI-RESORTS.
    MEMBER IS LIFTS.
END.
```

Figure 7-7: Simplified schema description for network-model ski information database.

shown in Figure 7–8, we can represent this more complex relationship. Another possibility is to add information to group ski patrollers by their ranks: junior instructor, senior instructor, assistant director, director. Figure 7–9 shows the addition of a RANKS record type which stores the rank information and owns the group of ski patrollers who are of that rank. Figure 7–10 shows the schema diagram additions for the LINKS

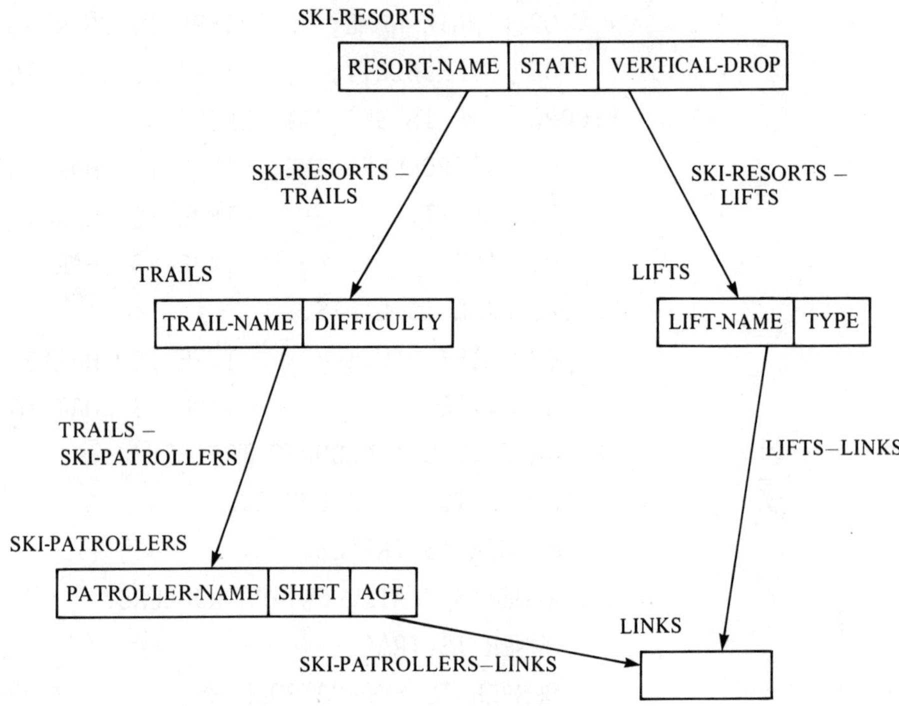

Figure 7-8: Schema diagram for network model-ski information database with LINKS information.

and RANKS information. The full network model has many additional features for organizing information, searching efficiently, storing records, controlling privacy, checking integrity and facilitating data administration. Network data model implementations include Honeywell's IDS–II, Cullinane's IDMS, UNIVAC's DMS/1100 and DEC's DBMS–10.

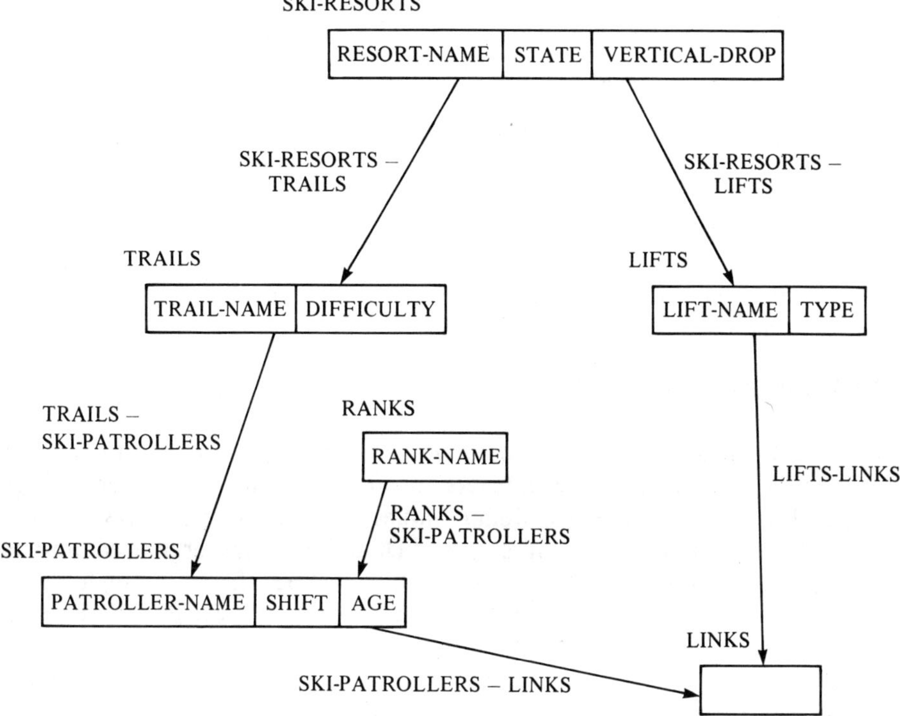

Figure 7-9: Schema diagram for network-model ski information database with LINKS and RANKS information.

```
RECORD NAME IS LINKS.
    02  TRAIL-NAME;        TYPE IS CHAR 35.
    02  LIFT-NAME;         TYPE IS CHAR 5.
RECORD NAME IS RANKS.
    02  RANK;              TYPE IS CHAR 20.
SET NAME IS TRAILS-LINKS.
    OWNER IS TRAILS.
    MEMBER IS LINKS.
```

Figure 7-10: Additions for schema of Figure 7-7 to include new relationships.

```
SET NAME IS LIFTS-LINKS.
    OWNER IS LIFTS.
    MEMBER IS LINKS.
SET NAME IS RANKS-SKI-PATROLLERS.
    OWNER IS RANKS.
    MEMBER IS SKI-PATROLLERS.
```

Figure 7-10 *Cont.*

7.1.3 The Relational Model

In the relational model, data values are chosen from domains such as the real numbers, the integers from 1 to 100, character strings of length less than 40, positive dollar values, Celsius temperatures from -273 to 1000 degrees, or a list of colors. Data items are organized into tabular structures where each column contains values from a single domain. The column may be given a name such as EMPLOYEE-NAME, SALARY, AGE, or EMP-ID, and the relation is given a name such as EMPLOYEE. The rows of the relation are called *tuples*. The relational model has three simple organizational rules:

1) no two tuples are the same
2) the order of the tuples is immaterial
3) the order of the columns is immaterial, assuming that the column name is kept with the column values.

A relation is a tabular representation of a file where each tuple represents a record instance and the record instances are unordered. A relational database consists of a group of one or more relations. Tabular structures are easy to comprehend, yet complex data relationships can be modeled. Links are by data values in common domains, not by physical pointers. Figure 7-11 shows the relation headers (schema diagram) for the ski information database. The linkage between the SKI-RESORTS and the TRAILS relations is accomplished by the shared RESORT-NAME column. The instance diagram, Figure 7-12, represents the same information shown in Figures 7-3 and 7-6. Although there is redundancy in the instance diagram, the physical implementation need not have redundant data entries. Figure 7-13 shows a simplified relational schema definition. The LINKS information in Figure 7-8 can be stored in a LINKS relation with TRAILS-NAME and LIFTS-NAME domains.

The *key* of a relation is a column or set of columns which uniquely identify the tuple within the relation. No two tuples can have the same

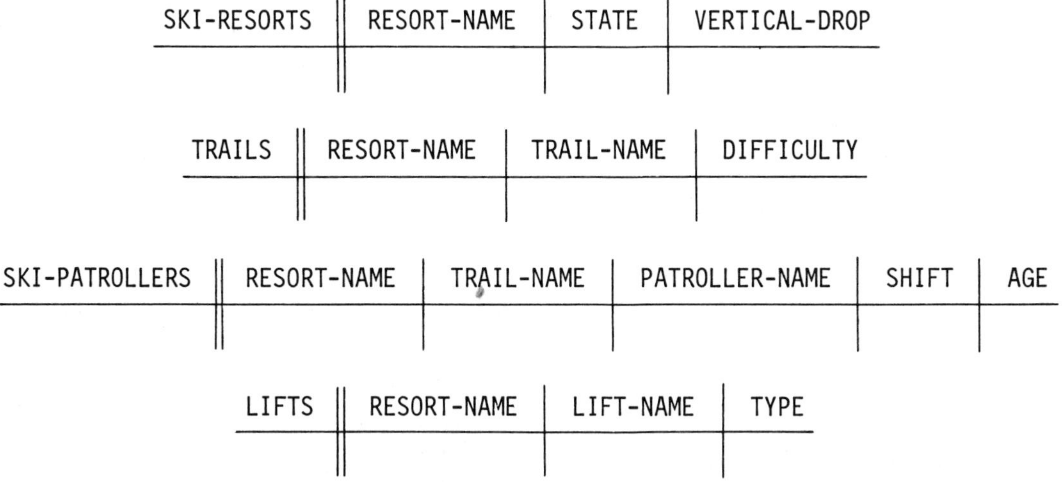

Figure 7-11: Schema diagram for relational ski information database.

SKI-RESORTS	RESORT-NAME	STATE	VERTICAL-DROP
	ASPEN	CO	3300
	HUNTER	NY	1600
	.	.	.
	.	.	.
	.	.	.

TRAILS	RESORT-NAME	TRAIL-NAME	DIFFICULTY
	ASPEN	DIPSY DOODLE	INTERMEDIATE
	ASPEN	RUTHIE'S RUN	INTERMEDIATE
	ASPEN	LITTLE NELL	EASY
	HUNTER	K-27	EXPERT
	HUNTER	BELT PARKWAY	INTERMEDIATE
	HUNTER	CLAIR'S	EXPERT
	HUNTER	THE BATTERY	NOVICE
	.	.	.
	.	.	.
	.	.	.

SKI-PATROLLERS	RESORT-NAME	TRAIL-NAME	PATROLLER-NAME	SHIFT	AGE
	ASPEN	DIPSY DOODLE	PIERRE	1	21
	ASPEN	DIPSY DOODLE	EDDIE	2	24
	ASPEN	DIPSY DOODLE	HANS	2	28
	ASPEN	DIPSY DOODLE	HELENE	3	32
	ASPEN	RUTHIE'S RUN	CLAUDE	1	39

Figure 7-12: Relational version of ski information database.

ASPEN	RUTHIE'S RUN	MEIRA	2	37
ASPEN	LITTLE NELL	SUZIE	1	28
ASPEN	LITTLE NELL	NORMAN	2	29
ASPEN	LITTLE NELL	DAVID	3	28
HUNTER	K-27	ROGER	1	30
HUNTER	K-27	KAREN	2	30
HUNTER	BELT PARKWAY	MARK	1	25
HUNTER	BELT PARKWAY	JOAN	2	31
HUNTER	BELT PARKWAY	MEL	3	31
HUNTER	CLAIR'S RUN	GUY	1	31
HUNTER	CLAIR'S RUN	GEORGE	2	31
HUNTER	THE BATTERY	NANCY	1	34
⋮	⋮	⋮	⋮	⋮

LIFTS	RESORT-NAME	LIFT-NAME	TYPE
	ASPEN	1-A	CHAIR
	ASPEN	2	CHAIR
	ASPEN	3	CHAIR
	HUNTER	PL	POMA
	HUNTER	T-1	TBAR
	HUNTER	R1	ROPETOW
	HUNTER	D	CHAIR
	⋮	⋮	⋮

Figure 7-12 *Cont.*

```
SCHEMA NAME IS SKI-INFORMATION.
DOMAINS.
    RESORT-NAME       CHAR 30.
    STATE             CHAR 2.
    VERTICAL-DROP     CHAR 4.
    TRAIL-NAME        CHAR 35.
    DIFFICULTY        CHAR 10.
    PATROLLER-NAME    CHAR 25.
    SHIFT             CHAR 1.
    AGE               CHAR 2.
    LIFT-NAME         CHAR 5.
    TYPE              CHAR 10.
RELATIONS.
    SKI-RESORTS.
```

Figure 7-13: Schema definition for relational ski information database diagram.

```
        KEY            RESORT-NAME.
        NON-KEY        STATE, VERTICAL-DROP.
      TRAILS.
        KEY            RESORT-NAME, TRAIL-NAME.
        NON-KEY        DIFFICULTY.
      SKI-PATROLLERS.
        KEY            RESORT-NAME, TRAIL-NAME, PATROLLER-NAME.
        NON-KEY        SHIFT, AGE.
      LIFTS.
        KEY            RESORT-NAME, LIFT-NAME.
        NON-KEY        TYPE.
  END.
```

Figure 7-13 *Cont.*

values for the key columns. In the SKI-RESORTS relation the key is the RESORT-NAME column. In the SKI-PATROLLERS relation the key columns are the RESORT-NAME, TRAIL-NAME, and PATROLLER-NAME.

The elegant relational model avoids implementation details and promotes data independence, the separation of physical and logical issues. The relational model, based on the sound mathematical principles of the relational algebra and predicate calculus, has attracted strong academic interest. Although efficient commercially viable relational database systems have not appeared, every area of database research and development has been influenced by the relational model (Date, 1977).

7.1.4 Other Data Models

Other data models have attracted academic interest and may lead to or influence future commercial systems. Senko's (Senko et al., 1973) binary relations model decomposes relations into their domains and maintains only binary relations, that is, relations between two domains. This guarantees mathematical purity, but the wealth of detail may be overwhelming for humans. Chen's entity-relationship model (1975) requires the real world to be modeled as entities connected by relationships and guides database administrators in creating a schema based on trees, networks, or relations. Smith and Smith (1976, 1977) propose a *data abstraction* model based on *aggregation* and *generalization*. Aggregation is the clustering of different items, such as ROOM-NUMBER, TIME, COURSE-NUMBER, and PROFESSOR, to form an aggregate entity called COURSE-OFFERING. Generalization is the clustering of related items such as PROFESSORS, SECRETARIES, JANITORS, and ADMINISTRATORS to form a generic entity called EMPLOYEES. These three data models facilitate accurate real world representation with explicit integrity constraints and precise rules for insertion, deletion, and updating.

7.1.5 Subschemas and Views

Database administrators use data definition languages to describe an application schema containing dozens of segments, records, or relations involving hundreds, of fields, items or domains. Since schema design involves consideration of complex integrity constraints, privacy protection, machine efficiency, and the satisfaction of the needs of a large community, the schema may be more complex than individual users need. To cope with this problem, database designers created the hierarchical or network *subschema* and the relational *view*. A subschema or view is a portion of the schema which meets the needs of a specific application community. The purpose of subschemas or views is to improve security/integrity and to simplify human interaction even at the expense of machine efficiency or database system internal complexity.

For example, if the ski information database were available for public use, a manufacturer of chairlifts might be interested in the SKI-RESORTS and LIFTS portions only. The database administrator could create a subschema containing only these two segments, and the manufacturer could do marketing research on these segments without worrying about the others. Figure 7-14 shows the three subschemas and views for the manufacturer in each of the three popular data models. A national association of ski patrollers might want a subschema showing only the SKI-RESORTS and which SKI-PATROLLERS worked there. Figure 7-15 shows the subschemas and views for the association. Subschemas not only improve the human factors but aid in privacy protection since users need not be aware of the entire database contents to use only a portion of it.

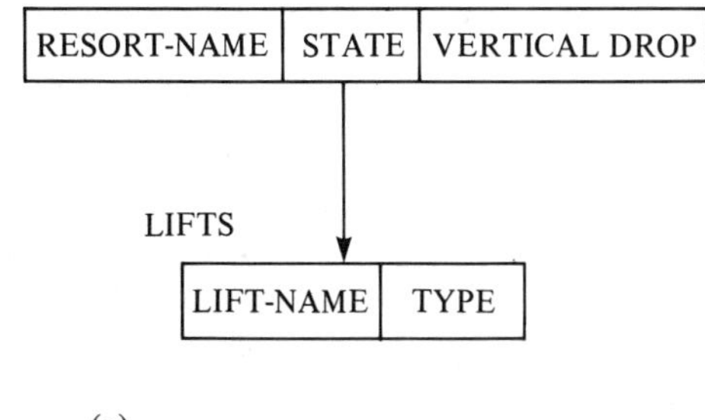

(a)

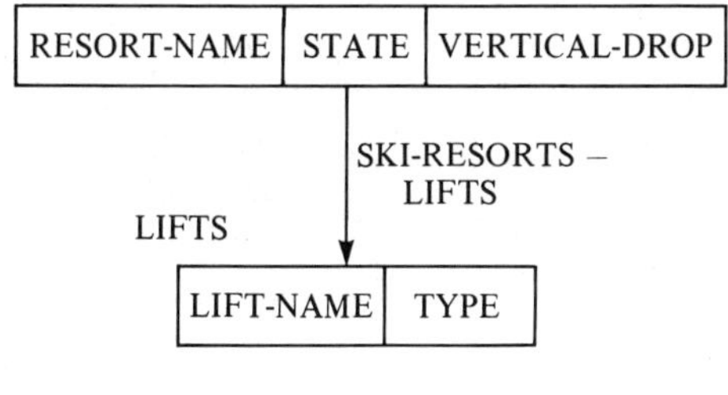

(b)

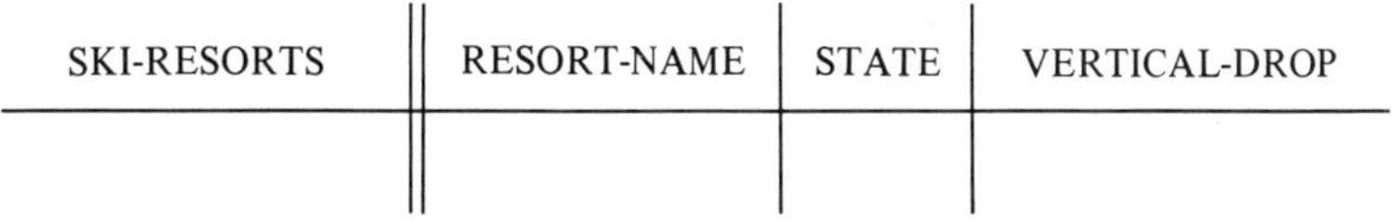

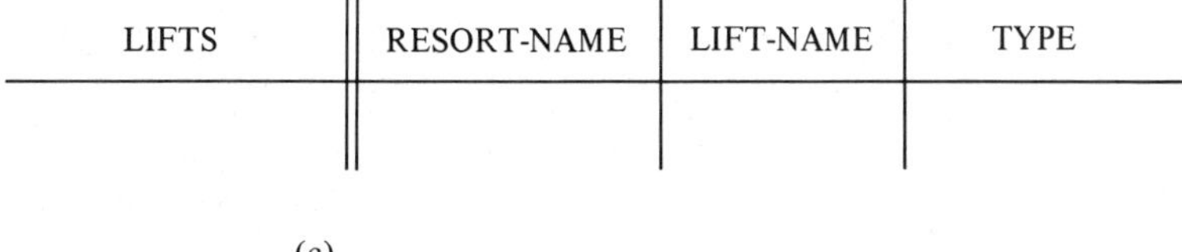

(c)

Figure 7-14: Subschemas for chair lift manufacturers: (a) tree subschema; (b) network subschema; (c) relational view.

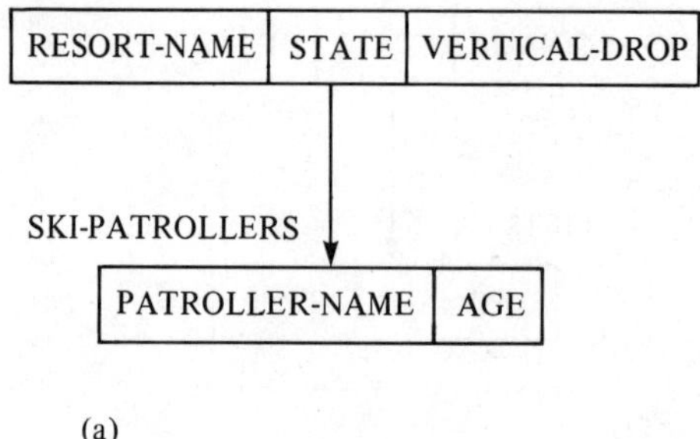

(a)

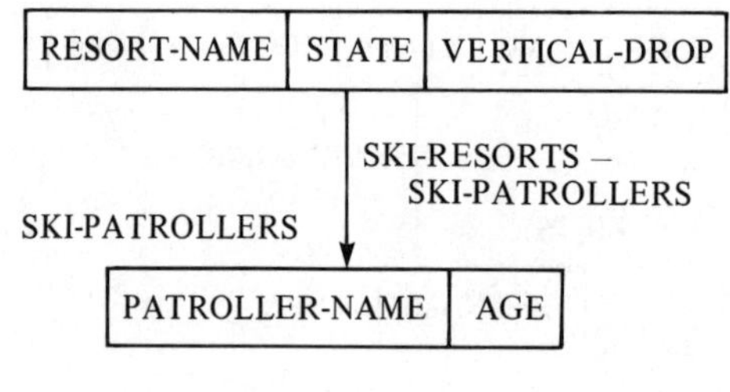

(b)

SKI-RESORTS	RESORT-NAME	STATE	VERTICAL-DROP

SKI-PATROLLERS	RESORT-NAME	PATROLLER-NAME	AGE

(c)

Figure 7-15: Subschemas for ski patrollers' association: (a) tree subschema; (b) network subschema; (c) relational view.

7.2 DATA MODEL SELECTION

The heated debates (Rustin, 1974) of the past years over the relative merits of proposed data models have cooled down. Developers are more concerned with the efficient implementation and effective incorporation of schema-oriented database systems in realistic environments. Supporters of each model have adopted features from competitors, but each model's advantages are becoming clearer.

McGee (1976) gives a set of criteria for evaluating data models, based largely on human factors considerations, including:

Simplicity. A model should have the smallest possible number of structure types, composition rules, and attributes.

Elegance. A model should be as simple as possible for a given direct modeling capability.

Picturability. Model structures should be displayable in pictorial form.

Modeling directness. A model should not provide equivalent direct modeling techniques.

Overlap with co-resident models. A model should mesh smoothly with other co-resident models.

Partitionability. A model should have structures which facilitate the administrative partitioning of data.

Nonconflicting terminology. A model should use terminology which does not conflict with established terminology.

These ill-defined qualitative criteria are a useful starting point, but few guidelines are offered for measuring the simplicity or elegance of a data model. Picturability appears to be a useful attribute, but how can we be sure? Another problem with these criteria is that we may get conflicting impressions from different users of the relative simplicity of two data models. In short, we need the more precise, replicable, and generalizable results which can be obtained from controlled experiments.

Tree-structured data models appear to be most successful when the data is perceived to have a natural tree structure, but is cumbersome otherwise. The relational model is elegant, but critics have complained that it is too arbitrary and that models which can represent more semantic information are preferred. The network model permits sophisticated structures to be described, but the concomitant complexity increases the difficulty of usage. These subjective impressions culled from the literature and comments from colleagues need to be clarified and verified. I suspect that no model will emerge as the best, but that several data models will be necessary to satisfy the variety of users and problems.

Durding, Becker and Gould (1977) experimentally studied the structure people use to organize data. Undergraduate subjects were asked to organize sets of 15–20 words and present them on paper. The word sets had a natural organization pattern such as a tree, network, list or table: for example, a tree structure would be natural for the words 'occupations,' 'professional,' 'laborer,' 'doctor,' 'lawyer,' 'miner,' 'plumber,' and 'farmer.' The experiments demonstrated that the subjects could recognize each of the four organization patterns and use them effectively. When compelled to use structures which did not match the natural pattern of the data, subjects had serious difficulty. Durding et al., conclude that 'the structure of the database...should conform to the semantic relationships among the data elements; and, second, that the language used to interrogate the data base should allow for the direct expression of the different types of relations.' These reasonable conclusions support the conjecture that no one data model is universally superior, but that different problems may require different data models.

An experiment (Brosey and Shneiderman, 1978) on 38 undergraduates found that the tree model was somewhat easier to use than the relational model for a university course/student database which had a natural tree structure. This experiment was designed to test data models independently of query facilities. Computer science students with two or three terms of programming (beginner group) and students with six terms of programming (advanced group) were given a schema and instance diagrams for the tree and relational models in this counterbalanced within subjects experiment. Figures 7–16 and 7–17 show the databases presented to subjects. The subjects had to:

1) Execute 16 queries on the instance diagram
2) Prepare questions in English to respond to a problem solving situation: You would like to consider a major in one of the many departments of the university. You can review and compare departments by asking questions. What questions would you ask that could be answered by the information shown in the diagram?
3) Memorize the schema diagram and recall it immediately.

Figure 7–18 shows the graphs of the results for the three experimental tasks. These results, which significantly (at least 1 percent level) favored the tree model for the comprehension and memorization tasks, suggest that if the database has a natural tree-structured pattern, then the tree model is convenient. In this example, the relational model suffered from its weakness in showing interrelationships among relations. The tree-structured pattern of the schema must be discovered by tracing common domains in the relations. The appealing graphical presentation of the tree model might be adopted to show linkages in the relational model.

```
DEPT(D-NAME,HEAD,BLDG,COLLEGE
COURSE(COURSE#,TITLE,D-NAME,DESC)
PREREQ(PREREQ#,P-DEPT,P-TITLE,COURSE#,D-NAME)
OFFERING(O-DATE,LOCATION,FORMAT,COURSE#,D-NAME)
TEXT(T-TITLE,AUTHOR,DATE-P,PUBL,COURSE#,D-NAME)
TEACHER(IDEN,T-NAME,RANK,O-DATE,LOCATION,COURSE#,D-NAME)
STUDENT(STU#,S-NAME,GRADE,O-DATE,LOCATION,COURSE#,D-NAME)
```

(a)

COURSE

COURSE#	TITLE	D-NAME	DESC
001	Basic Prog	CmpSc	...
102	Comp Org	CmpSc	...
450	Info Theory	CmpSc	...
260	Num Anal	CmpSc	...

OFFERING

O-DATE	LOCATION	FORMAT	COURSE#	D-NAME
F77	New Ken	F3	001	CmpSc
W77	York	F2	001	CmpSc
Sp77	Hershey	F2	001	CmpSc
Su76	DuBois	F3	102	CmpSc
W76	York	F3	102	CmpSc
W76	Hershey	F2	102	CmpSc
F77	New Ken	F3	260	CmpSc
Sp76	Pitts	F2	260	CmpSc
F77	DuBois	F2	260	CmpSc
Su77	York	F1	450	CmpSc
F77	York	F2	450	CmpSc
Sp77	New Ken	F2	450	CmpSc

DEPT

D-NAME	HEAD	BLDG	COLLEGE
CmpSc	Rhodes,F	Brown	Science

PREREQ

PREREQ#	P-DEPT	P-TITLE	COURSE#	D-NAME
010	Math	Alg & Trig	001	CmpSc
101	CmpSc	Fortran IV	102	CmpSc
110	CmpSc	Num Anal	260	CmpSc
212	Phil	Logistics	260	CmpSc
318	Stat	Stat	260	CmpSc
260	CmpSc	Adv Num Anal	450	CmpSc
071	Math	Lin Alg	450	CmpSc

STUDENT

STU#	S-NAME	GRADE	O-DATE	LOCATION	COURSE#	D-NAME
1122	Shaw,K	B	W77	York	001	CmpSc
1134	Arbuckle,P	A	W77	York	001	CmpSc
8909	Levey,K	C	W77	York	001	CmpSc
8997	Cramer,T	A	W77	York	001	CmpSc
2389	Fox,L	A	F77	New Ken	001	CmpSc
2390	Cruley,D	B	F77	New Ken	001	CmpSc
5135	Norris,P	A	W76	York	102	CmpSc
6111	Riley,K	B	W76	York	102	CmpSc
6544	Staugh,L	C	W76	York	102	CmpSc
9110	Meckley,L	B	W76	York	102	CmpSc
4567	Witte,C	B	Su76	DuBois	102	CmpSc
4911	Trimmer,L	C	Su76	DuBois	102	CmpSc
6410	Ulmer,A	A	Su76	DuBois	102	CmpSc
7766	Trottle,B	A	Su76	DuBois	102	CmpSc
3323	Abel,F	D	Sp76	Pitts	260	CmpSc
4872	Curran,G	C	Sp76	Pitts	260	CmpSc
8018	Platt,B	B	Sp76	Pitts	260	CmpSc
9155	Poff,E	A	Sp76	Pitts	260	CmpSc
6123	Spoon,L	A	F77	New Ken	260	CmpSc
7432	Wrebe,C	A	F77	New Ken	260	CmpSc
9786	Eaton,A	A	F77	New Ken	260	CmpSc
2998	Acher.P	B	F77	York	450	CmpSc
3110	Miller,F	B	F77	York	450	CmpSc
4932	Bixler,R	B	F77	York	450	CmpSc
3572	Houser,A	A	Su77	York	450	CmpSc
4421	Zebb,F	A	Su77	York	450	CmpSc
4485	Hott,F	B	Su77	York	450	CmpSc
5600	Miller,K	B	Su77	York	450	CmpSc
6799	Quinn,P	C	Su77	York	450	CmpSc
3455	Weston,D	C	Sp77	Hershey	001	CmpSc
6547	Amato,J	B	Sp77	Hershey	001	CmpSc
5010	Trone,T	C	W76	Hershey	102	CmpSc
8410	Starz,N	C	W76	Hershey	102	CmpSc
8596	Mears,L	D	W76	Hershey	102	CmpSc
2998	Webb,E	B	F77	DuBois	260	CmpSc
4166	Sterner,A	A	F77	DuBois	260	CmpSc
4801	Gaines,G	B	F77	DuBois	260	CmpSc
6913	Shory,P	B	F77	DuBois	260	CmpSc
4010	Geisey,L	B	Sp77	New Ken	450	CmpSc
5002	Duke,P	B	Sp77	New Ken	450	CmpSc
6123	Spoon,L	B	Sp77	New Ken	450	CmpSc
8018	Platt,B	B	Sp77	New Ken	450	CmpSc

TEXT

T-TITLE	AUTHOR	DATE-P	PUBL	COURSE#	D-NAME
Computers	Jon	1976	Wiley	001	CmpSc
Intro to CS	Chia	1977	McG	001	CmpSc
BAL/370	Koff	1975	Brown	102	CmpSc
Intro to BAL	Lang	1971	Aver	102	CmpSc
Adv Num Anal	Kott	1974	McG	260	CmpSc
Num Compt	Reed	1975	PSU	260	CmpSc
Info theory	Shott	1973	Hay	450	CmpSc

TEACHER

IDEN	T-NAME	RANK	O-DATE	LOCATION	COURSE#	D-NAME
2345	Wolf,J	Assoc	W77	York	001	CmpSc
4366	Kicks,J	Prof	W77	York	001	CmpSc
8970	Mottle,A	Asst	W77	York	001	CmpSc
1111	Kimmel,J	Inst	F77	New Ken	001	CmpSc
2377	Lott,L	Asst	F77	New Ken	001	CmpSc
6999	Myers,O	Asst	W76	York	102	CmpSc
7474	Pyle,F	Asst	W76	Hershey	102	CmpSc
2234	Johns,M	Asst	Su77	DuBois	102	CmpSc
2345	Wolf,J	Assoc	Sp76	Pitts	260	CmpSc
3678	Miller,Z	Prof	Sp76	Pitts	260	CmpSc
8855	Klopp,M	Assoc	Sp76	Pitts	260	CmpSc
1011	Stopp,L	Prof	F77	New Ken	260	CmpSc
4545	Aaron,J	Assoc	F77	New Ken	260	CmpSc
3579	Wine,S	Inst	F77	York	450	CmpSc
4102	Pricer,M	Asst	F77	York	450	CmpSc
6999	Myers,O	Asst	Su77	York	450	CmpSc
7474	Pyle,F	Asst	Su77	York	450	CmpSc
6788	Gerk,S	Inst	Sp77	Hershey	001	CmpSc
6900	Mills,O	Asst	Sp77	Hershey	001	CmpSc
6788	Gerk,S	Asst	W76	Hershey	102	CmpSc
6900	Mills,O	Asst	W76	Hershey	102	CmpSc
2234	Johns,M	Prof	F77	DuBois	260	CmpSc
6999	Myers,O	Asst	F77	DuBois	260	CmpSc
2236	Dunker,F	Prof	Sp77	New Ken	450	CmpSc
2377	Lott,L	Asst	Sp77	New Ken	450	CmpSc

(b)

Figure 7-16: Relational instance diagram used in experiment (Brosey and Shneiderman, 1978): (a) table format; (b) table instance diagram.

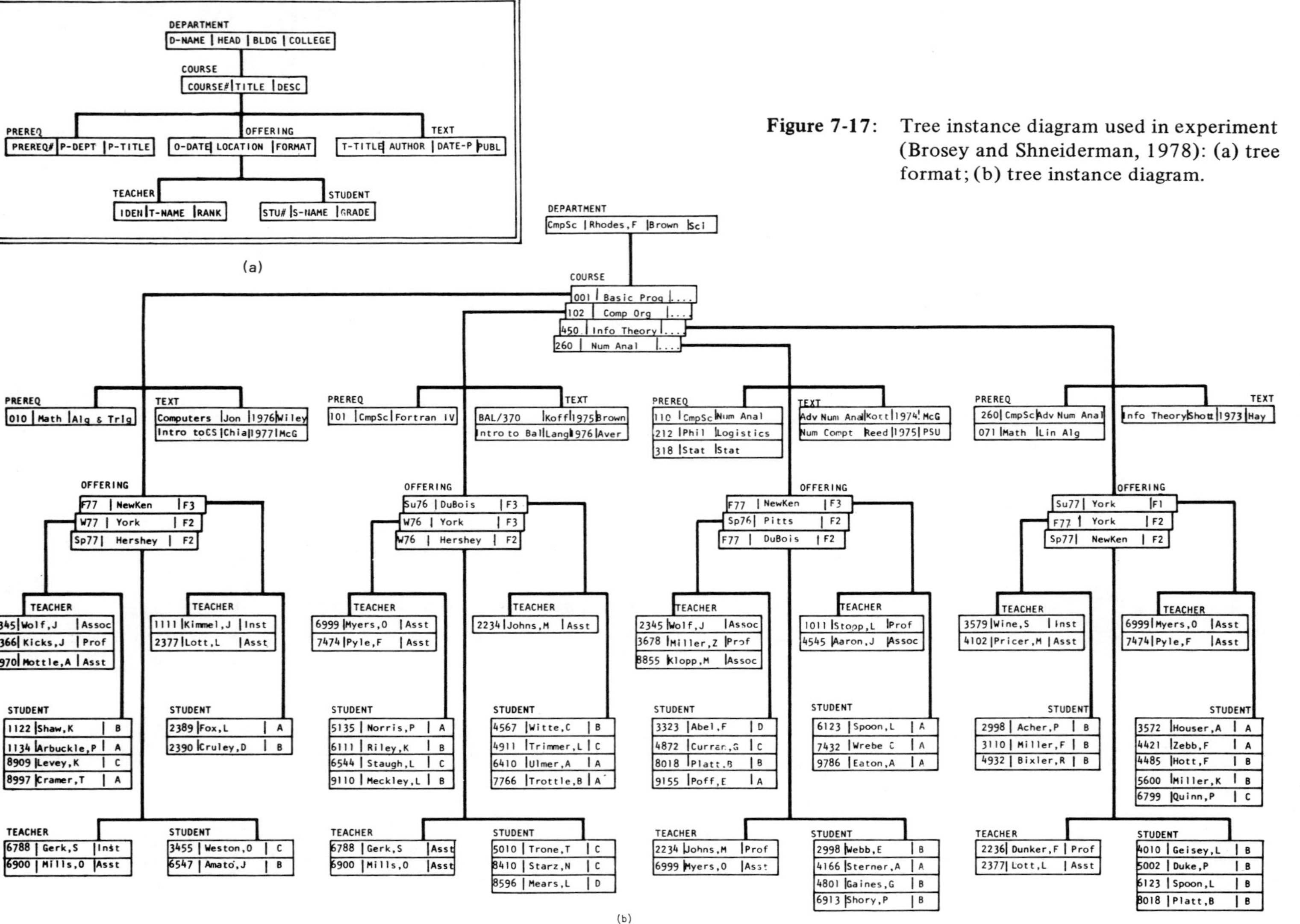

Figure 7-17: Tree instance diagram used in experiment (Brosey and Shneiderman, 1978): (a) tree format; (b) tree instance diagram.

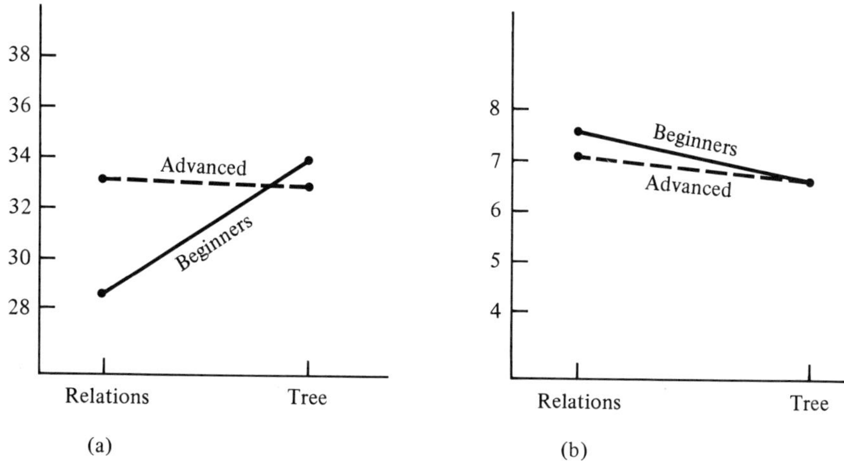

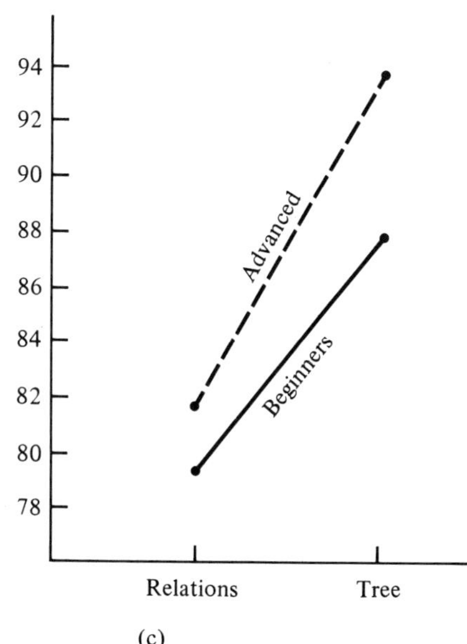

Figure 7-18: Results of relation and tree data model comparison (Brosey and Shneiderman, 1978): (a) comprehension means for group by model; (b) situation problem means for group by model; (c) memorization means for group by model.

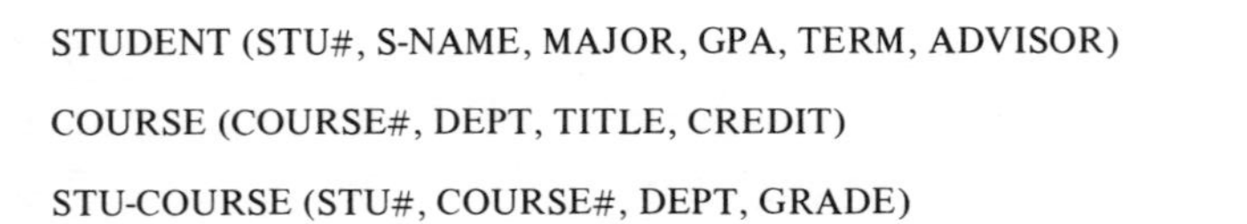

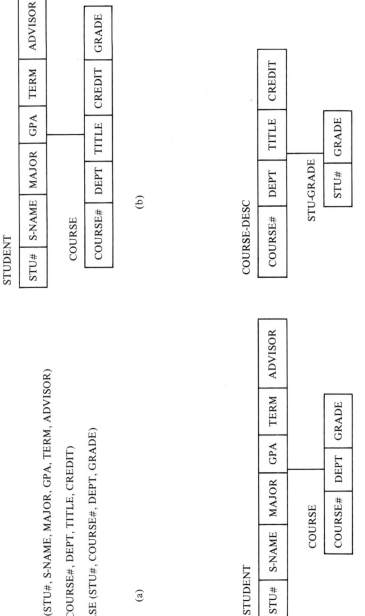

STUDENT (STU#, S-NAME, MAJOR, GPA, TERM, ADVISOR)

COURSE (COURSE#, DEPT, TITLE, CREDIT)

STU-COURSE (STU#, COURSE#, DEPT, GRADE)

(a)

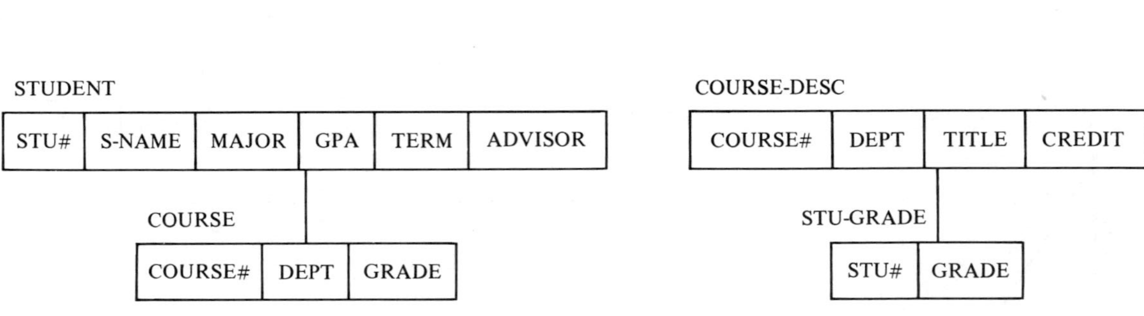

Figure 7-19: Schemas for second experimental study of data models: (a) table format; (b) tree-1 format; (c) tree-2 format.

In a second experiment requiring only comprehension and memorization tasks, 75 undergraduate subjects were assigned to three groups so as to balance grade point averages. A reduced university data base (Figure 7-19) was prepared in the relational model (Table format), the tree model (Tree-1 format) and the tree model organized into two trees (Tree-2 format). The goal of this experiment was to compare performance for these three approaches in presenting structural patterns. Table 7-1 shows the Tree-2 format was easier to use for the comprehension section which required query execution (1 percent level) but significantly more difficult to memorize (5 percent level) due to the greater volume of detail.

Data Model	Comprehension Score (16 questions at 8 points per question)	Memorization Score (Perfect score = 100)
Table	90.0	88.4
Tree-1	99.8	90.5
Tree-2	103.2	79.9

Table 7-1: Scores for second experimental comparison of relational and tree data models (Brosey and Shneiderman, 1978).

These two experiments reveal that, although the relational model is mathematically purer and possibly a convenient notation in general, there exist circumstances in which the tree model is easier to use. Furthermore, the relational model might be made more usable by a visual presentation of the interrelationships among relations. Astute application systems designers should recognize the applicability of each data model for a particular schema pattern and user group.

7.3 SUBSCHEMA DESIGN

Once a data model has been selected for an application, the database designer/analyst must create the schema. Although machine efficiency issues may intervene, every effort should be made to provide the easiest to use schema.

In the relational model, since operations involving several relations increase query complexity, it may be preferable to have fewer relations with more columns. Unfortunately, these relations may exhibit update anomalies (Heath, 1972), causing conflicting facts to enter the database when an update is made or permitting useful information to be lost.

For example, Figure 7-20 shows airline schedule information

AIRLINE	FLT #	MONTH	DATE	DAY	PILOT	RANK	PLANE
	102	4	1	MON	SIBLEY	SENIOR	747
	102	4	2	TUE	GRAVE	FIRST	727
	102	4	3	WED	SIBLEY	SENIOR	747
	107	4	2	TUE	DERMAN	SECOND	DC10
	107	4	3	WED	GRAVE	FIRST	L1011
	108	4	3	WED	CODD	FIRST	747
	.	.	.	.	.	.	.
	.	.	.	.	.	.	.
	.	.	.	.	.	.	.

Figure 7-20: Simple single-relation database.

an easy to understand and query form, but dependencies among the domains obscure the meaning of the data and make insertion, deletion, and update perilous. The DAY is dependent on the MONTH and DATE columns and the RANK column is dependent on the PILOT column. A change in RANK would have to be made in every tuple which referred to a specific pilot. If a PILOT was not scheduled for a specific month, the RANK information would probably still be required. To resolve these problems the database might be kept in the form shown in Figure 7-21 which explicitly demonstrates dependencies. An elegant database design might provide a subschema in the form of Figure 7-20 for query purposes while insertions, deletions, and updates might be made through a subschema in the form of Figure 7-21. Analogous transformations can be made in the network and tree structure data models.

A second issue in subschema design is the difference in views held by different user communities. For example, in cataloging journal articles, librarians may think of a database of JOURNALS consisting of VOLUMES containing ARTICLES written by AUTHORS and having KEYWORDS (Figure 7-22). The library users probably prefer the database to show KEYWORDS referencing a collection of ARTICLES which are written by a group of AUTHORS (Figure 7-23).

Another problem that arises in tree structures is depth versus breadth tradeoffs. Organizational DIVISIONS may be parent to DEPARTMENTS which are parents to EMPLOYEES (Figure 7-24), or DIVISIONS may be parent to EMPLOYEES directly with department included as a field of the employee segment (Figure 7-25). Although this

CALENDAR	MONTH	DATE	DAY
	4	1	MON
	4	2	TUE
	4	3	WED
	.	.	.
	.	.	.
	.	.	.

CREW	PILOT	RANK
	SIBLEY	SENIOR
	GRAVE	FIRST
	DERMAN	SECOND
	CODD	FIRST
	.	.
	.	.
	.	.

SCHEDULE	FLT #	MONTH	DATE	PILOT	PLANE
	102	4	1	SIBLEY	747
	102	4	2	GRAVE	727
	102	4	3	SIBLEY	747
	107	4	2	DERMAN	DC10
	107	4	3	GRAVE	L1011
	108	4	3	CODD	747
	.	.	.	.	.
	.	.	.	.	.
	.	.	.	.	.

Figure 7-21: Three-relation form of the database of Figure 7-20.

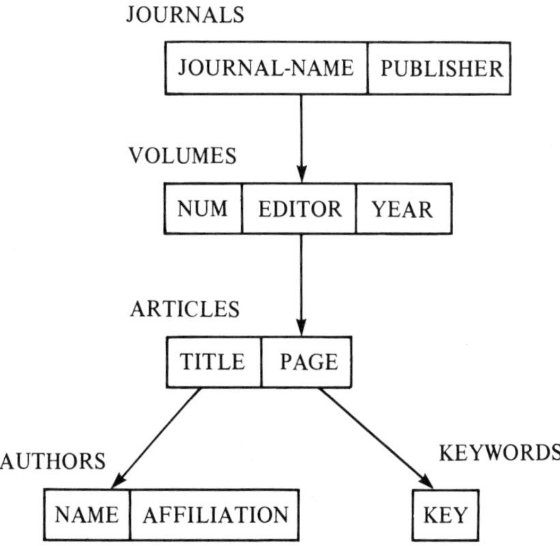

Figure 7-22: Librarian view.

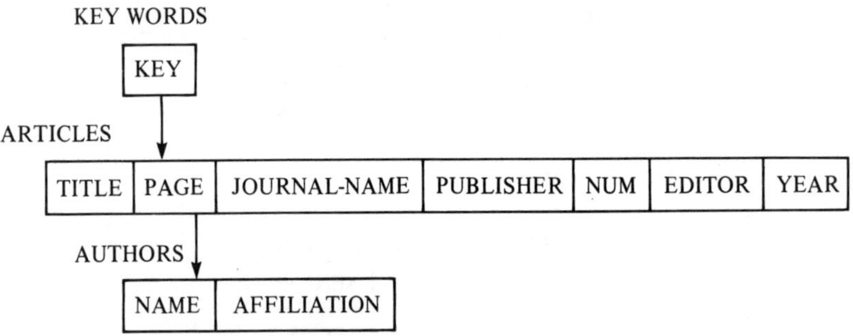

Figure 7-23: User's view of Figure 7-22.

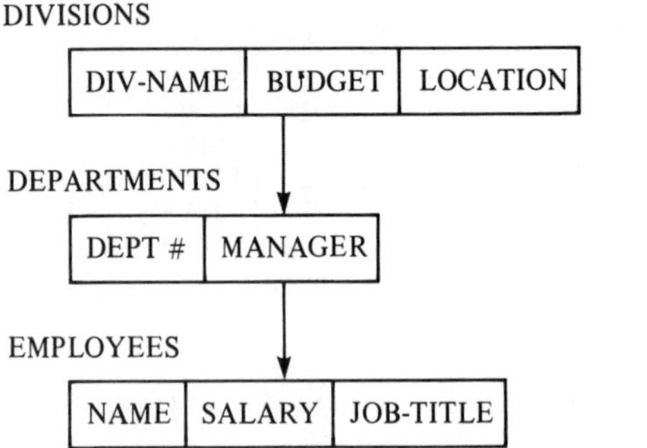

Figure 7-24: Three-level database schema.

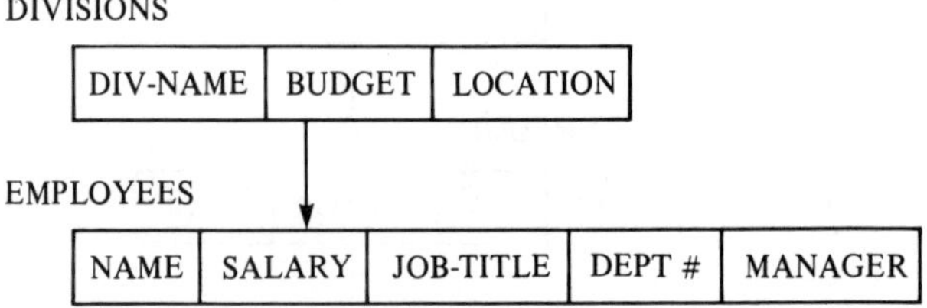

Figure 7-25: Two-level version of database schema of Figure 7-24.

problem involves machine performance considerations, the human factors component is important. These and other design considerations should be studied experimentally.

Network models which require currency pointer maintenance present additional difficulties for programmers. Record types which have more than one owner record type and cyclic schema structures are particularly confusing to novices.

The binary relational model (Senko et al., 1973) has an elegant and simple basis, but the complexity of schema diagrams can lead to confusion. Studies need to be performed to assess ease of use of binary relations which do not have the convenience of a grouping structure such as a record or a segment.

Since variable names are critical in conveying the meaning of the data, experiments should be performed with the intended user population to ensure that the proper meaning has been conveyed. Even domain values, such as job titles ('secretary' has at least two meanings at the Department of Defense) or student grades (not everyone is familiar with each of the grade codes: A, B, C, D, F, I, W), should be tested to ensure user comprehension.

7.4 PRACTITIONER'S SUMMARY

The lively debate over the primacy of the relational, network, and hierarchical data models has subsided as proponents improve the capabilities of their model and recognize the advantages of each model for specific application domains, user classes, and data manipulation demands. System designers should carefully select from these models or incorporate more than one of these models in their system. Pilot designs should be tested on several models before a choice is made. Within a given data model, care should be taken in designing subschemas to suit user needs. Multiple subschemas can be optimized to meet divergent needs, but proliferation of subschemas can disrupt cooperation.

7.5 RESEARCHER'S AGENDA

The data models are still primitive and refinements are possible. More precise techniques for formal definition and comparison of data models are necessary to support continuing evaluation efforts. Schema definition languages are often crude and likely candidates for improvements. Metrics of subschema complexity, such as, depth, breadth, or number of fields, should be developed to assist designers in preparing easy to use subschemas. These metrics should be verified with user experiments.

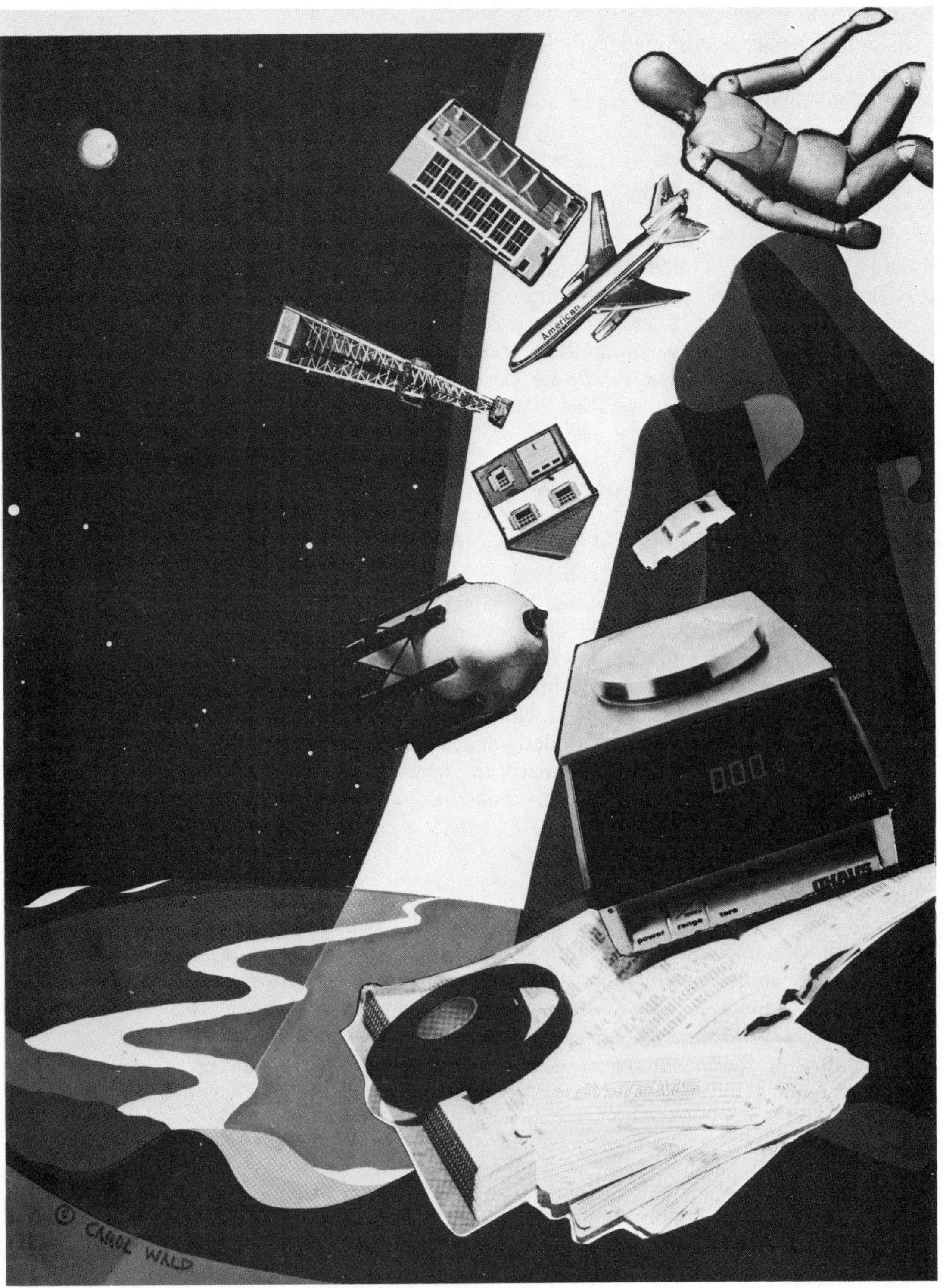
American
OHAUS
power
range
tare
SYSTEMS
© CAROL WALD

8

DATABASE QUERY AND MANIPULATION LANGUAGES

At any given instant, innumerable images are decaying, dropping into the black immensity of the forgotten. Others are entering the system, being processed and filed. At the same time, we are retrieving images, using them and returning them to the file, perhaps in a different place. We are constantly comparing images, associating them, cross-referencing them in new ways and repositioning them.

Alvin Toffler, *Future Shock* (1970)

Frameworks for evaluation and design of database query and manipulation facilities – functions – tasks – query features – language samples – host-embedded vs. self-contained – specification vs. procedural languages – linear keyword vs. positional languages – experimental results

8.1 INTRODUCTION

Users of database systems require data manipulation languages for operating on the data described by the schema. Hundreds of proposals have been made for query and data manipulation languages and a large portion of these have been implemented. The keen competition has produced rapid evolutionary refinements, but historical inertia is often a more powerful force than survival of the fittest. Having learned one approach, programmers and managers are likely to stick to that approach, just as they have remained with their first programming language. Still, there is room for new ideas; programmers will accept refinements to their language and new facilities when the advantages are obvious.

The exciting aspect of database query languages is that usage will expand dramatically to nonprogrammers through information utilities and home computer systems. These new users will not be influenced by historical precedent, but will gravitate to the easiest to use facility. Since the background of these nonprogrammers is radically different from the background of programming language designers, controlled experiments on user performance may be helpful in guiding development.

Zloof (1978) offers nine requirements for design of a user-friendly data manipulation language for nonprogrammers:

1) Minimum concepts required to get started: simple operations should be simple.
2) Minimum syntax: simple syntax, even for complex operations.
3) Consistency: operators should have consistent semantics in all contexts.
4) Flexibility: language should 'capture the user's thought process, thus providing many degrees of freedom in formulating a transaction.'

5) Not sensitive: a small change in the query should produce a small change in the query language expression.
6) Easy to extend and modify: views, snapshots and reorganizations.
7) Minimum exception rules: uniform language structure.
8) Easy detection of errors: minimize possibility of error and provide good error messages.
9) Unified language: same syntax for query, update, insert, delete, definition, and security control.

This list is a useful set of high-level goals for evaluating or designing a data manipulation or query language. The detailed set of issues to aid evaluation and design is presented in the next section.

8.2 ISSUES IN DATABASE USAGE

The wide variety of applications and users of database systems may produce confusion in the designer's mind and result in a system which is optimized for only a limited subset of the application domain. The ensuing categories may help organize the design process, provide a guide to evaluation, and suggest directions for experimental research. These categories are not entirely independent and the sections in each category represent discrete partitions of a continuum. An attempt has been made to be thorough, but no claim for completeness is made. The issues include the operational functions, user tasks, and query features.

8.2.1 Functions

Functions are the operations that users perform on the database. An item may be a field, record, collection of records, file, or the entire database. Primary transaction-oriented functions include:

1) *Insertion* of one or more items. This operation typically includes the specification of the keys and related data.
2) *Deletion* of one or more items. This operation requires the user to specify a key which is used to search the database. If a record with the key is found, the record is deleted.
3) *Retrieval* of information from the database. The user provides a query and the database returns required information. A retrieval may be as complex as the copying of the entire database.

Ancillary functions include:

4) *Locking and unlocking* of items to provide for integrity during concurrent processing.
5) *Privacy check* to ensure that the user is permitted to perform the function requested.
6) *Utility functions* include database administration operations such as an initial load, physical reorganization, logical restructuring, data translation, performance statistics collection, and data validation.
7) *Data description* to create the schema. The user provides detailed descriptions of fields, record structures, and relationships among records.

8.2.2 Tasks

Tasks are components in the performance of the previously mentioned functions. To accomplish one of the functions, the user must perform one or more of these tasks:

1) *Learning* the syntax and semantics of the function specification. A typical goal is to reduce the learning time for a function. Database facilities which are easy to learn may be convenient for only a limited subset of the functions. The traditional tradeoffs in programming languages of ease of learning and power of expression apply here. For example, BASIC is considered to be relatively easy to learn, but it has weak control and data structure facilities.

2) *Composition* of the syntax required to perform a function. Composition includes writing a program or query, formulating a natural language query, or even responding to a menu selection frame on an interactive terminal. We hope that facilities which are easy-to-learn are also easy to compose with, but this is not always the case. An easy-to-learn facility may be so limited that composing useful functions is difficult.

3) *Comprehension* of function syntax composed by someone else. It is often necessary to read syntax composed by others for learning purposes. Easily composed syntax may not be easy to comprehend. Comprehension is often a component of other tasks.

4) *Debugging* of syntax written by oneself or others to correct errors. Debugging requires comprehension and composition ability but includes other complex cognitive skills. Database application programs may be debugged using traditional programming techniques, but natural language, menu selection, and query language programs will require novel debugging strategies. The central problem will be to provide users with feedback to help them determine whether the semantics of the function they invoke correspond with their intentions.

5) *Modification* of a function written by oneself or others to convert to a new transactions request. Existing database queries will often be the basis of new queries. The modification task requires composition and comprehension skills.

This categorization is taken directly from previous work on programming languages, but it seems to be appropriate. Learning and composition may be more important in database applications, but the full range of tasks will be required. New techniques for debugging database requests in query languages are an attractive research area.

8.2.3 Query Features

The variety and complexity of features suggests the need for a finer categorization. The following is based on Reisner's (1977) list of features in relational query languages:

1) *Simple mapping* returns data values when a known data value for another field is supplied. An example would be: Find the names of employees in Department 50. Comparison operations such as equal to, less than, or greater than may be included in the specification of the simple mapping.

2) *Selection* gives all the data values associated with a specified key value, for example: Give the entire record for the employee whose name is John Jones.

3) *Projection*, in the relational model, selects an entire column or domain of a relation, for example: Print the names of all employees.

4) *Boolean queries* are those which permit AND/OR/NOT connectives such as: Find the names of employees who work for

Smith and are not in Department 50.

5) *Set operation* queries are those which permit intersection, union, symmetric difference, or other set operators. Boolean queries can be converted to set operation queries.

6) *Built-in-functions* provide special-purpose library functions to aid in question formulation, such as MAXIMUM, MINIMUM, AVERAGE, COUNT, and SUM. For example: Print the average salary in department 50.

The query types described thus far are an easy-to-learn subset which has been used in our pilot studies and Reisner's (Reisner et al., 1975; Reisner, 1975) work. She found that even nonprogrammer subjects scored better than 70 percent correct in composing these query types using SEQUEL. Programmers scored better than 80 percent correct.

More complex query features include:

7) *Combination* queries are the result of using the output of one query as the input for another. Reisner uses the term 'composition.' An example would be: Find the names of all departments which have more than 30 employees and then print the department managers' names.

8) *Grouping* collects items with a common domain value, such as department number, for example: Print the names of departments where the average salary is greater than 15,000. The employees must be grouped by departments before the averaging can take place.

9) *Universal quantification* corresponds to the 'for all' concept of the first order predicate calculus. This operation is difficult for most users to comprehend and work with. The ambiguous use of the word 'all' in English and the subtlety of set equivalence and set containment contribute to the difficulties (Thomas, 1976a).

The query features discussed thus far are available in most query languages that have been designed for the binary, tree, and relational models of data.

Codd (1971) defines relational completeness of a query language as the property of having the descriptive power of the first-order predicate calculus. Relational completeness has been used as a primitive measuring rod for the selective power of a query language. Two problems come to mind with this yardstick in evaluating the human factors aspect of a language:

1) Many queries that can be written with a relationally complete language are extremely difficult to compose or comprehend. Few people claim to have a thorough understanding of first-order predicate calculus.

2) Many common, useful, simple to understand, and potentially easy to express queries are outside the bounds of relational completeness. For example, in a table of distances between adjacent cities, finding the shortest path between two remote cities is not included in relational completeness (Figure 8-1). Similarly, in a table of employees and their managers, finding the names of all the employees who make more than any of their managers going up the organizational structure, is not a relationally complete query.

DISTANCE	CITY-A	CITY-B	MILES

Relationally complete: Find the distance from NYC to Phil.

Not relationally complete: Find the distance from NYC to LA (assume no direct connection).

Not relationally complete: Find the itinerary with the shortest distance between NYC and LA.

EMP	NAME	SALARY	MGR-NAME

Relationally complete: Find the names of employees who make more than their manager.

Not relationally complete: Find the names of employees who make more than any of their managers going up the organizational structure.

Figure 8-1: Examples of relationally complete and not relationally complete queries.

As an alternative to relational completeness, we need a taxonomy of queries which orders queries from simple to complex. Reisner and others have argued for a level-structured or layered query facility which allows users to compose simple queries and gradually increase their capacity for composing more complex queries. Reisner's feature list and her theoretical linguistic model are a beginning but much work remains.

```
CALL PLITDLI(4,'GUbb',QUERY_PCB,SKI_RESORTS_IO_AREA,'SKI_RESR(STATEbbb=NY)');
DO WHILE(PCB.STATUS_CODE='bb');
CALL PLITDLI(4,'GNPb',QUERY_PCB,TRAILS_IO_AREA,'TRAILSbb(DIFFICULT=EXPERT)');
IF PCB.STATUS_CODE='bb' THEN PUT DATA(RESORT-NAME);
CALL PLITDLI(4,'GNbb',QUERY_PCB,SKI-RESORTS_IO_AREA,'SKI_RESR(STATEbbb=NY)');
END;
```

Figure 8-2: PL/I statements to invoke the PL/I facility of IMS.

```
     GET UNIQUE  SKI-RESORTS   (STATE='NY')
                 TRAILS        (DIFFICULTY='EXPERT')
     Print RESORT-NAME
LOOP GET NEXT    SKI-RESORTS   (STATE='NY')
                 TRAILS        (DIFFICULTY='EXPERT')
     Print RESORT-NAME
     GO TO LOOP
```

Figure 8-3: Simplified version of Figure 8-2.

8.3 LANGUAGE SAMPLES

An overwhelming variety of database query and manipulation languages have been implemented or proposed. This section includes sample syntax ranging from low-level host-embedded operations to elegant self-contained languages to elaborate graphics-oriented facilities. Where reasonable, the syntactic form is modeled after Date (1977).

These samples are based on the ski information database of Chapter 7 and are for the query: Print the names of ski resorts in New York state which have at least one expert trail. Executing this query requires the database system to find the name of New York ski resorts and then check to see if the difficulty of any of the trails is expert. If an expert trail is found, then the name of the ski resort is printed.

Figure 8-2 shows the PL/I code required for the query when the DL/I language facility of IMS is used for the schema shown in Figure 7-1. Figure 8-3 shows a syntactically 'sugared' version. In either form, the first instance is treated separately from other instances. The GU code stands for 'Get Unique,' which means find the first, and GN stands for 'Get Next.'

Figure 8-4 shows the COBOL statements for the DBTG network schema of Figure 7-4. The first statement of the loop finds the New York State resorts and then a check is made to see if any of the TRAIL member records have an expert designation.

Both the IMS and DBTG examples are simplified. The application programmer would have to establish lengthy data declarations for the record types and for database systems communications areas, and would have to include additional status checking.

```
      MOVE 'NY' TO STATE IN SKI-RESORTS.
LOOP  FIND DUPLICATE SKI-RESORTS.
      IF NOTFOUND='YES' GO TO QUIT.
      MOVE 'EXPERT' TO DIFFICULTY IN TRAILS.
      FIND TRAILS WITHIN SKI-RESORTS-TRAILS
           CURRENT USING DIFFICULTY IN TRAILS.
      IF ENDSET = 'YES' GO TO LOOP.
      GET SKI-RESORTS.
      Print RESORT-NAME
      GO TO LOOP
```

Figure 8-4: COBOL statements for DBTG network approach.

Figure 8-5 shows the code for the self-contained language of Model 204. Figure 8-6 contains the simple query form of System 2000's Immediate Access Language.

Figures 8-7 through 8-11 show relational model languages based on querying the schema shown in Figure 7-10. In order, these query languages are the relational algebra, the relational calculus, SEQUEL, Query-by-Example, and CUPID. The relational algebra has high-level

```
OPEN SKI-RESORTS
OPEN TRAILS
BEGIN
1.  IN SKI-RESORTS FIND ALL RECORDS FOR WHICH STATE = 'NY'
2.  FOR EACH RECORD IN 1
    2.1.  NOTE RESORT-NAME
    2.2.  IN TRAILS FIND ALL RECORDS FOR WHICH RESORT-NAME = VALUE IN 2.1
          AND DIFFICULTY = 'EXPERT'
    2.3.  PRINT RESORT-NAME IN 2.2
END
```

Figure 8-5: Model 204's self-contained code.

```
PRINT RESORT-NAME
   WHERE  STATE='NY'
   AND    DIFFICULTY='EXPERT'
```

Figure 8-6: System 2000 Immediate Access Language.

```
INTERSECT (PROJECT (SELECT SKI-RESORTS WHERE STATE = 'NY')
                   OVER RESORT-NAME
           AND
           PROJECT (SELECT TRAILS WHERE DIFFICULTY = 'EXPERT')
                   OVER RESORT-NAME)
```

Figure 8-7: Relational algebra.

```
RANGE SKI-RESORTS SX
RANGE TRAILS      TX
GET W (SKI-RESORTS, RESORT-NAME):
      ∃SX (SX.STATE='NY'
       ∧ ∃TX (SX.RESORT-NAME = TX.RESORT-NAME
             ∧ TX.DIFFICULTY = 'EXPERT'))
```

Figure 8-8: Relational calculus.

```
SELECT      RESORT-NAME
FROM        SKI-RESORTS
WHERE       STATE = 'NY'
INTERSECT
SELECT      RESORT-NAME
FROM        TRAILS
WHERE       DIFFICULTY = 'EXPERT'
```

Figure 8-9: SEQUEL (now called SQL).

SKI-RESORTS	RESORT-NAME	STATE	VERTICAL-DROP
	P.X	NY	

TRAILS	RESORT-NAME	TRAIL-NAME	DIFFICULTY
	X		EXPERT

Figure 8-10: Query by example.

procedural operations which act on entire relations. These operations include SELECT for selecting rows of a relation, PROJECT for choosing columns of a relation, and JOIN for combining two relations to form a new relation. The relational calculus is based on the predicate calculus and is more specification oriented then the relational algebra. Users describe the result they want rather than operations for producing the result, for example, GET NEW-EMP(EMP.NAME, EMP > ID) WHERE (EMP.YEARS-EMPLOYED < 2). The algebra and calculus are not intended as user languages, but they have been used as the basis for several. SEQUEL (Chamberlin et al., 1976) and Query-by-Example (Zloof, 1975a, 1978) were intended to be user-oriented and both of these are in continuing development and testing. SEQUEL's keyword approach is natural to programmers who can use it in batch or interactive modes. Query-by-example is designed for an interactive environment where the relational headers are produced by the system and the user merely fills in the boxes. Zloof favors the abstract positional approach and feels that keywords clutter thinking.

CUPID (McDonald and Stonebraker, 1975) depends on interactive graphics to aid the user in producing the diagram which represents the query.

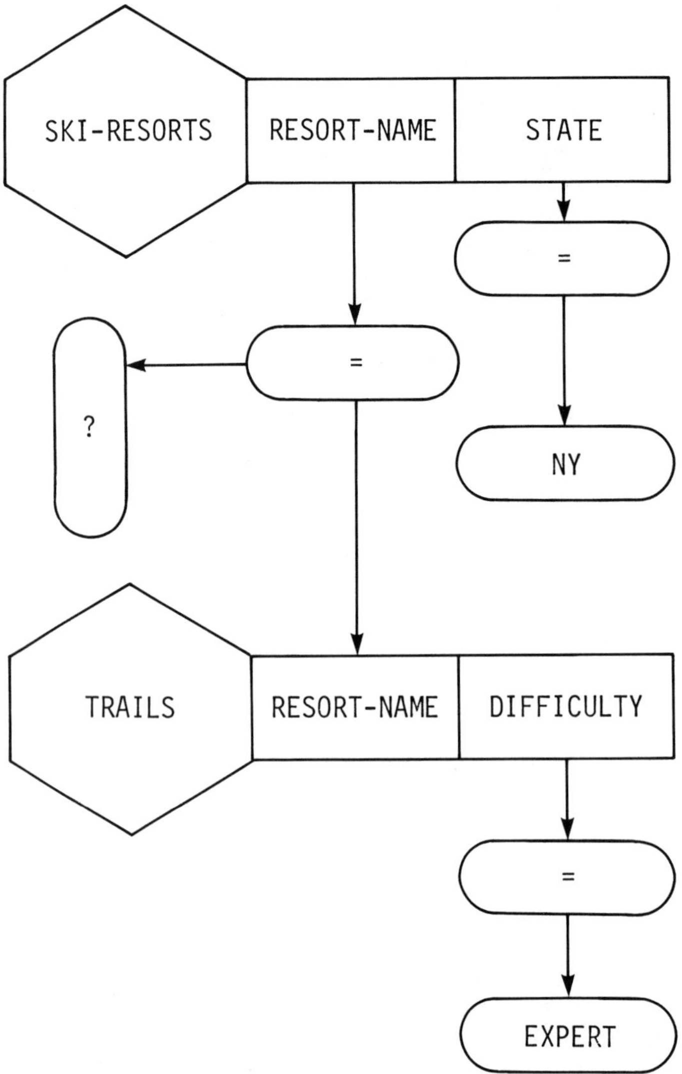

Figure 8-11: CUPID.

Finally, Figure 8-12 shows the FORAL and FORAL LP (lightpen) versions of this query (Senko, 1977). The impressive power of FORAL LP permits rapid expression of extremely complex queries by merely making lightpen touches to the on screen version of the binary relationship diagram.

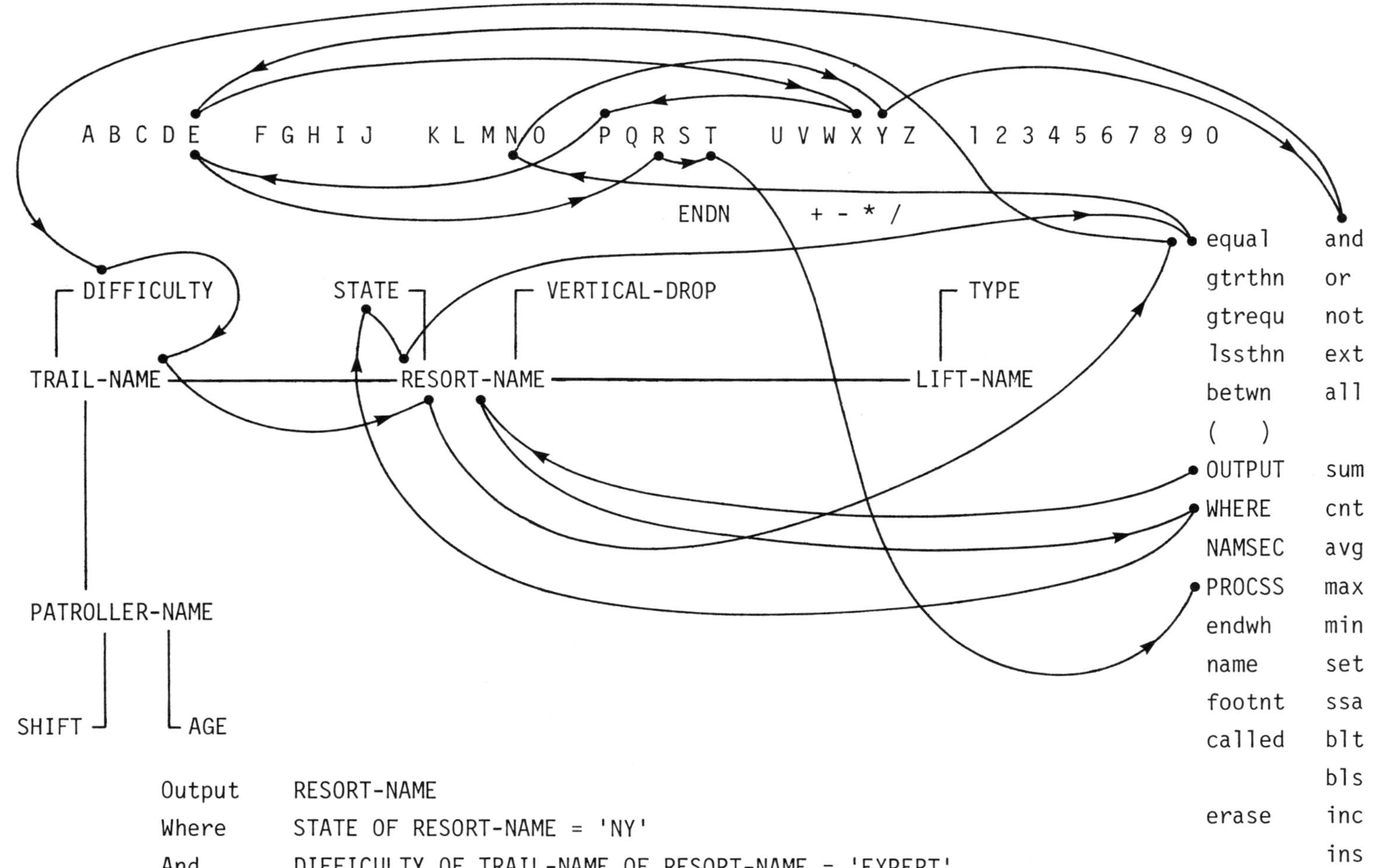


```
Output    RESORT-NAME
Where     STATE OF RESORT-NAME = 'NY'
And       DIFFICULTY OF TRAIL-NAME OF RESORT-NAME = 'EXPERT'
```

Figure 8-12: FORAL LP and FORAL statement.

8.3.1 Host-Embedded vs. Self-Contained

Commercial database systems have used a limited number of operations, such as FIND, GET or STORE, which may be embedded in a host language such as COBOL, PL/I, FORTRAN or Assembler. These data manipulation operations are usually translated by a precompiler into host language procedure calls. Some commercial systems such as IBM's GIS, Computer Corporation of America's Model 204 and the Immediate Access Language of MRI's System 2000 have *self-contained languages* which do not require embedding in a host language. UNIVAC's DMS/1100, which is based on the network model, has, like System 2000, both a self-contained language and a set of operations which can be embedded in a high-level procedural programming language.

Programs written in self-contained languages tend to be shorter and less cluttered with machine oriented details, but they require that programmers learn an entirely new way of manipulating databases. Self-contained languages do not have the flexibility that high-level programming languages such as COBOL or PL/I afford, but they are easier to comprehend and easier for novices to learn. In the long run, self-contained languages will probably prove dominant since automatic optimization, verification, and transformation are possible, and improved comprehensibility implies higher reliability and maintainability.

Proposed languages for the relational model reflect the two possibilities. The low-level 'tuple at a time' approach mirrors the 'record at a time' processing of host-embedded languages while the higher-level languages based on the relational algebra or calculus resemble the self-contained languages.

Advocates of host embedding claim that such facilities are easy for programmers to learn, build on previous knowledge, allow detailed error checking, and provide precise efficient control, but critics claim that the profusion of details leads to complexity which produces errors and makes maintenance difficult. Supporters of self-contained languages argue that fewer more powerful primitives increase programmer productivity even though a whole new way of thinking must be learned. Self-contained languages are probably easier for nonprogrammers to master since the layered or spiral approach permits simple queries to be expressed simply. Even if the execution time is increased, self-contained languages probably lower the overall cost for returning a fraction of the database. Large production runs, which require efficient implementation, will probably always be written in lower-level languages.

8.3.2 Specification vs. Procedural Languages

Database query languages provide a new domain for the controversy between specification languages, which describe the goal, and procedural languages, which describe a process for arriving at the goal. This classification is not discrete: a language fits in the continuum between the extremes. Specification languages are usually viewed as being of higher-level and having shorter length than procedural languages. In database querying, specification languages may be more appealing since the database functions are brief and lend themselves to specification.

The relational algebra is seen as being more procedurally oriented than the relational calculus or calculus based languages such as QUEL, SQUARE, SEQUEL, and Query-by-Example. Commercial query languages like those for System 2000 or Model 204 also blend procedural and specification concepts.

All of these languages are more specification oriented than host-embedded systems which usually require programmed logic control and record-at-a-time processing. CODASYL DBTG network systems have host-embedded operations providing 'navigation' through the database (Bachman, 1974, 1975).

The psychological foundations of this issue are intriguing. Are there cognitive style variables which might indicate which method is preferable for certain subjects or tasks? Could composition be easier with procedural languages but comprehension be easier with specification languages? Some programmers may prefer multiple lower-level procedural navigation to a simple high-level complex specification. Paper and pencil studies seem appropriate here since only semantic issues are involved and syntactic or terminal interface problems are secondary.

8.3.3 Linear Keyword vs. Positional Languages

Some proposals for database query languages, such as QUEL or SEQUEL, are keyword oriented, basing their structure on traditional programming language design. Other proposals include a two-dimensional notation in which positioning is critical: SQUARE, Query-by-Example, CUPID, and FORAL LP. In the latter class of languages, very few keywords are used and a graphics support system may be required.

Supporters of keyword-oriented languages argue that the keywords help in learning and query composition, by associating query semantics with familiar terminology. Supporters of two-dimensional positional query languages claim that confusion can be reduced by using positional notation or special shapes to indicate components of queries.

In Query-by-Example, users are provided with a screen display of relational skeletons. Queries are composed by filling in columns with literals or underlined examples. A keyboard controlled cursor makes placement of items easy. In CUPID, lightpen touches enable users to move shapes and generate diagrams which represent a query. In FORAL LP, the user employs a lightpen to select operations and elements displayed as a binary network on the screen.

The fundamental psychological issue of keyword use versus abstract shape notation is unstudied. For each of the five tasks, does English language knowledge confuse or facilitate users? An early pilot study of ours suggests that high SAT (Scholastic Aptitude Test) Verbal nonprogrammers preferred the keyword based approach of SEQUEL, while high SAT Math nonprogrammers preferred the math-like positional notation of Query-by-Example. Users who emphasize right brain visual intuitive thinking may have different preferences from those who prefer left brain verbal deductive thinking.

8.4 EXPERIMENTAL RESULTS

Gould and Ascher (1975) conducted an experiment on 17 female nonprogrammers' use of a query language patterned after IBM's Interactive Query Facility (IQF). They investigated performance during the formulate, plan, and code stages of problem solving with special attention to the learning processes of these subjects. After lengthy training (range: 4 to 24.5 hours) subjects composed 15 queries from English statements such as: 'List the average salary of employees who were in Chicago, have at least a Bachelor's degree, and are married; and the average salary of engineers over 50 years of age working in St. Louis.' These subjects produced only 37 percent correctly coded queries. Query complexity increased the total times and errors. Poorly stated problems lengthened formulation times but not planning or coding times. No comparison of languages or data models was attempted.

Reisner, Boyce and Chamberlin (1975) and Reisner (1977) present a comparative study of SEQUEL and SQUARE, two languages keyed to the relational model of data. Twenty-nine programmers and 35 nonprogrammers were taught SEQUEL or SQUARE for 12 to 14 hours over a two week period. Subjects were required to compose 40 SEQUEL or SQUARE queries presented to them in English. These queries were graded as 'correct,' 'minor error,' or 'major error' (Table 8-1). Careful records of errors (Tables 8-2 and 8-3) were kept and these led to seven

	Square	Sequel	Mean
Nonprogrammers	54.7	65.0	59.8
Programmers	77.7	77.5	77.6
Mean	66.2	71.2	68.7

Table 8-1: Mean percentage essentially correct in query composition tasks (Reisner, 1977).

	Sequel		Square	
	Nonprogrammers	Programmers	Nonprogrammers	Programmers
Ending	60	39	80	64
Spelling	53	61	55	45
Synonym	33	50	40	18
Quotation mark	47	50	20	8
Other punctuation	20	22	85	54

Table 8-2: Percentage of subjects making at least one minor error of given type on final exam (Reisner, 1977).

	Sequel		Square	
	Nonprogrammers	Programmers	Nonprogrammers	Programmers
Mapping	91	98	88	91
Selection	87	89	90	91
Projection	73	100	90	100
Assignment	87	94	75	100
Built-in functions	88	89	65	87
And/or	77	82	65	80
Set operations	70	88	71	87
Composition	53	74	25	67
Free variable (sq)	-	-	11	48
Group by (seq)	46	61	-	-
Correlation var. (seq)	12	33	-	-
Computed var.	7	44	8	64

Table 8-3: Mean percentage essentially correct scores on final exam, basic features questions (Reisner, 1977).

recommendations for improving the SEQUEL language including: a layered language approach should be used to make simple query facilities available to novice users, online aids should catch minor spelling or syntax errors, training should focus on difficult components, and the syntax should match user's expectations. The revised SEQUEL II language (Chamberlin et al., 1976), now called SQL, was directly influenced by this experiment. Reisner (1977) presents a model of query writing which measures transformational complexity, that is, the number of operations necessary to transform the English presentation of a query into SEQUEL statements. This model may be used to predict errors in query composition.

Thomas and Gould (1975) studied the Query-by-Example language (Zloof, 1975a) to demonstrate the 'ease and accuracy with which nonprogrammers learned and used this powerful Query-by-Example language.' Further motives were to find the challenging parts of the language to improve training and online aids. Thirty-nine subjects received 105 minutes of training, a 20 question composition test, 70 minutes of additional instruction, and finally a second 20 question composition test. Timing and confidence measures were obtained for each query. The detailed performance and error analysis have provided valuable insights on user behavior. A linear multiple regression, based on the numbers of columns, different operators, rows, and linking variables in the correct answer, show good correlation ($r = -.74$) with the proportion of correctly written queries. Thomas and Gould concluded that the advantages of Query-by-Example are: the user has an explicit representation of the data to work with, the tabular model is helpful, the absence of keywords avoids confusion, the system is easy to learn, and the language is 'behaviorally extendable' (same as layered approach).

Greenblatt and Waxman (1978) compared three relationally oriented database query languages: Query-by-Example, a SEQUEL variant, and a relational algebra based language. Undergraduate subjects provided background data on age, sex, high school average, college grade point average, and number of college computer courses (Table 8-4). Greenblatt and Waxman reported 'Query-by-Example had the highest proportion correct and the highest mean confidence ratings and took less than one-half the mean time per question than the closest competitive language.' Only the time measures were significantly different and there was an uneven distribution of subject backgrounds, raising some doubts about the strength of the findings (Table 8-5). These comparative language studies are interesting because they reveal the impact of the query language independently of data model.

Welty (1978) compared performance of undergraduates in an accounting course where 35 learned SQL, a specification-oriented relational language, and 37 learned TABLET, a procedurally-oriented relational language. Twelve-lesson manuals for each language were read outside of class and questions were answered during 14 class meetings. Composition tasks from quizzes during the course, a final at the end of the course, and a retention test three weeks after the final were graded and analyzed. One of the significant results is that for difficult queries the subjects did better using the procedurally-oriented TABLET language. Performance differences between students with and without programming background are also reported, supporting Reisner's results that programming language experience improves query language ability.

	Query by Example	Sequel	Algebraic Language
No. of subjects participating	7	17	13
Mean age	19.3	24.8	20.9
Mean high school average	90.8	82.8	87.4
Mean college GPA (students with over 32 credits. A = 4.0)	3.3	3.4	2.9
Mean no. of previous college computer courses	1.0	1.9	3.5
Percent male	71.4	52.9	53.9

Table 8-4: Subject background data for relational query language experiment (Greenblatt and Waxman, 1978).

	Query by Example	Sequel	Algebraic Language
Training time (hours : minutes)	1:35	1:40	2:05
Mean total exam time (minutes)	23.3	53.9	63.3
Mean correct queries (%)	75.2	72.8	67.7
Mean time/Query (minutes)	0.9	2.5	3.0
Mean confidence/Query (1 to 5)	1.6	1.9	1.9

Table 8-5: Results from relational query language experiment (Greenblatt and Waxman, 1978).

Lochovsky and Tsichritzis (1977) and Lochovsky (1978) describe two experiments which compared the three most popular data models (relational, network, and hierarchical) while keeping the interface facility constant. The Educational Data Base System (EDBS), developed at the University of Toronto, provided three groups of users with similar APL-oriented facilities for accessing data. The three data manipulation languages were designed to reflect the typical network approach, the IMS hierarchical approach, and the relational calculus (Figure 8-13). Although all three data models were embedded in APL, there were strong variations in the power and format of the operators. Performance measures included coding accuracy, coding time, debug time, query comprehension, and query correction. Three different application areas and problems

```
        Given a patient number, determine the type of
        medication that the patient is taking.
```

Hierarchical Model

```
        QUERY1 PNO
[1]  GU 'PATIENT WHERE (PATIENT_NO=',PNO,')'
[2]  ->0 IF STATUS≠0
[3]  LOOP: GNP 'MEDICATION'
[4]  ->0 IF STATUS=5
[5]  READ 'MEDICATION.TYPE'
[6]  ->LOOP
```

Network Model

```
        QUERY1 PNO
[1]  GET 'FIRST PATIENT RECORD WHERE (PATIENT_NO=',PNO,')'
[2]  ->0 IF STATUS≠0
[3]  'PATIENT_MEDICATION' CTC 'PATIENT'
[4]  LOOP:GET 'NEXT PATIENT_MEDICATION SET'
[5]  ->0 IF STATUS=3
[6]  READ 'MEDICATION.TYPE'
[7]  ->LOOP
```

Relational Model

```
        QUERY1 PNO
[1]  GET 'MEDICATION.TYPE
          WHERE (MEDICATION.PATIENT NO=',PNO,')'
[2]  ->0 IF STATUS≠0
[3]  '' READ 'ALL'
```

Figure 8-13: Queries on medical records database (Lochovsky, 1978).

were used by each data model group: airlines schedules, medical records, and Canadian government (Figure 8-14). The results indicate that the EDBS relational calculus facility produced better performance on many measures in two large experiments (Tables 8-6 and 8-7).

An intriguing portion of Lochovsky's experimental writeup is the section describing coding errors. As might be expected, users of hierarchical and network models which require navigation through the database made errors in handling currency pointers and testing status codes, while relational model users had difficulty with join operations to link relations. All three groups had trouble with the command syntax and made minor errors such as misspelling domain names even though the names were available to them. Lochovsky identified five factors affecting database user performance:

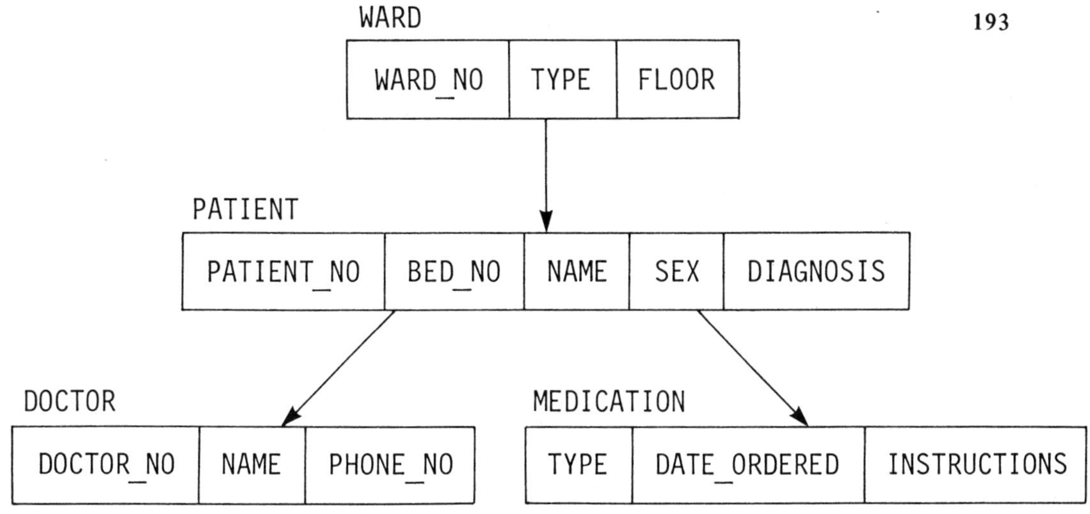

(a) Hierarchical schema

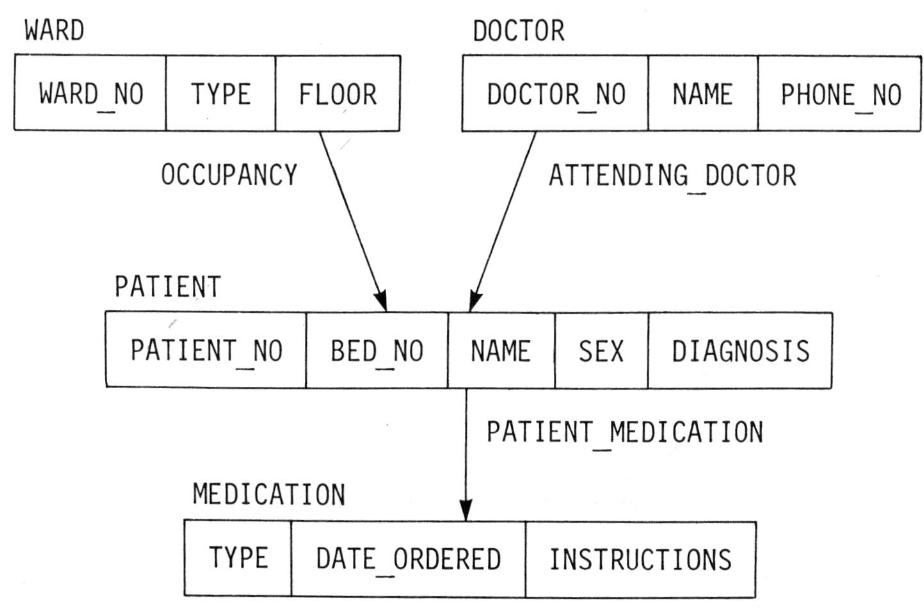

(b) Network schema

```
WARD(WARD_NO, TYPE, FLOOR)
PATIENT(PATIENT_NO, NAME, SEX, DIAGNOSIS, ATTENDING_DOCTOR,
        WARD_NO, BED_NO)
DOCTOR(DOCTOR_NO, NAME, PHONE_NO)
MEDICATION(PATIENT_NO, TYPE, DATE_ORDERED, INSTRUCTIONS)
```

Figure 8-14: Schemas for medical records database (Tsichritzis and Lochovsky, 1977).

	Hierarchical	Network	Relational
Airline schedules	20.0	60.0	48.1
Medical records	43.3	44.4	57.8
Canadian gov't	45.0	53.3	77.2

Table 8-6: Average normalized score in program composition task (Lochovsky, 1978).

	Computer Science Students		
	Hierarchical	Network	Relational
First coding	32.9	26.7	67.5
Second coding	58.6	62.2	76.7
Comprehension	97.3	96.4	94.0
Correction	87.0	82.9	97.8
	Management Students		
	Hierarchical	Network	Relational
First coding	24.4	41.3	72.0
Second coding	42.2	57.3	93.3
Comprehension	99.2	99.0	88.1
Correction	56.1	61.1	89.3

Table 8-7: Average normalized scores for several database manipulation tasks (Lochovsky, 1978).

1) Increasing the number of details such as data language commands or status conditions increases the number of errors.
2) Uniformities in the data description and manipulation languages improve performance and reduce errors.
3) Currency pointers are an important component of system design and they should be 'neither totally implicit nor too explicit. Some user control is required, but the level of control should be determined by the user.'
4) The 'syntax of a command should reflect the semantics and not mislead the user.'

5) The choice of data model influences user performance. Hierarchical and network model users had difficulty translating schemas into instances and processing them correctly while relational model users had difficulty with relationships among the relations.

8.5 PRACTITIONER'S SUMMARY

The variety of query and data manipulation languages, makes comparative evaluation a difficult task for system designers. The efficiency requirements of large-scale production systems suggest that host-embedded facilities will remain in widespread use until effective self-contained facilities can be developed. Professional programmers can cope with the complexity of host-embedded facilities, but as database access is granted to a wider class of users, self-contained facilities will become more appealing.

Self-contained query languages should be evaluated for their effectiveness in providing the necessary functions, facilitating the required tasks, and supporting each of the query features. Finally, they should be tested with typical users to ensure acceptability.

8.6 RESEARCHER'S AGENDA

The descriptions of the functions, tasks, and query features need refinement to support the reductionist experimental approach. A taxonomy of queries should be developed to avoid the issue of relational completeness and group queries by perceived complexity. Such a taxonomy would enable language designers to evaluate the capacity of their proposals to cope with each query class and guide instructors in presenting query features.

The development of 'user friendly' query facilities offers an opportunity for extensive experimentation with competing proposals. Tests are critical because the background of typical users is very different from the background of query language designers and because these users will be reluctant to accept future modifications. Fundamental issues such as specifications vs. procedurality and linear keyword vs. positional notation should be investigated from the perspective of cognitive psychology.

AUTH
CLEAR
1 2 3 4 5 6 7 8 9 0
ITEM 1
ITEM 2
ITEM 3
ITEM 4
ITEM 5
13
9
40 1 2 3 4 5 41 4

9

NATURAL LANGUAGE

Those who are so fascinated by the computer's lifelike feats – that they would turn it into the voice of omniscience, betray how little understanding they have of either themselves, their mechanical-electrical agents or the potentialities of life.

Lewis Mumford, *The Myth of the Machine* (1970)

Natural language 'dialog' with computers from technical feasibility and practical utility points of view - examples of natural language systems - advantages and disadvantages - experimental results - human knowledge requirements for use of natural language systems

9.1 NATURAL LANGUAGE SYSTEMS

All through history humans have constructed mechanical imitators of human behavior. From the earliest stone and clay idols, to the medieval clockwork automatons, to Walt Disney's audio-animatronic creatures, there has been a dream of creating mechanical versions of humans. Writers who could not build automatons, wrote about them: the Golem of the 13th century rabbi of Prague, the robots of Karl Capek's play *R.U.R.* , the monster created by Dr. Frankenstein, and the armies of science fiction robots.

Each generation looks quaintly back on the fantasies of the previous generation, but manages to create newer modern fantasies. In this generation the emergence of complex electronics permitted visionaries to dream of 'intelligent' computers which reproduce aspects of human behavior. The term artificial intelligence has been applied to work whose goal is in part, to give computers human skills and knowledge.

In the early 1950's, the major area of artificial intelligence research was natural language translation. Researchers believed that with a sufficiently large online dictionary and a set of linguistic transformation rules, it would be possible to translate, say, Russian into English. While the early results were encouraging, the output quality never reached satisfactory levels. Although researchers argued that larger storage and faster processing units were the solution, the real problem was the lack of a suitable theory of language. Noam Chomsky and his colleagues made some progress in language theory during the late 1950's and 1960's, but an adequate theoretical basis is still lacking. In spite of the failure to develop a complete language translation system, IBM was proud enough of its efforts to demonstrate an online Russian-English translation system at the 1964 New York World's Fair. Currently available translation systems are commercially useful for professional translators of technical journals. The computer system provides a first draft which is reworked by a human knowledgeable in the languages and technical domain. The gulf between the computer as a high speed typist and the human who 'understands' is still wide.

A second early effort was toward the construction of natural language understanding programs. These programs could accept human instructions in English for operating the computer, thereby simplifying the programming process. Researchers who pursued this goal followed two routes: the creation of complex programs which would understand arbitrary English statements and the design of programming languages which were English-like. Those in the first group faced and were defeated by the same problems that confronted the natural language translators. Without an adequate theory of language, it is just too much of an exercise in complex programming to create a system which correctly interprets instructions given in English. Those in the second group created languages like ENGLISH (Barnett, 1969) which permitted programs such as:

```
SET THE GRAND TOTAL TO 0. READ A RECORD. CALL
THE 1-ST CHARACTER OF THE RECORD THE TAG.
(GROUP START) COPY THE TAG AND CALL IT THE
LAG. SET THE GROUP TOTAL TO 1. (LOOP START) IF
THE INPUT IS EXHAUSTED CONTINUE WITH THE
FINAL ENDING, OTHERWISE CONTINUE AS FOLLOWS.
READ A RECORD. IF THE TAG IS THE SAME AS THE
LAG INCREASE THE GROUP TOTAL BY 1, AND REPEAT
FROM THE LOOP START, OTHERWISE CONTINUE AS
FOLLOWS. (GROUP ENDING) PRINT 'THE NUMBER OF
NAMES BEGINNING WITH ' THEN THE LAG THEN ' IS
' THEN THE GROUP TOTAL. INCREASE THE GRAND
TOTAL BY THE GROUP TOTAL. REPEAT FROM THE
GROUP START. (FINAL ENDING) PRINT 'THE NUMBER
OF NAMES BEGINNING WITH ' THEN THE TAG THEN '
IS ' THEN THE GROUP TOTAL. INCREASE THE GRAND
TOTAL BY THE GROUP TOTAL. PRINT 'THE TOTAL
NUMBER OF NAMES IS ' THEN THE GRAND TOTAL.
EXECUTE.
```

Reading and comprehending an English-like programming language is relatively easy, but writing syntactically correct code is a challenge. The closeness of ENGLISH to English makes it difficult to remember the grammar of ENGLISH: an elegant demonstration of *proactive interference*, the confusion between what you know and what you are trying to learn. The more ENGLISH resembles English, the greater the proactive interference.

Although ENGLISH and other English-like languages did not have wide success, the belief in the utility of English-like languages influenced the design of COBOL. By using numerous English words in COBOL, the developers hoped that managers and other nonprogrammers would be able to comprehend application programs.

A third field of exploration has been natural language generation programs. These include simple poetry generators of haiku, iambic pentameter, and sonnets which select words from lists according to a specified grammar pattern. *Creative Computing* magazine (September-October 1976) offered a variety of computer generated poems including this one by Margaret Chisman:

MYSELF MANIFEST

My head thrives on pain
Unseen by guilt
Not relaxing not seducing
Comfort if controlled
Corrupts

My eye quickens with grief
Bleak with doubt yet true
Rarely hoarding rarely aching
Sorrow if withheld
Consoles

My hand delights in rejection
Eager for despair ever calm
Beyond quarreling beyond dreaming
Friendship if followed
Refreshes

Other natural language generators can produce simple sentences or 2500 word mystery stories with modest character and plot development. These programs are more sophisticated than an array of monkeys poking at typewriter keyboards, but not much. Some practical uses can be found for natural language generation programs. For example, at least one program successfully converts coded medical data into complete English sentences which are comprehensible by nurses and doctors.

The second and third fields of investigation -- programs for understanding and generating natural language -- are combined with database ideas in pursuing natural language question-answering systems. Instead of writing a program to obtain information from a database, the user would ask questions by typing in English at a computer terminal and would receive a response in English. Early scenarios suggested that the computer program would immediately comprehend and respond correctly, but recent efforts include the notion of *clarification dialog* to resolve ambiguity.

One early system, called BASEBALL, was capable of responding properly to questions about American League games in a particular year. Typical questions were: Where did the Red Sox play on July 7? What teams won ten games in June? or How many games did the Yankees play in July? A more intriguing system was STUDENT (Bobrow, 1972) which could handle high school algebra word problems such as:

> The gas consumption of my car is 15 miles per gallon. The distance between Boston and New York is 250 miles. What is the number of gallons used on a trip between New York and Boston?

> Mary is twice as old as Ann when Mary was as old as Ann is now. If Mary is 24 years old, what is Ann's age?

These primitive natural language systems were replaced by more sophisticated systems such as SHRDLU (Winograd, 1972) which allowed users to give a robot hand and eye system instructions about picking up and moving blocks (Figure 9-1). Although the scope of knowledge is narrow, the system's capacity for coping with this 'blocks world' is impressive.

Human: pick up the red block.
Computer: OK.
Human: grasp the pyramid.
Computer: I DON'T UNDERSTAND WHICH PYRAMID YOU MEAN.
Human: find a block which is taller than the one you are holding and put it into the box.
Computer: BY 'IT,' I ASSUME YOU MEAN THE BLOCK WHICH IS TALLER THAN THE ONE I AM HOLDING. OK.
Human: what does the box contain?
Computer: THE BLUE PYRAMID AND THE BLUE BLOCK.
Human: what is the pyramid supported by?
Computer: THE BOX.
Human: how many blocks are not in the box?
Computer: FOUR OF THEM.
Human: is at least one of them narrower than the one which i told you to pick up?
Computer: YES, THE RED CUBE.
Human: is it supported?

Computer: YES, BY THE TABLE.
Human: can the table pick up blocks?
Computer: NO.
Human: can a pyramid be supported by a block?
Computer: YES.
Human: can a pyramid support a pyramid?
Computer: I DON'T KNOW.

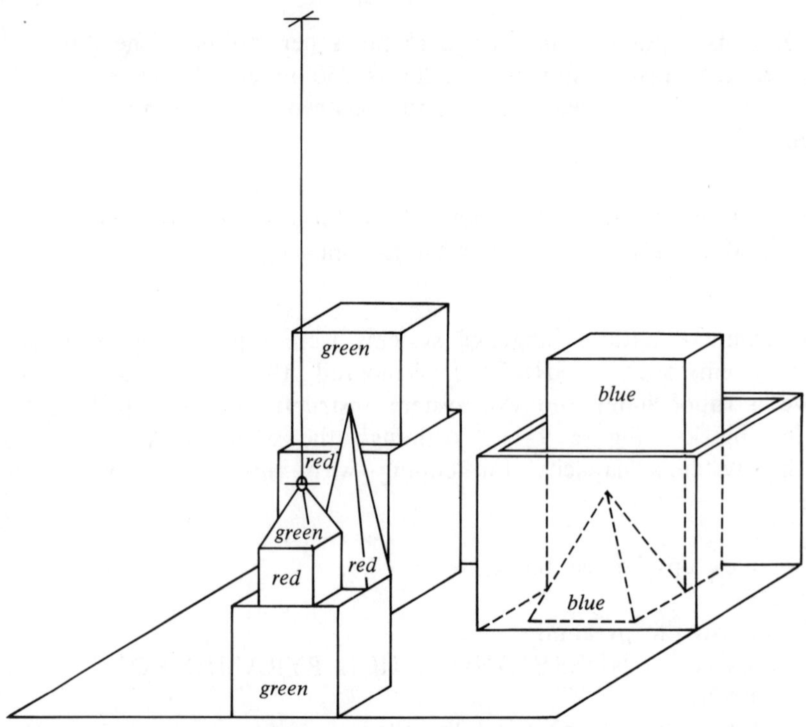

Figure 9-1: Blocks world with robot arm in position over green pyramid (Winograd, 1971).

An appealing system without clarification dialog is LUNAR (Woods et al., 1972; Woods, 1973) which responds to lunar geologists' questions about the rocks brought back by the Apollo 11 moon flight. At the Second Annual Lunar Science Conference in 1971, LUNAR was presented with 111 actual requests: 10 percent could not be parsed or interpreted, 12 percent 'failed due to trivial clerical errors' (which were corrected immediately after the conference) and 78 percent were handled satisfactorily. Successfully handled queries included:

Give me the average SM analysis of Type A rocks
Give me the oxygen analysis in S10084
What samples contain chromite
Give me the EU determinations in samples which contain ILM

Woods reports that 'a class of graduate students in information retrieval given an appropriate introduction spent an hour and a half asking it questions and found only two that failed.' A psychology graduate student had to pose six questions before constructing one with which the system could cope. These different experiences underline the impact of user background in using natural language systems.

Two systems which emphasize clarification dialog are Waltz's PLANES (1978) and Codd's RENDEZVOUS (1978). PLANES deals with a relational database on military aircraft maintenance:

Human: which skyhawks logged less than 10 hours
Computer: PLEASE ENTER A SPECIFIC TIME PERIOD
Human: between jan. 1 and jule 1 '73
Computer: I DON'T KNOW THE MEANING OF JULE
PERHAPS IT'S MISSPELLED?
PLEASE ENTER A NUMBER CORRESPONDING TO THE FOLLOWING
1. JUNE
2. JULY
3. NONE OF THE ABOVE

Codd's RENDEZVOUS system is also relationally based. Version 1 deals with a supplier-parts-projects database:

Computer: PLEASE TYPE IN YOUR QUERY:
Human: i want to find certain projects. pipes were sent to them in feb. 1975.
Computer: THIS IS WHAT THE SYSTEM UNDERSTANDS YOUR QUERY TO BE: PRINT THE NAME OF EVERY PROJECT TO WHICH A SHIPMENT OF A PART NAMED PIPE WAS SENT DURING FEBRUARY 1975.

IS THE SYSTEM'S UNDERSTANDING
1 CORRECT AND COMPLETE
2 NOT YET COMPLETE
3 INCORRECT
SELECT EXACTLY ONE ITEM BY NUMBER
Human: 1

```
Computer: THE ANSWER TO YOUR QUERY IS:
            ------------
             PROJECT
               NAME
            ------------
             SAN LUIS
             HYDRO
             SONOMA
            ------------

          IN REGARD TO YOUR PRESENT QUERY, WHAT
          ADDITIONAL INFORMATION WOULD YOU LIKE TO
          HAVE?  IF NONE, JUST HIT THE 'SEND' KEY.
Human:      give me their locatio also
Computer: IS THE WORD 'LOCATIO' INTENDED TO BE:
          LOCATION?
          (YES OR NO)
Human:      YES
Computer: THIS IS WHAT THE SYSTEM UNDERSTANDS YOUR
          QUERY TO BE:

          PRINT THE NAME AND LOCATION OF EVERY
          PROJECT TO WHICH A SHIPMENT OF A PART
          NAMED PIPE WAS SENT DURING FEBRUARY 1975.
```

Both Waltz's and Codd's relationally oriented clarification dialog systems attempt to provide feedback to users about what the computer interprets as the query. This component of these systems requires sophisticated sentence generation procedures which are very different from the sentence comprehension procedures.

The ROBOT system (Harris, 1977) is the first commercial venture in natural language front ends for database systems. The database is managed by the ADABAS system and the front end is a cleverly designed natural language processing system which makes use of five types of information:

1) the meaning of individual English words
2) the syntactic structure of English as represented by a grammar in the form of an augmented transition network
3) advice from the database administrator in the form of detailed definitions of domains and files
4) information contained in the database, such as domain values

5) the user, through clarification dialog or question rephrasing.

The innovative practical approach used in ROBOT allows interpretation of complete sentences or fragments. A query such as NEW YORK SECRETARIES? could be answered since the system knows that NEW YORK is only contained in the CITY domain and SECRETARIES is only contained in the JOB domain. Previously stored recommendations from the database administrator might indicate that NAMES and EMPLOYEE-NUMBERS should be printed for this sort of query. More than ten commercial sites are using ROBOT and 'the acceptance rate for experienced users is above the 90 percent level.' Apparently users find a linguistic niche which satisfies them and is acceptable for ROBOT. These initial commercial successes should be encouraging to supporters of natural language systems.

No presentation of natural language systems is complete without a visit with DOCTOR and the underlying system ELIZA (Weizenbaum, 1966, 1976). This program was designed to play the role of a Rogerian psychotherapist who makes no judgments, but merely guides patients in exploring their concerns. Weizenbaum's cleverly designed program manages to carry on a reasonable discussion for a while, but does not develop the relationship which is necessary for therapy.

Human: men are all alike.
Computer: IN WHAT WAY
Human: they're always bugging us about something or other.
Computer: CAN YOU THINK OF A SPECIFIC EXAMPLE
Human: well, my boyfriend made me come here.
Computer: YOUR BOYFRIEND MADE YOU COME HERE
Human: he says i'm depressed much of the time.
Computer: I AM SORRY TO HEAR YOU ARE DEPRESSED
Human: it's true. i am unhappy.
Computer: DO YOU THINK COMING HERE WILL HELP YOU NOT TO BE UNHAPPY
Human: i need some help, that much seems certain.
Computer: WHAT WOULD IT MEAN TO YOU IF YOU GOT SOME HELP
Human: perhaps i could get along with my mother.
Computer: TELL ME MORE ABOUT YOUR FAMILY
Human: my mother takes care of me.
Computer: WHO ELSE IN YOUR FAMILY TAKES CARE OF YOU
Human: my father.
Computer: YOUR FATHER
Human: you are like my father in some ways.

Computer: WHAT RESEMBLANCE DO YOU SEE
Human: you are not very aggressive but i think you don't want me to notice that.
Computer: WHAT MAKES YOU THINK I AM NOT VERY AGGRESSIVE
Human: you don't argue with me.
Computer: WHY DO YOU THINK I DON'T ARGUE WITH YOU
Human: you are afraid of me.
Computer: DOES IT PLEASE YOU TO BELIEVE I AM AFRAID OF YOU
Human: my father is afraid of everybody.
Computer: WHAT ELSE COMES TO MIND WHEN YOU THINK OF YOUR FATHER
Human: bullies.
Computer: DOES THAT HAVE ANYTHING TO DO WITH THE FACT THAT YOUR BOYFRIEND MADE YOU COME HERE

Weizenbaum is completely aware of the shallowness of his program as a therapist and is clear that he only intended an exploration of natural language processing. Unfortunately, some people felt that 'it demonstrated a general solution to the problem of computer understanding of natural language' and some psychiatrists felt it was a first step towards automated therapy. Weizenbaum is shocked by this suggestion and comments:

> What can the psychiatrist's image of his patient be when he sees himself, as therapist, not as an engaged human being acting as a healer but as an information processor following rules.

9.2 PROS AND CONS

The artificial intelligentsia who support development of natural language systems argue that since humans already know their natural language, use of computers would be facilitated if natural language systems were available. Users would not have to invest in learning programming or database query languages and struggle in translating their thoughts into an artificial language. The developers of natural language systems believe that they can produce reliable and easy-to-use systems which will be commercially viable in replacing human information providers and programmers. Waltz claims that a 90 percent answer rate without rephrasing is acceptable and would be sufficient to maintain user interest while providing practical, useful systems, but acknowledges the need to test this conjecture. One wonders whether telephones, televisions, cars or computers would be acceptable if they operate only nine out of ten times. Failing to operate is not nearly as dangerous, though, as operating incorrectly -- televisions shocking the viewer, cars slipping into reverse, and computers providing incorrect information.

Petrick (1976) presents the pros and cons of natural language systems. He analyzes the weaknesses of current systems and is cautiously optimistic that practical systems will emerge in a few years. Montgomery (1974) is also concerned about the utility of natural language systems in her paper 'Is natural language an unnatural query language.' After showing some serious challenges to natural language comprehension she ends optimistically: 'I feel strongly that (developers) can provide a systematic framework for dealing with natural language as an instrument of communication in automated systems, thus overcoming even my own reservations concerning the naturalness of natural language in an automated context.' Chai (1974) details his concerns about the capacity of a computerized system to resolve ambiguities in English commands and offers a keyword oriented query language as an alternative. Finally, it is a pleasure to recommend reading Hill's charming paper (1972) entitled 'Wouldn't it be nice if we could write computer programs in ordinary English -- or would it?' With an amusing light-hearted style he catalogues dozens of ambiguous English statements taken from real situations. Near the end, he drops his arguments for a moment and allows us to assume that a natural language programming system could be built:

> Would things really be any easier? The main difficulty in programming lies in deciding *exactly* what is the right thing to do. To put it into a programming language is relatively trivial. This would lead to the idea that any fool could write a program -- and we have quite enough rubbishy programs clogging up the works even now.
>
> And would we not have to throw away one of the greatest advantages of computers? Namely that they can be instructed to do exactly what you want without argument or misunderstanding.

I agree! When people want a discussion they go to other humans, when they want precision and speed they go to a computer. The special notation of a precise concise artificial language can be a helpful tool in guiding thought processes. The long and successful history of notation systems such as mathematics, chemical formulas, and music, suggests that structured notation helps clarify problems and aids creative work.

Natural language systems must overcome at least these problems:

1) Unrealistic expectations of the computer's power. Users might pose questions such as: How can I improve profits? or Is the defendant guilty? These questions involve value judgments and complex ideas which computers cannot and probably should not be relied upon to answer (Weizenbaum, 1974).

2) Attempts to request information not contained in the database, thus wasting time and effort, while increasing frustration. Natural language users may not be aware of the contents and semantics of the database. In a corporate database it may be reasonable to inquire about departmental average salaries but comparisons with industry-wide salaries may be inappropriate.

3) By allowing, users to use natural language without training we allow the ambiguities of English syntax to pollute the query process, driving developers to design long and tedious clarification dialogs. This clarification dialog will have to take place even for sophisticated users who are careful in their selection of words. Particularly annoying are difficulties with existential and universal quantification (use of SOME, ALL or NOT in formal logic).

4) Typical users may not be aware of the semantics of question asking. Although they may know English syntax, they may not have thought of what kind of questions could be answered by a database system. By teaching users a concise and precise artificial language we are also teaching the semantics of question asking. Having the tool of a well-learned query language may enable users to compose complex queries which may not have occurred to them otherwise. The Bauhaus motto 'Form is Freedom' is relevant: the structure of a query language may help users in query formulation.

5) Finally, the overhead of creating and maintaining a natural language interface will always be larger than for a concise query language or a menu selection process.

These criticisms don't imply that natural language interfaces are useless, only that their domain of applications may be less broad than has been suggested.

In any case, why pursue the game of trying to force computers to act like people. Computers have impressive speed, storage and accuracy which are bypassed if we use natural language. Building computers that behave like people is like trying to build planes that flap their wings.

The syntactic/semantic model suggests a possible role for natural language systems. Figure 9-2 shows a division of users based on their syntactic and semantic knowledge. Those lacking either kind of knowledge will be stymied by natural language systems because these users don't even know where to begin asking questions and might not be a reasonable partner in clarification dialog. Those with only syntactic knowledge would also lack the semantic structure to actively pursue a dialog. Those with rich syntactic and semantic knowledge would probably prefer the precise concise query facility. The remaining group, those who have semantic knowledge of a problem domain yet are not knowledgeable in the query language syntax, is the most likely to be served by a natural language system. In this same group are infrequent users who cannot maintain syntactic knowledge, but are knowledgeable about the problem domain.

9.3 EXPERIMENTAL STUDIES

Social psychologists have studied human communication among individuals and small groups. Experimental factors have included competition vs. cooperation, the communication medium, group pressure to conform, dominant vs. subordinate power relationships, grammatic structure and word usage.

Several experimenters have required individuals to give natural language instructions to a computer. Miller and Becker (1974) had subjects play the role of a file clerk who had to program the computer for tasks such as 'Make a list of those employess who make more than 8 dollars per hour and also are over 50 years old. List should be organized by

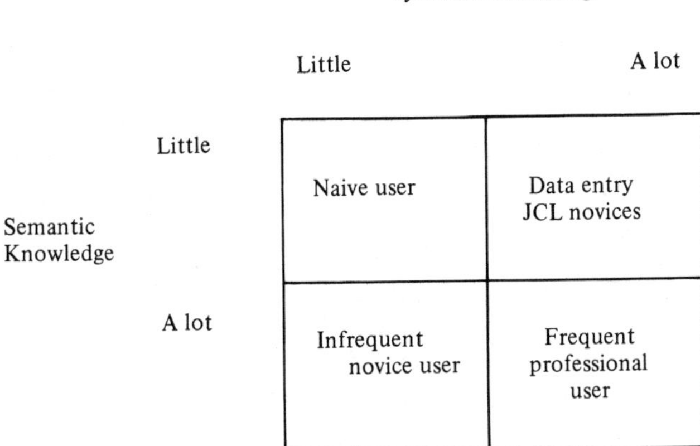

Figure 9-2: Syntactic/semantic knowledge of users.

employee name.' The resulting instructions suggest that people think and write in structures quite different from those found in popular programming languages. Subjects were far less precise than is required in using programming languages and numerous contextual assumptions were made.

Thomas (1976a) describes an experiment in which subjects specified order-handling and invoicing procedures to an interactive natural language system. An experimental aide played the role of the natural language system by carrying on the computer's half of the dialog from a remote terminal. The variety of dialog styles indicates the difficulty of building a truly automated system. Thomas (1976b) raises further questions about the possibility of natural language query systems in a wide-ranging discussion which reveals the confusion that most humans have over universal and existential quantification.

Recent results from Small and Weldon (1977) raised further doubts about the advantages of natural language query facilities. In that experiment, twenty subjects were required to compose queries in natural language English and a subset of SEQUEL. Answers were marked on sample relational databases with some notation (underlining, arrows, circles, etc.) to indicate the origin of the answers, and subjects were required to compose the queries at interactive terminals. Experimental aides in a separate room played the role of the natural language or subset-SEQUEL processor and provided error messages as needed. Users of natural language had to follow the tabular patterns, but had syntactic and naming freedom. Each subject performed in both interaction modes and counterbalanced orderings were used in this repeated measure design. Times to first response and to correct response both indicated that subset-SEQUEL was superior. Those using SEQUEL in the latter half of the experiment were the highest scoring group.

Small and Weldon conclude with a bold statement:

> The common assumption that ordinary, everyday English is the ideal way to communicate with computers is not supported by the present results. Subjects were not reliably more accurate using English than using SEQUEL. They were reliably faster using SEQUEL, suggesting that the structured language is easier to use.

We felt that requiring subjects to provide queries in this constrained format did not measure a subject's capacity to resolve problems by formulating queries. Secondly, requiring subjects to understand the patterns of table usage did not represent true natural language usage. To resolve these two problems we decided to offer subjects a situation problem where they had to formulate questions on their own. Natural language users were told about a department store employee database and were asked to pose questions to help them decide in which department to work. Subset-SEQUEL users were given brief training, a seven item comprehension test and were told to pose questions in subset-SEQUEL. The criterion of success was the number of relevant queries that each subject asked. A counterbalanced within-subjects design was used, so each subject worked in both modes.

The subjects were 22 students enrolled in an undergraduate COBOL programming and information systems course, some of whom may have had previous programming experience. Subjects were tested in the eighth week of the fifteen week course. The SEQUEL Instruction booklet contained four double-spaced pages with sample SEQUEL queries and responses. Single-table databases were assumed, thus eliminating the need for the FROM clause, and only simple mappings, AND/OR logic, and five arithmetic functions (SUM, COUNT, AVG, MAX, MIN) were shown.

The situation problem results were graded as invalid or valid. Valid queries had to be answerable from the database and relevant to the task of deciding in which department to work. Minor spelling or syntactic errors were accepted in both forms, as long as the intent was clear.

Table 9-1 presents the results. T-tests showed no significant differences, even at the 0.10 level, between valid English and valid SEQUEL queries. The order effect was not significant. However the number of invalid queries did differ significantly (1 percent level) between the English and SEQUEL groups. The order effect for invalid queries was also significant (1 percent level): the NAT-SEQ group had more invalid queries than the SEQ-NAT group.

Since the invalid queries provided the significant differences, an informal review of the kinds of invalid queries was undertaken. Those using English often let their imagination go and came up with interesting and relevant questions which could not be answered from the database.

	Language Used					
Order	Subset-SEQUEL		Natural language		Combined Score	
	Valid	Invalid	Valid	Invalid	Valid	Invalid
Natural-SEQUEL	2.54	0.36	2.45	2.90	2.49	1.64
SEQUEL-Natural	3.54	0.09	2.64	0.90	3.09	0.49
Combined	3.04	0.23	2.54	1.91	2.79	1.07

Table 9-1: Mean number of queries posed in situational problem.

Typical examples include:

What is the starting salary for each department?
How often are raises awarded?
Are the managers lenient concerning tardiness and absences?
Do people like working in (the) department?
What is the personality of the managers?
What type of clientele does the department cater to?

The lack of significant differences in the number of valid queries in the natural language and subset SEQUEL groups can support advocates of natural language facilities or precise, concise artificial languages. Adherents of artificial languages might argue that with only 15 minutes of training in SEQUEL, the performance is impressive and that with additional experience, SEQUEL users should be able to surpass natural language users. Learning additional features of the SEQUEL language should also improve performance.

Supporters of natural language front ends might complain that the SEQUEL training period helped subjects by providing examples to follow. They might also complain that natural language users were not given a chance to become familiar with the application domain.

Future experiments will have to determine the importance of:

1) familiarity with the application domain
2) familiarity with the data items stored in the computer
3) amount of prologue needed to prepare natural language users to deal with the computer
4) the capacity of the system and the user to produce effective clarification dialogs
5) typing skill for communication at a terminal
6) understanding data model ideas (one-to-many, one-to-one, many-to-many relationships)
7) understanding query formulation (linking domains, set comparison, etc.)

The significant differences on the invalid query tally do support those with reservations about natural language use. Natural language users were far more likely to pose unanswerable queries. Only three of the 22 subjects posed invalid queries during their SEQUEL sessions while twelve of the same 22 subjects posed invalid queries during their natural language sessions. Nine of the eleven who had natural language first made invalid queries in natural language, but only three of eleven subjects who had natural language second made invalid queries in natural language. These results suggest that the structuring during SEQUEL use was learned and applied during the natural language session. These results reflect the meaningful learning and language independence of semantic knowledge and the reduced importance of syntax for problem solving.

These results should not be interpreted as a condemnation of natural language usage, but as an aid in determining which applications are suitable for natural language front ends and what training users should be given. User knowledge of the application domain seems to be critical: without this prerequisite, natural language usage would be extremely difficult. Secondly, user knowledge of the structure of the data in the computer and what each item means appears to be vital. Finally, experience in asking questions against a specific database is probably helpful. Thus, the ideal candidate for natural language usage may be the experienced frequent user of a manual information system, but these users are likely to appreciate the simplicity, brevity and precision of a structured query language. The casual user with little knowledge of the application area, understanding of the data structure and experience in posing queries may find natural language facilities more confusing. Realistic applications for natural language would be situations where people have familiarity with the application area, data structure and queries but are infrequent users. Typical situations that fit this description include library card catalogs, airline schedules or banking transactions. More research is necessary to support these hypotheses.

The future is not yet clear. There is no proof of the ineffectiveness or the ease of use of natural language systems. I keep an open mind to the possibility of their widespread use but believe that in many instances there are better ways to operate this tool called a computer.

9.4 PRACTITIONER'S SUMMARY

Although a great deal of effort has been spent on natural language computer systems, the capacity of computer programs to cope with natural language is modest. Improvements may be made, but in the short run, systems designers must be cautious about relying on natural language facilities. As products are tested in the commercial marketplace the technology will improve, although errors of omission and commission should be carefully monitored. Even as research results improve, application systems should be thoroughly tested to assure user acceptance. Users may prefer a concise artificial language or a menu selection approach instead of the wordy and time-consuming 'clarification dialog.'

9.5 RESEARCHER'S AGENDA

Research on natural language systems should be pursued with careful attention to psycholinguistic principles and an understanding of user psychology. The role of user comprehension of knowledge domains, data organization, query formulation, and mathematical principles should be the starting point for research and designs. Experimental testing should be conducted in a controlled environment with typical users and realistic situations.

CAROL WALD

10

INTERACTIVE INTERFACE ISSUES

The wheel is an extension of the foot, the book is an extension of the eye, clothing, an extension of the skin, electric circuitry, an extension of the central nervous system.

Marshall McLuhan and Quentin Fiore, *The Medium is the Massage* (1967)

Design issues for interactive use of computer systems via personal terminals – hardware considerations – keyboard layout – hard and soft copy – cursor control – audio output – speech recognition – graphics – psychological issues – short and long term memory – closure – attitude and anxiety – control – response time – time sharing and batch preference – error handling – error messages – help facilities

10.1 INTRODUCTION

Prophets of the new computer age celebrate online interactive person-computer use as if this technologically sophisticated approach will by itself solve problems. But these prophets are only oldtimers who remember the batch processing past; the youngsters see terminal access and instant response as normal. The newcomers are more discriminating, they want more than just instant response, they want a 'good' system.

A good system not only wins respect and makes you want to use it, but it generates satisfying feelings and confidence in your capacity to use it effectively. These good systems can be everything from a well-designed hand calculator to a customer bank terminal to a complete programming system. The attributes that create the image of a quality system include: easy to learn, easy to use, easy to remember, prompt, reliable, courteous, helpful when difficulties arise, and effective as a tool in solving user problems. This chapter covers critical issues in the design of a quality interactive interface.

10.2 HARDWARE OPTIONS

The hundreds of terminals commercially available present a dizzying array of options for the system designer. Peripheral devices and custom features compound the problem, but they provide appealing opportunities for the creative designer.

10.2.1 Keyboards

Keyboard selection presents numerous difficult questions. The spacing between keys, number of special keys, availability of a numeric pad for fast keying of numeric data, the angle, shape and surface texture of the keys, pressure and distance required to depress the keys, tactile or auditory feedback on reaching bottom, placement of frequently used keys, and the clarity of the characters on the keys all contribute to the appeal of a keyboard. With the exception of cheap models with hard to push keys or extremely compact keyboards, mass production has enabled vendors to produce relatively high-quality keyboards. Classic human factors research covers keyboard design (Rupp and Hirsch, 1977; Hart, 1976). Figure 10-1 shows interesting results on the workload distribution of each finger using the standard keyboard and the error percentage for each finger.

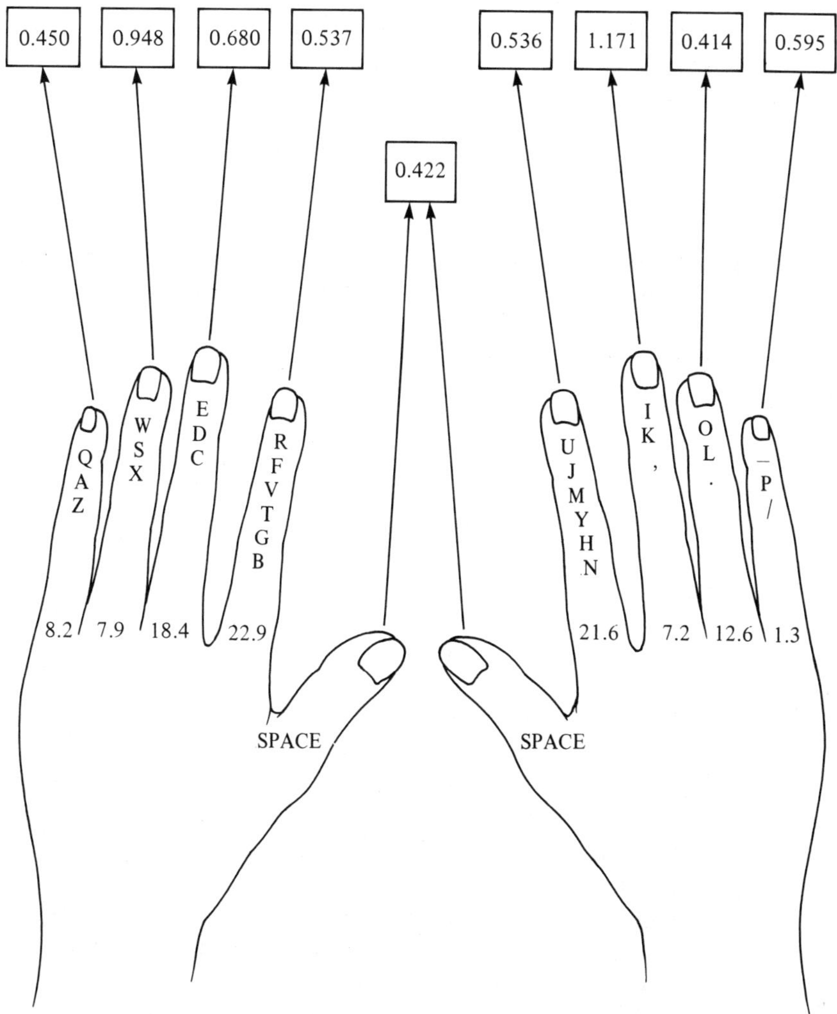

Figure 10-1: Percent errors by fingers. Errors as a percentage of all characters struck by each finger, based on 515,966 effective keystrokes (Hirsch, 1976). Numbers on fingers are percent of workload (Hart, 1976).

Some studies have investigated the advantage of alternative keyboard layouts such as alphabetically ordered ones for nontypists who make only limited entries. For professional typists, it is possible to redesign key layout to increase typing speed for English language text (A. Martin, 1972; Kroemer, 1972). The 19th century layout was done in order to balance the mechanical loads, but with electric typewriters the layout can be based on digram frequencies for English. Although such typewriters were built and proved their worth in experimental studies, it is unlikely that they will overcome the widespread acceptance of the traditional typewriter keyboard layout. Here is another example of the *historical imperative*, that is, people's unwillingness to give up what they already know unless the improvement is substantial.

10.2.2 Soft vs. Hard Copy

Hard copy displays provide permanent records of the terminal session, while soft copy displays provide an electronic window and eliminate costly and polluting paper consumption. The choice is largely dependent on the application, but the lower cost, higher reliability, quieter operation, and potentially higher speeds of soft displays give them some advantages. At least two experiments (Walther and O'Neil, 1974; Carlisle, 1970) showed that users made fewer typing errors at hard copy displays — apparently the sound provides reassuring feedback, while soft copy displays require visual attention to verify that the information has been accepted.

Hard copy can be produced by noisy impact devices, such as Selectric balls, 'daisy' wheels, cylinders, or a matrix of pins; or by quiet nonimpact thermal, electrostatic or ink spray printers. Typical terminal print speeds are 15-80 characters per second. The imprint clarity and typing surface visibility, which may be obscured by the typing device or cover, play important roles in user acceptability.

Soft copy can be produced by the popular cathode ray tube (CRT), light emitting diodes (LED), liquid crystal diodes (LCD), or a flat plasma screen (which permits rear projection of photographic quality images). Display rates can be thousands of characters per second. Glare from the screen, flickering images, lack of contrast and limited number of lines may detract from CRT usage. However, silent operation, unlimited character sets, blinking, multiple intensity levels, black/white reversal, color images, erasing, insertion, cursor action, scrolling and multiple windows are attractive features.

In all display devices the type size, available fonts, sharpness, contrast, platen width, and vertical spacing influence acceptability.

Dramatic improvements are still being made in terminal design and price continues to fall. As standardization occurs and production volume increases, we may expect continuing increases in quality and decreases in cost.

10.2.3 Cursor Control Devices

Some applications require position definitions by cursor movement in two-dimensional space. Positioning can be accomplished by keystrokes from a standard keyboard, but this can be slow and annoying. Several cursor moving devices have been developed, such as:

- a lightpen which is used to move a cursor to the proper position on the screen
- a sonic pen which is moved to a position on a special board equipped with microphones which sense the click emitted when the sonic pen touches the board
- a mouse, which is a small mouse-sized box with rubber wheels which are rolled on the table to activate potentiometers and sense changes in position
- a touch-sensitive screen with embedded sensing wires or a grid of light beams
- a touch-sensitive plate used as a writing surface
- a joystick which can be rotated about two axes.

Work needs to be done to determine the utility of these relatively cheap devices for differing applications. They all face the 'third hand problem' -- the user must lift at least one hand from the keyboard to indicate the position. Lightpens and touch-sensitive screens have the advantage that the user works directly with the image, but the disadvantage that the screen becomes obscured by the user's hand and that it is tiring to continuously raise a hand and hold it close to a vertical screen.

10.2.4 Audio Output

Computer activated tape recording devices are being replaced by more sophisticated speech generation systems which can be programmed to take stored phrases and generate arbitrarily complex sentences. These impressive and inexpensive speech generation systems, when programmed carefully, produce comprehensible speech. They have been employed by the phone company for automatic generation of changed number messages and by stock exchanges for current quotes in response to telephoned requests. Sophisticated devices which scan typewritten or printed text and speak the material to blind people are appearing on the market. Talking toys and teaching devices are appealing consumer oriented applications.

Another form of audio output is to have a terminal ring a bell or sound a chime to indicate special conditions. This seems a simple and effective procedure if not overused. Audio tones to signal error conditions should not be used when the terminal is in a public place, since it may lead to embarrassment.

10.2.5 Speech Recognition Systems

The image of the computer as a secretary which is competent at taking dictation and producing a typewritten letter, has persisted from the earliest days of computing. Early attempts at discrete word recognition showed promising results. Systems constructed in the mid-1960's could recognize words spoken in a laboratory setting, taken from a dictionary of one thousand words with more than 90 percent accuracy. The words had to be spoken for entry into the computer's storage by the same person who later used the system. Hobbyists can now buy a speech recognition device which records up to 64 words and achieves 90 percent accuracy for about $200. Commercial systems with 100 to 1000 word vocabularies are in the $10,000 to $20,000 range. Discrete word recognition might be useful in giving single word directives in controlling manufacturing equipment, wheelchairs, aircraft, operating room equipment, etc., when both hands are required for other tasks.

Continuous speech recognition in typically noisy environments with a variety of speakers presents a much greater challenge. Researchers at Carnegie-Mellon University have developed a series of systems, DRAGON, HEARSAY-I and HARPY, to cope with continuous speech recognition (Reddy, 1975; Lowerre, 1976). In one of the experiments, the vocabulary was restricted to 37 words dealing with programming for a desk calculator, and four different people provided sample sentences. The system accurately recognized more than 90 percent of the words and 80 percent of the sentences. Research continues at other universities and industrial sites such as IBM's Yorktown Heights, New York labs.

These results suggest that continuous speech recognition is still a difficult task, and the probability of near term success in developing a commercial system is low. Noisy office environments, changes in speech style over time and across individuals, variety of syntactic forms, and the large number of words and names makes this task very difficult. A 90 percent or 95 percent recognition score may not be sufficient for commercial applications. Errors of commission (incorrect recognition) must be made extremely small, but errors of omission (failure to recognize with a request for clarification) may be more acceptable.

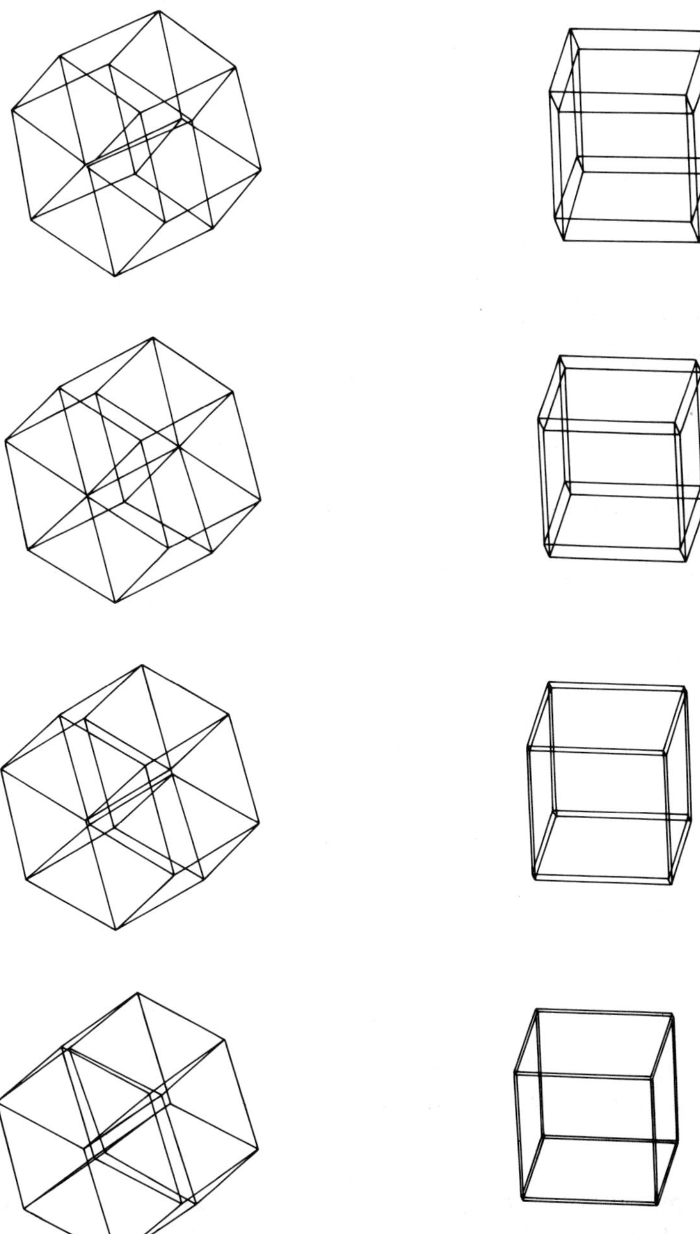

Figure 10-2: Four-dimensional hypercubes projected into three-space and drawn as a series of frames in two-space.

10.2.6 Graphics Output, Input, and Interaction

Since a picture is worth a thousand words, system designers have sought to provide graphic input and output. Perceptual psychologists have amply demonstrated the advantage of imagery over words or numbers for certain applications. Error rates and time can be reduced substantially when a proper graphic representation can be found.

Early users of computer systems produced graphs, histograms, scattergrams, and crude drawings using line printer characters. CRT screens, electrostatic printers, ink pen plotters, and other devices allowed continuous line drawings with resolution, on the order of one hundred lines per inch. Contemporary displays allow two to four times the resolution and color displays further enhance image quality.

The difficulty has always been to develop software which makes image production convenient. Most graphics equipment manufacturers provide only basic software. Special-purpose graphics languages such as ARTSPEAK, EXPLOR, graphic ALGOL, BUGSYS, and Computer Animated Movie Language have been developed. Special purpose graphics hardware reduces the central processing unit load and permits rapid operations such as real-time rotation in three space, contrast enhancement, filtering, color substitution, and size changes (zooming in or out). Graphics systems can provide a window on worlds that never existed or are invisible. Graphics applications have included views of:

- a universe where gravity does not operate on the inverse square law
- human heart functioning with injuries or diseases
- crystal growth
- wind tunnel flows
- four-dimensional objects projected onto the third dimension (Figure 10-2 shows several projections of a hypercube)
- demographic data on a map as it changes over time
- travel at speeds approaching the speed of light.

Graphic input is becoming less of a problem. Point by point digitizers facilitate manual insertion of images and TV camera input is becoming more available. Weather and reconnaissance satellite images are dramatic evidence of the success of computer image processing. Software to transform images and perform pattern recognition is improving and has been commercially applied for detecting deviation from manufacturing standards, as in the development of integrated circuit chips.

Interactive computer graphics applications (Newman and Sproull, 1979) include electronic circuit design, map making, surveying, architecture, automobile design, numerical control of machine tools, textile pattern layout, newspaper layout, and police or firefighter dispatching. Graphics interaction is particularly effective if a basic pattern is to be entered and modifications can be made on line. The success of graphics interaction depends on a narrow application domain, natural representation of the real world phenomenon, and the acceptability of the set of operators. Foley and Wallace (1974) support graphics interaction but caution users and developers about five problem areas:

1) Boredom - improper pacing
2) Panic - unexpectedly long delays
3) Frustration - inability to convey intentions or inflexible and unforgiving system
4) Confusion - excessive detail or lack of structure
5) Discomfort - inappropriate physical environment.

Bennett (1977) gives a set of guidelines for graphics systems developers:

1) Arrange text and graphic symbols on each presentation to establish an explicit context for user action
2) When a user process is not known in advance, concentrate on displayable data representations and then design operations to act upon these representations
3) Design the system to provide an explicit framework for representations. The framework gives a uniformity of structure within which the user can synthesize problem solutions. This framework can be developed even though problems themselves are unstructured.

More experimental research is needed to refine our understanding of the advantages and environments suitable to graphics interaction. In summary, the graphics system should provide a familiar representation and standard operations. If graphics interaction provides 90 percent of what is possible manually, users may still be unhappy about losing 10 percent of their operations. A natural evolution for new technologies is to duplicate old technology performance before opening up new possibilities.

10.3 PSYCHOLOGICAL ISSUES

10.3.1 Short- and Long-Term Memory

Current models of the human memory system include at least three components (Lindsay and Norman, 1977; Tracz, 1979). The *sensory information storage* processes visual, tactical, auditory, or other raw sensation and maintains it for only a few tenths of a second before passing it on and replacing it with new sensations. The fraction of a second maintenance of an image allows us to perceive a television or movie as continuous.

The *short-term memory* processes the sensation and holds interpreted units of information for up to thirty seconds, but this period can be extended by continued rehearsal or repetition. For example, a telephone number, a stranger's face, or a melody will quickly fade from short-term memory unless purposefully repeated or reviewed. The size of the short-term memory has been much discussed ever since George Miller's (1956) classic paper 'The magical number seven -- plus or minus two' described a number of experiments which suggested that information perceived by any sensory organ was limited to seven units. The nature of the units or *chunks* in short-term memory are a function of experience and training. To one person a string of 21 binary digits may be difficult to memorize, but someone else may be able to recode the binary digits into seven octal digits which are easier to cope with. An American can probably memorize seven English words as easily as seven letters, but would have a hard time recalling seven Russian letters and a harder time still, recalling seven Russian words. Similarly, a novice programmer has a hard time recalling a computer program, but an experienced programmer recognizes and recodes the program into fewer but larger chunks.

Transferring chunks from the short-term to the *long-term memory* requires time and effort. The long-term memory appears to be permanent, although some kinds of information may become more difficult to retrieve as time goes by. The organization and the continuing reorganization of information in the long-term memory is poorly understood, but the seemingly unlimited capacity, durability of knowledge, and rapid recall enable us to perform remarkable feats.

For terminal interaction, the magical number seven plus or minus two implies that the processing capacity of individuals is extremely small and in constant danger of overload. Soft copy terminal interactions which start with a frame requiring the user to memorize twenty options will probably overload the user's short-term memory. A printed list of options or offline training to embed the knowledge in long-term memory might be preferable. If training is to be accomplished online, then the options should be presented one at a time, with intervening exercises to test comprehension and to retain the knowledge. Requiring users to keep newly learned information in short-term memory severely restricts capacity for problem solving. Users must constantly rehearse their knowledge to maintain the information.

10.3.2 Closure

One of the byproducts of the limitation on human short-term memory is that there is great relief when information no longer needs to be retained. This produces a powerful desire to complete a task, reduce our memory load, and gain relief. *Closure* is the completion of a task leading to relief. Since terminal users strive for closure in their work, interactions should be defined in sections so completion can be attained and information released. Every time a user completes editing a line or ends an editing session with an EXIT or SAVE command, there is relief associated with completion and attaining closure.

The pressure for closure means that users, especially novices, may prefer multiple small operations to a single large operation. Not only can they monitor progress and ensure that all is going well, but they can release the details of coping with the early portions of the task. One informal study showed that users preferred three separate menu lists, rather than three menus on the screen at once. Although more typing and more interactions were required for the three separate menus, the users preferred doing one small thing at a time. With three menus at a time, the information about the first menu decision must be maintained until the system acknowledges or the RETURN key is hit. Similarly, word processor users may make three separate changes on adjacent words, when one large change command could have accomplished the same results with fewer keystrokes.

10.3.3 Attitude and Anxiety

Several studies have demonstrated that user attitudes can dramatically impact learning and performance with interactive systems. Novices with negative attitudes towards computers learned editing tasks more slowly and made more errors (Walther and O'Neil, 1974). Anxiety, generated by fear of failure, may reduce short-term memory capacity and inhibit performance. If users are insecure about their ability to use the system, worried about destroying files or the computer itself, overwhelmed by volumes of details or pressured to work rapidly, their anxiety will lower performance. Programmers who must meet a deadline tend to make more errors as they frantically patch programs in a manic attempt to finish. Of course, mild pressure can act as a motivator, but if the pressure becomes too strong the resultant high levels of anxiety interfere with competent work.

In designing a system for novices, every attempt should be made to make the user at ease, without being patronizing or too obvious. A message telling users not to be nervous is a bad idea. Users will feel best if the instructions are lucid, expressed in familiar terms, and easy to follow. They should be given simple tasks and gain the confidence that comes with successful use of any tool or machine. Diagnostic messages should be understandable, nonthreatening, and low-key. If the input is incorrect, avoid blaring phrases such as 'ERROR 435 - NUMBERS ARE ILLEGAL' and merely state what is necessary to make things right 'MONTHS ARE ENTERED BY NAME'. Try to avoid meaningless, condemning messages such as 'SYNTAX ERROR' and give helpful, informative statements such as 'UNMATCHED RIGHT PARENTHESIS'. Constructive messages and positive reinforcement produce faster learning and increase user acceptance.

10.3.4 Control

A driving force in human behavior is the desire to control. Some individuals have powerful needs to attain and maintain control of their total environment; others are less strongly motivated in this direction and are more accepting of their fate. With respect to using computers, the desire for control apparently increases with experience. Novice terminal users and children are perfectly willing to follow the computer's instructions and accept the computer as the controlling agent in the interaction. With experience and maturity, users resent the computer's dominance and prefer to use the computer as a tool. These users perceive the computer as merely an aid in accomplishing their own job or personal objectives and resent messages which suggest that the computer is in charge.

The Library of Congress recognized this distinction in changing the prompting message from the authoritarian 'ENTER NEXT COMMAND' to the servant-like 'READY FOR NEXT COMMAND.' A large bank offers a banking terminal which displays the message 'HOW CAN I HELP YOU?' This is appealing at first glance, but after some use, this come-on becomes annoying. The illusion that the machine is just like a human teller is perceived as a deception and the user starts to wonder about other ways in which the bank has been deceptive. The attempt to dominate the interaction by implying that the terminal will help the user and by emphasizing the 'I', violates common rules of courtesy. If a starting message is used at all, it probably should focus on the customer, for example 'WHAT DO YOU NEED?' followed by a list of available operations. Preferably, the user should initiate the operation by hitting a button labeled 'START', thus reinforcing the idea that the user is in control of the machine.

Early computer-assisted instruction systems heaped praise on the student and 'wisely' guided the student through the material at a computer-selected pace; more recent systems merely display performance scores and provide an environment where the student chooses the path and pace. Only children appreciate praise from a computer, most people achieve internal satisfaction if their performance is satisfactory. Instead of the lengthy 'VERY GOOD, YOU GOT THE RIGHT ANSWER,' the simple display of '++' signals a correct answer to a problem.

Reinforcement for these ideas comes from Jerome Ginsburg of Equitable Life Assurance Society who prepared a set of guidelines for developing interactive applications systems. He makes the powerful claim that:

> Nothing can contribute more to satisfactory system performance than the conviction on the part of the terminal operators that they are in control of the system and not the system in control of them. Equally, nothing can be more damaging to satisfactory system operation, regardless of how well all other aspects of the implementation have been handled, than the operator's conviction that the terminal and thus the system are in control, have 'a mind of their own,' or are tugging against rather than observing the operator's wishes.

Being in control is one of the satisfying components of time-sharing and of programming in general. Systems which are designed to enhance user control are preferred. One explanation of why word processing systems have come into widespread use in only the last few years is that mini and micro computers give users a powerful feeling of being in control compared to the time-shared usage of a large machine. Files kept on floppy disks are tangible when compared to disk files on an unseen remote machine. Although failures, loss of files, and faulty disks probably occur more often on the stand-alone minis and micros than on larger systems, the users of minis and micros have the satisfaction of controlling their own destiny.

10.4 RESPONSE TIME

Most designers recognize that a simple limit on response time, the time it takes for the system to respond to a command, like two seconds, is an unreasonably crude specification. Some systems have design specifications of two second response time for 90 percent of the commands and ten second response time for the remaining 10 percent. A more informed view is that the acceptable response time is a function of the command type. Users are not disturbed to wait several seconds for the loading of a file or large program, but they expect immediate response to editing commands or emergency requests. R. B. Miller (1968) provides a list of seventeen command types and reasonable response times (Table 10–1).

User Activity	"Maximum" Response Time
Control activation (for example, keyboard entry).	0.1 SECOND
System activation (system initialization).	3.0
Request for given service:	
simple	2
complex	5
loading and restart	15-60
Error feedback (following completion of input).	2-4
Response to ID.	2
Information on next procedure.	<5
Response to simple inquiry from list.	2
Response to simple <u>status</u> inquiry.	2
Response to complex inquiry in table form.	2-4
Request for next page.	0.5-1
Response to "execute problem."	< 15
Light pen entries.	1.0
Drawing with light pens.	0.1
Response to complex inquire in <u>graphic</u> form.	2-10
Response to dynamic modeling.	-
Response to graphic manipulation.	2
Response to user intervention in automatic process.	4

Table 10-1: System response time as a function of user activity (R. B. Miller, 1968).

We may disagree with specific entries or suggest new entries, but the idea of having different response times seems acceptable. In fact, one possible approach is to guarantee that more complex and expensive commands require longer waits. This will shape user behavior in the direction of faster, cheaper commands.

A contrasting design goal is to minimize the variance of response time. It has been suggested and confirmed by experiment (L. H. Miller, 1977) that increasing the variability of response time generates poorer performance (Figure 10-3) and lower user satisfaction (Figure 10-4). Users

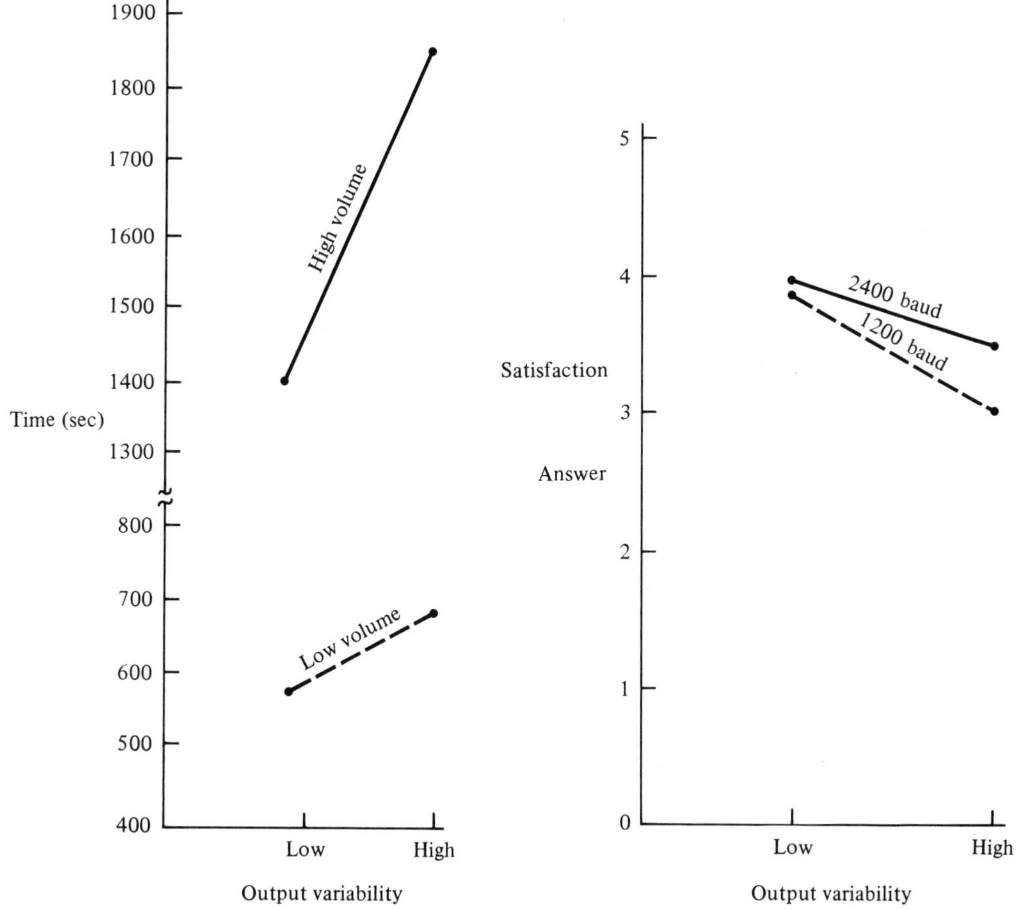

Figure 10-3: Graph of time to complete tasks vs. output variability for low and high volume (L. H. Miller, 1977).

Figure 10-4: Graph of average response to post-test questionnaire vs. output variability for 1200 and 2400 baud (L. H. Miller, 1977).

may prefer a system which always responds in 4.0 seconds to one which varies from 1.0 to 6.0 seconds, even though the average in the second case is 3.5. Apparently users can devote 3.9 seconds to planning if they are sure that the time is available. If attention has to be maintained on the screen, users will not use the response time for planning work. Some users even report surprise and disruption if the response is too prompt. Holding responses to minimize response time variance may actually improve user performance and satisfaction. For extremely long response times, more than 15 seconds, the user should be informed of the time required. One graphics system shows a clock hand ticking backwards to count off the seconds until the system will respond. Even if the response is ready earlier, the system continues its countdown to zero.

Installers of time-sharing systems report user dissatisfaction in two situations where response time variance is a factor. In the first case, when a new time-sharing system is installed and the work load is light, response times are low and users are pleased. As the load increases, the response time will deteriorate to normal levels and produce dissatisfaction. By slowing down the system when it is first installed, the change is eliminated and users seem content. A second case occurs when the load on a time-sharing system varies substantially during the day. Users become aware of the fast and slow periods and try to cram their work into the fast periods. Although this approach does help to balance the load, users tend to make errors while working quickly to beat the crowd. Anxiety is increased, complaints rise, and programmers or terminal users may even be unwilling to work during the slow periods. By eliminating the variance in response time, service is perceived to be more reliable and one source of anxiety can be reduced.

In summary, response time is an intriguing issue whose complexities have not yet been unraveled. We are left with several conflicting design goals:

- response time should be reduced under all conditions
- response time should match the complexity and cost of the command
- variance of response time should be reduced even at the expense of some increase in the mean response time
- system performance should be invariant over time.

In an experiment studying the effect of system response time on performance in a multiparameter optimization task, solution time increased significantly with system response time (Goodman and Spence, 1978). Subjects modified five parameters with light pen touches till a curve matched requirements. Each of the 30 subjects performed the task with fixed system response times of 0.16, 0.72, and 1.49 seconds. Figure 10–5 shows that decreasing the response time from 1.49 to 0.72 seconds reduces the solution time for this task.

Grossberg, Wiesen and Yntema (1976) studied four subjects performing 36 interactive tasks involving calculations on numeric arrays. Response times were varied from 1 to 4 to 16 to 64 seconds. As the response time increased subjects became more cautious, used fewer commands, took longer time between commands, but the total time consumed showed surprising invariance with respect to the response time increase. The subjects changed their working style as the response time increased by becoming more cautious and by making heavier use of hard copy printouts. The difference in results between this experiment and the previous one may be a product of the available commands, required tasks or subject experience.

A related aspect of response time is the think time of the terminal user. For complex decision making, there is some evidence that locking the terminal for a short period, say 25 seconds in one pilot study, may improve user performance on the decision and increase user satisfaction.

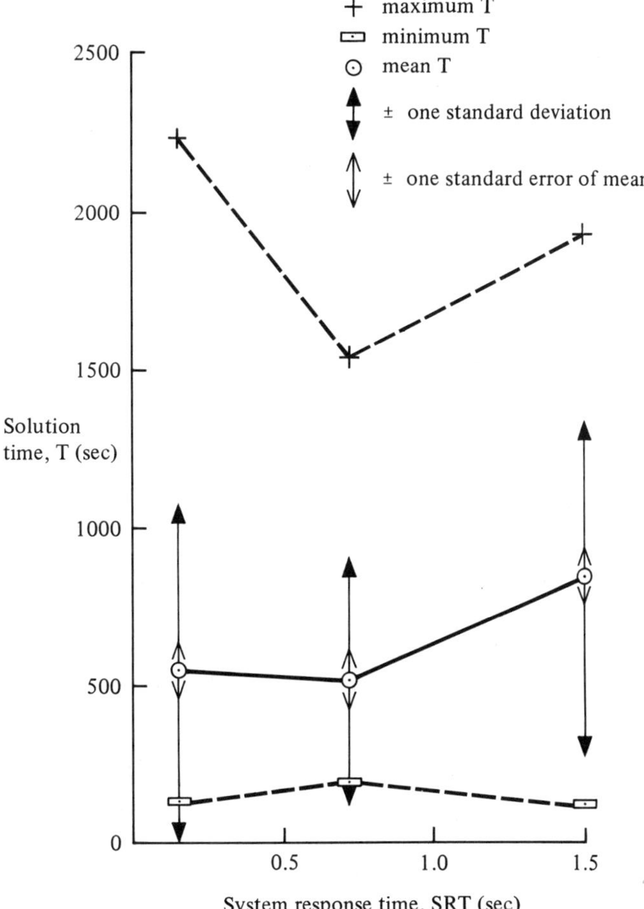

Figure 10-5: Solution time (T) vs. System Response Time (SRT) for 30 subjects (Goodman and Spence, 1978).

An open keyboard and partial attention to the display can distract the users and interfere with problem solving while increasing anxiety. The illusion of 'dialog' may compel users to keep their end of the 'conversation' going. A decision making study (Boehm, Seven and Watson, 1971) with longer lockout times (5 and 8 minutes) revealed that subjects with no lockout used twice as much computer time and, as might be expected, the lockout groups expressed dissatisfaction with restricted access. The high variance in performance of the 20 subjects made it impossible to assess the impact of lockout, although the highest performance mean was achieved by the five minute lockout group. Possibly if users perceive the computer as a tool they may be more willing to take their time and reflect on decisions. If users feel they are involved in a 'dialog' in which they must respond promptly, anxiety and poorer performance may result. Maybe we should eliminate the term 'dialog' and switch to 'utilog' to convey the impression that the user is utilizing the system as a tool.

10.5 TIME-SHARING vs. BATCH PROCESSING

As technological developments allowed programmers to use interactive terminals for preparing and executing their programs, a controversy arose over the relative merits of interactive usage and traditional batch submittal. Time-sharing adherents argued that waiting for processing by batch oriented computer systems was annoying, disruptive, and slowed production. Others felt that time sharing encouraged sloppy and hasty programming which led to more errors and poorer quality work.

Two of the earliest studies comparing online and offline processing were by Schatzoff, Tsao and Wiig (1967) and Gold (1969). The former study showed a 50 percent higher total cost for time-sharing, and a 50 percent greater elapsed time for batch, with no difference in computer time. More compilations were made online, suggesting less time is spent in desk checking. Gold indicated that the 'user's attitude appears to be one of the variables which may influence the user's immediate behavior and usage of computer systems.' Both studies agreed that there exists a variation in performance which may be attributable to programmer and problem differences.

Smith (1967) examined the effects of conventional batch versus instant batch (less than 5 minutes). With respect to elapsed time (time from the start of a problem to its completion) and student reaction, instant surpassed conventional.

Summarizing five studies comparing online to offline problem solving (including the two mentioned above), Sackman (1970) stated that time-sharing had a 20 percent advantage over batch in hours used, whereas batch surpassed time-sharing with a 40 percent advantage in central processor time. In regard to cost, neither mode outperformed the other.

He suggested that 'the comparison...is becoming academic as the contest converges toward interactive time-sharing and fast or even instant batch.' These studies need to be reevaluated and redone since hardware speeds and software capabilities have changed substantially in the last decade.

As a result of experimentation with junior college students, the use of time-sharing was recommended to alleviate the high drop-out rate from the introductory computer science courses (Boillot, 1974). The immediate feedback of time-sharing was seen as positively reinforcing.

The decrease in literature comparing the two modes of program development and the increase in articles on time-sharing systems give the illusion that the controversy has ended and the superiority of online processing is accepted. But some managers and researchers suggest that the time-sharing mode encourages hasty program development and increases the number of errors. They feel that the slower turnaround of batch processing produces more careful program design and thorough desk debugging.

In a related application of interactive systems, J. Hansen (1976) investigated performance differences for two management decision making tasks using time-sharing and batch approaches. Both problems, stochastic capital budgeting and product demand forecasting, were not solvable by a mathematical algorithm, but required heuristic approaches where feedback from each interaction would suggest new decision rules. The results (Table 10-2) demonstrate that in this environment time-sharing access significantly improved the quality of the decisions.

In short, the experimental results suggest that a good time-sharing system is better than a bad batch system. Correcting minor errors quickly in time-sharing mode speeds productivity and reduces irritation. For more fundamental work, some programmers may abuse the rapid access of time-sharing, make hasty patches, and produce poor quality code.

In all the experimental results, the influence of individual differences

	Group A (Batch/online) (5 subjects)	Group B (Online/batch) (5 subjects)
Problem 1 (capital budgeting)	82.0 (batch)	88.4 (online)
Problem 2 (product demand forecast)	90.6 (online)	84.6 (batch)

Table 10-2: Decision-making performance averages using time-sharing and batch modes (J. Hansen, 1976).

apparently played a major role. The high variance in performance and conflicting anecdotal evidence suggest that unmeasured factors such as personality may influence preference and performance. Whether or not a programmer wants to use interactive equipment may be an important consideration. Merely because many programmers, perhaps even a majority, prefer interactive mode does not mean that all programmers should utilize that mode. Those individuals who feel more secure with a deck of keypunch cards are just as necessary to an organization.

Many variables enter into a programmer's preference for a particular computer communication alternative. In an effort to identify specific personality traits influencing preference, we studied (Lee and Shneiderman, 1978) locus of control and assertiveness.

Locus of control concerns the perception individuals have of their influence over events. Internally controlled individuals perceive an event as contingent upon their own actions, whereas externally controlled people perceive a reinforcement for an action as being: more a result of luck, chance, or fate; under the control of other powerful people; or as unpredictable.

Assertive behavior 'allows an individual expression in a manner that fully communicates his personal desires without infringing upon the rights of others (Winship and Kelly, 1976). Assertive individuals exhibit the ability to state their feelings, whereas nonassertive people have difficulty with this type of communication.

Many programmers learned the use of keypunch equipment prior to being introduced to time-sharing. It would be less anxiety provoking for

Locus dimension:	Batch 0	1	2	3	Time Sharing 4	Mean	Total Observations
Internal	0	0	2	2	2	3.0	6
External	0	0	8	4	0	2.3	12
							18

Assertiveness dimension:	Batch 0	1	2	3	Time Sharing 4	Mean	Total Observations
Low	0	0	5	3	0	2.4	8
High	0	0	5	3	2	2.7	10
							18

Table 10-3: Preference scores by personality factors (Lee and Shneiderman, 1978).

them to remain with a mode of program entry which is familiar, i.e., keypunch, than to attempt online communication with its many problems, e.g., signing on or possible loss of an editing session. It seems that individuals who view themselves as more effective and powerful, or internally controlled, would master online interaction with the computer, while those who see themselves as less powerful and not very independent or effective, or externally controlled, would continue to process by batch.

Likewise, more assertive programmers would not let the intimidating terminal inhibit them from learning and using interactive equipment. They would be able to ask for help when needed, thus promoting their learning process. The nonassertive individual might look for a means of program entry which allows him/her least contact with others, including avoidance of equipment which could require a great deal of help and guidance during the familiarization stage. Weinberg (1971) conjectures that 'humble programmers perform better in batch environments and assertive ones will be more likely to shine online.'

Subjects for our exploratory study were programmers from a Control Data Corporation installation, which allows the choice of either card or terminal entry. Three questionnaires, one to measure locus of control, one to ascertain assertiveness, and another to determine online or offline preference were distributed via interoffice mail.

When the eighteen responses were grouped by preference scores (Table 10-3), the batch group did not differ significantly from the interactive group on either personality dimension: locus of control or assertiveness. However, when the sample was grouped by both internal-locus/high-assertive and external-locus/low-assertive (Table 10-4), there was a significant difference in mean preference scores. Similar studies need to be carried out with more subjects in a wide variety of programming environments.

Although our findings in this exploratory study showed mixed results, the import lies in the attempt to identify variables entering into a pro-

	Internal-locus/ High-assertive	External-locus/ Low-assertive
Mean Preference Score	3.34	2.54
Variance	0.399	0.108
Number of subjects (total number was 18)	4	6

Table 10-4: Average preference scores for personality groups (Lee and Shneiderman, 1978).

grammer's preference for either batch or time-sharing. If programmers are allowed to use the mode they prefer, their performance and job attitude could improve. If preference is affected by the type of task, the availability of different modes may again improve performance. When recruiting programmers for a time-sharing environment, managers may find that those who desire to work online will produce better products in that environment than those who prefer working in a batch environment.

10.6 TEXT EDITOR USAGE

A rapidly growing mode of computer use is by way of text editors, document preparation systems, and word processing equipment. These tools allow users to construct files containing programs, alphanumeric data, correspondence, or general textual information. The diversity of user experience and the range of user patterns is enormous. Sophisticated frequent users differ from infrequent users, who are all very different from novice users. The variety of hardware and software environments further increases the choices for text editor designers and users.

Experimental comparisons of text editors are providing information about usage patterns, suggesting directions for development projects, and aiding development of a cognitive model. Walther and O'Neil (1974) report on an experiment with 69 undergraduate computer science students; 41 percent never used an online system, 38 percent had some experience and 22 percent had much experience. The three experimental factors were: flexibility (one version of the editor was inflexible, while the second version permitted abbreviations, default values, user declaration of synonyms, a variety of delimiters, and other features), display device (cathode ray tube and impact teletype both at ten characters per second), and attitude (three subjective tests indicating attitude towards computers and anxiety). The subjects performed 18 corrections to a text file while errors were tabulated and timing data was collected. Experienced users worked faster with the flexible version but inexperienced users were overwhelmed by the flexible version. The inexperienced users made fewer errors and worked faster with the inflexible version. The impact teletype users worked faster and made fewer errors, suggesting that the feedback from the impact may facilitate performance. Those with negative attitudes made more errors. Walther and O'Neil offer interaction effects, conjectures, potential design rules, and research directions.

Sondheimer (1979) describes an experiment with more than 60 professional programmer users of a text editor. With active participation of the subjects, five features were chosen for addition to the text editor. Announcements, documentation, and training were provided but after some initial testing, usage of the features dropped off substantially. Sondheimer concludes that 'the results of the experiment seem to indicate the persistence of individual usage habits.' This experiment has implications which go beyond the use of text editors, but it does emphasize that text editing is a skill which is deeply ingrained in the user's mind and difficult to change. Sondheimer conjectures that novice users of the text editor would more frequently employ the newly added features.

Card (1978) and Card, Moran and Newell (1979a, 1979b) provide detailed reports on text editor experiments and offer cognitive models of human performance. Their experiments emphasize in-depth study of a limited number of highly-trained subjects. Subjects performed manuscript editing tasks with a variety of line and display editors while precise timing measurements were made automatically. Text editing is characterized (Card, Moran and Newell, 1979b) as a 'routine cognitive skill' which 'occurs in situations that are familiar and repetitive, and which people master with practice and training, but where the variability in the task, plus the induced variability arising from error, keeps the task from becoming completely routine and requires cognitive involvement.' A cognitive model based on goals, operators, methods, and selection rules (GOMS model) is proposed and is claimed to represent the performance of expert users. User style in locating a line (by jumping ahead a given

```
READY FOR GRADE LEVEL:
1) FRESHPERSON
2) SOPHOMORE
3) JUNIOR
4) SENIOR
5) GRADUATE

? _
```

Figure 10-6: Menu selection example.

number of lines or by locating a character string) and correcting text (by substitution or by subcommands for modifying characters in a line) was compared among subjects with the goal of predicting behavior in future situations.

Card, Moran and Newell (1979a) use data from 28 subjects, on 10 systems, and over 14 task types to support the keystroke model of editor usage, which suggests that task performance time can be predicted from only the number of keystrokes required. This model has strict requirements: 'The user must be an expert, the task must be a routine unit task; the method must be specified in detail; and the performance must be error-free.' The timing data from a variety of users and systems reveals important differences such as the speed advantage of display editors over line editors (about twice as fast). The timing data from Card (1978) demonstrates the clear speed and accuracy advantages of a mouse for selecting text, when compared with a joystick, step keys, or text keys.

10.7 MENU SELECTION, FILL-IN-THE-BLANK AND PARAMETRIC MODES

Three easy to implement, frequently used interface modes are:

1) Menu selection: a terminal screen is filled with a set of numbered choices
2) Fill-in-the-blank: a user provides a word, number, or phrase response to a line of text
3) Parametric: a user provides a formatted set of numbers, codes, or words in response to a prepared line of text.

Martin (1973) shows detailed examples of these modes and their variants. Menu selection (Figure 10-6) requires little or no user training and has the advantage that users may be informed about the range of system features. A succession of menu selections can be used to produce a tree search. Choosing the terms in the menus, the number of items in each menu, and the sequencing of menus requires careful planning so as to minimize user error. A simple exit from the menu sequence, the opportunity to return to previous menus, and help frames should be provided. With a high speed communication line and terminal, menu selection does not lead to boredom and can be an effective method. Users should be allowed to respond to a menu as soon as it appears or as soon as their choice appears. Other advantages of menu systems include the ease with which error handling and user aids can be designed. The limited number of choices on any frame and the information about the sequence of frames which led to the current one provide a narrow context within which it is easy to design effective user aids.

Menu selection is used successfully in the PLATO computer-based education system and in the Problem Oriented Medical Information System (PROMIS) developed by the University of Vermont medical school. PROMIS provided high speed access to more than 30,000 information and selection frames. With rapid response, menu selection can be as appealing to knowledgeable users as it is to novices. Researchers at Carnegie-Mellon University are developing ZOG, a rapid response (0.05 seconds, 70 percent of the time) menu selection system (Robertson et al., 1977).

Fill-in-the-blank questions (Figure 10-7) require users to be aware of the reasonable responses, but the lengthy displays of menu selections are avoided. Some training may be required but with a bit of experience users become proficient quickly. Users must become aware of the format of the input, for example, which formats of a date are acceptable. The designer may resolve the date problem by dividing the date into three separately entered items with more explicit guidance, for example, 'ENTER MONTH AS TWO DIGITS', 'ENTER DAY OF MONTH AS TWO DIGITS' and 'ENTER YEAR AS FOUR DIGITS'. A second solution

```
READY FOR
GRADE LEVEL ? JUNIOR
GRADE POINT AVERAGE ? 3.47
MAJOR ?_
```

Figure 10-7: Fill-in-the-blank example.

is to offer a syntactic clue such as 'ENTER DATE AS MM.DD.YYYY' and hope that the user will understand. Format prompts can be complemented by range prompts, for example, a bank cash dispensing terminal might specify 'CASH DESIRED ($10 TO $200 IN $10 UNITS)'. Users should be allowed to enter a question mark in a blank to get more information. Multiple fill-in-the-blank questions might appear on the screen at once requiring cursor movement to respond to all questions. Error, diagnostic, and commentary messages could appear after each entry or after the complete set. Corrections could be entered by overwriting. Exit, backup, and help facilities should be provided.

Parametric systems (Figure 10-8) require still more training, but usage is extremely fast and user satisfaction is increased because users feel more in control. More complex error handling modules are required, but help frames which list the set of choices or commands are usually easy to prepare. When an error occurs with a novice user the system could default to a slower menu selection approach.

For example, in an airline reservation system the parametric command, 'A21AUGJFKLAX' might indicate a request for availability of flights on the 21st of August of the current year from Kennedy Airport in New York City to Los Angeles. The operator must learn the set of one letter operation codes, the pattern for entering dates (for example, all

```
@ACCOUNT  ENTER/SEATON,PASSWORD/ROBYN,FUNDS/500
    .
    .
    .
@CATALOG,M  BOOKS*FILES/BEN/BEN/,,,4
    .
    .
    .
@COPY,A,R  TAPE4,PRINTER6,50
```

Figure 10-8: Parametric control language examples establishing a computer account, cataloging a file with privacy keys, and copying the contents of a tape onto a printer.

dates are two digits and all months follow with three characters), and the three character codes for airports. Although it may take a novice some time to learn all the codes, the regular user need only enter a brief character string. A parametric system may offer novice users prompts such as 'READY FOR COMMAND (ODDMMM111222)' or assistance through menu selection if a question mark is entered.

Combinations of these three modes may be useful. If names, character strings, account numbers, large integers, fixed point values or floating point values are to be entered, fill in the blank is preferable. If the number of choices is limited, a menu selection may be appropriate.

With careful design a system could satisfy a broad range of users. Novices would get a set of menus. As the users gained experience, a fill-in-the-blank approach could be employed, but if users forgot the choices, a blank entry would produce the menu. Finally, the most experienced users could make parametric command strings and request fill-in-the-blank or menu approaches when they had difficulty.

In considering error handling and help facilities, the designer should be sensitive to the difference between syntactic and semantic knowledge. A novice user is not helped by brief prompts concerning syntax but needs a simple explanation of the terminology. These explanations must be carefully tested with actual users because the designer is the last to recognize a poor explanation. Designing a good interactive system is difficult and time-consuming.

Experimental tests need to be conducted to clarify the applications which are most suitable for these three modes. How many choices are appropriate for a single menu? Does a deep menu selection tree lead to loss of orientation? How many commands in a parametric system can users master if their usage is infrequent? What kind of frustrations are encountered in each of these three modes? How does variation in response time affect user satisfaction?

10.8 ERROR HANDLING

The error checking and handling components of an online system may occupy the majority of the programming effort. Well designed diagnostic facilities and error messages can make a system appealing. When user entries do not conform to expectations, diagnostic messages should guide the user in entering correct commands. Messages should be brief, without negative tones, and constructive. Avoid ringing bells and bold messages which may embarrass the user. Instead of meaningless messages like 'ILLEGAL SYNTAX', try to indicate where the error occurred and what may be done to set it right. If possible, allow users to modify the incorrect command rather than forcing a complete reentry. Command and programming languages should be designed so that a common error will not be interpreted as a valid command.

Error messages should be included in the system documentation, so that users know what to expect and so that designers cannot hide sloppy work in the system code.

The system should permit easy monitoring of error patterns so that system design can be modified in response to frequent errors. Simple tallies of error occurrences may suggest modifications of error messages, changes to command languages, or improved training procedures.

An intriguing issue in error handling is whether the error message should be issued immediately or when the end-of-line code (usually ENTER or RETURN key) is hit. A nicely designed study (Segal, 1975) suggests that human performance improves if errors are issued immediately and that the disruption of user thought processes by immediate interruption is not a serious impediment. Seventy undergraduate subjects in this counterbalanced within subjects experiment had to list 25 of the 50 states in the United States and list 20 permutations of 'abcde' such that 'c' occurs somewhere before the 'd'. The results of the permutation task strongly favor immediate interruption, but the results of the states task were mixed (Table 10-5). A powerful advantage of immediate interruption is that changes can be made simply by replacing the incorrect character.

A central problem in handling errors is providing the user with the right kind of information. Experienced frequent users need only an indication that an error has occurred, such as a locked keyboard, a light, or a special character. As soon as the error has been brought to their attention, they will probably recognize it and be prepared to make an immediate correction. Typical users familiar with the operations or semantics of the domain merely require a brief note to remind them of the

	States Task		Permutation Task	
	Error Correction Method			
	Immediate	End	Immediate	End
Percent error keypresses	2.55	1.99	4.54	4.48
Total time (seconds)	234.0	300.0	408.8	546.4
Two consecutive responses in error	1.17	1.17	1.09	2.77
Number of responses in error	4.29	3.77	4.46	4.83

Table 10-5: Average performance results for error correction styles (Segal, 1975).

proper syntax or the list of available options. Novice users whose semantic knowledge is shallow need more than prompting on syntax, they need explanations of possible commands and the required syntax. Since even experts may forget or be novices with respect to some portions of a system, a simple scheme based on recording user experience levels is unworkable. Probably the best approach is to give control to the user and provide options; maybe '?' for a brief prompt about syntax, a second '?' for a brief prompt about semantics and a third '?' for a more detailed explanation. Users could strike '??' or '???' initially to get complete information right away.

This question mark scheme is a simple approach to what are generally referred to as 'HELP' systems. Typing 'HELP' or merely 'H' the user can get some information; 'HELP FILES', 'HELP EDIT', 'HELP FORTRAN', etc. may invoke more extensive topic oriented HELP facilities. 'HELP HELP' should provide information about available facilities. The PLATO instructional system offers a special HELP key which offers appropriate guidance for the material currently on the screen.

10.9 PRACTITIONER'S SUMMARY

Hardware features can play a key role in system usability. If you can influence hardware choices, be thorough in reviewing alternatives for keyboards, displays, cursor control, audio input/output and graphics input/output. But, remember that an application system may be required to perform in a variety of hardware environments and that the application will probably survive into new generations of hardware. A modular approach which decouples the hardware from the required operations can help.

Do not violate the bounds of human performance imposed by limited short-term memory capacity. Design interactions in a modular fashion so that closure can be obtained providing satisfaction and relief for users. Be sensitive to user anxiety and desire for control. Provide novice users with the satisfaction of accomplishment and a sense of mastery, but avoid patronizing comments. Consider response time requirements as part of the design, not as an uncontrollable aspect of system performance.

Respect user preferences in choice of batch or interactive program development. Accept the personality and cognitive style differences among individuals and do not attempt to make everyone behave as you do.

Devote substantial energy to error design. Make messages constructive and give guidance for using the system in a courteous nonthreatening way. Prepare all messages as part of the system design and make them available in user manuals. Give users control over what kind of and how much information they wish at every point in the interaction. Do not require them to identify themselves at the start as novices. HELP facilities should be available for every command.

10.10 RESEARCHER'S AGENDA

Investigate the utility of hardware options for specific tasks. When are faster displays necessary? When is higher screen or cursor movement resolution important?

Relate the research on human perception to terminal design. Study short-term memory capacity for terminal interaction tasks. Develop explicit guidelines for designers to cope with psychological issues such as closure, anxiety, control, and personality differences. Study response time and think time variation by task. Explore the limits of menu selection with high-speed systems. Design systems that facilitate migration from menu selection to parametric commands. Investigate appropriate conditions for menu selection, fill-in-the-blank, and parametric approaches. Test different tutorial and help system strategies. Show how error handling styles influence performance and user satisfaction.

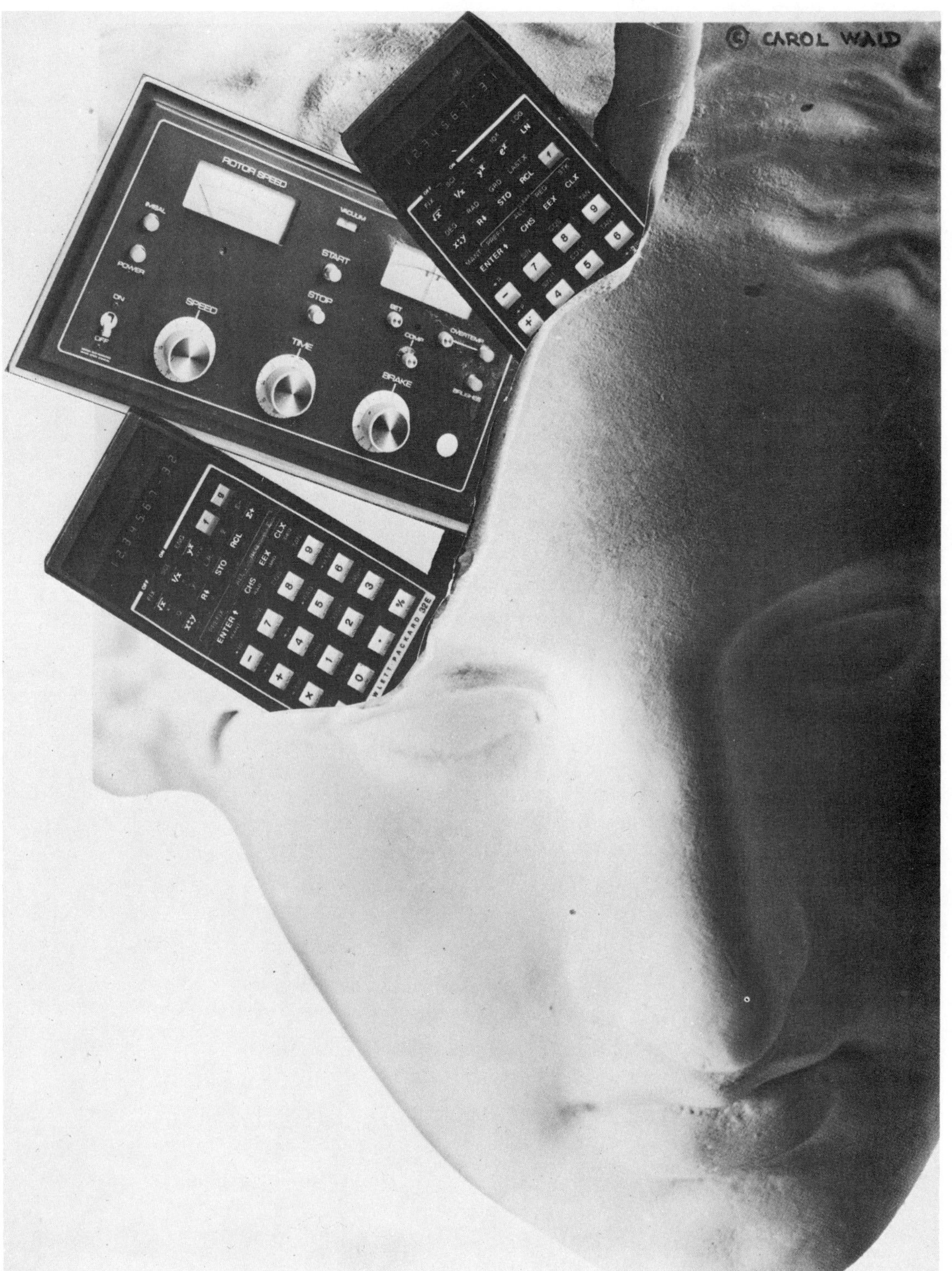
© CAROL WALD
ROTOR SPEED
VACUUM
POWER
START
STOP
ON
OFF
SPEED
TIME
BRAKE
COMP
OVERTEMP
ENTER
CHS
EEX
CLX
STO
RCL
LN
LOG
HEWLETT PACKARD 32E

11

DESIGNING INTERACTIVE SYSTEMS

The life-efficiency and adaptability of the computer must be questioned. Its judicious use depends upon the ability of its human employers quite literally to keep their own heads, not merely to scrutinize the programming but to reserve for themselves the right of ultimate decision. No automatic system can be intelligently run by automatons - or by people who dare not assert human intuition, human autonomy, human purpose.

Lewis Mumford, *The Myth of the Machine* (1970)

Design goals for interactive terminal systems - simplicity - power - user satisfaction - reasonable cost - design process for interactive systems - collect information - design semantic structures - specify physical devices - develop software - devise implementation plan - nurture the user community - prepare evolutionary plan

11.1 INTRODUCTION TO DESIGN

Successful industrial design gracefully unites esthetics and function while keeping costs low. Providing useful tools to computer users with a wide range of experience, problems, skills, and expectations is a challenge to scientific competence, engineering ingenuity, and artistic elegance. Systems designers are increasingly aware that ad hoc design processes, based on intuition and limited experience, may have been adequate for early programming languages and applications, but are insufficient for interactive systems which will be used by millions of people. Interactive computer-based consumer products for home, personal or office applications must be carefully designed to provide efficient, safe, reliable, and effective service while offering satisfaction to the user. Regular users quickly pass through the gadget fascination stage and become demanding users who expect the system to help them in performance of their work.

Unfortunately, it is not possible to offer an algorithm for optimal or even satisfactory design. Interactive systems designers, like architects or industrial designers, seek a workable compromise between conflicting design goals. Systems should be simple but powerful, easy to learn but appealing to experienced users, and facilitate error handling but allow freedom of expression. All of this should be accomplished in the shortest possible development time; costs should be kept low and future modification should be simple. Coping with these opposing design goals and managerial demands is a challenge.

Henry Dreyfuss (1955), a leading industrial designer responsible for plane, train, boat interiors, and dozens of familiar consumer items, provides useful guidance in *Designing for People*. He devotes a full chapter to the experience of designing the 500-Type Telephone, the standard rotary dial desk model. Measurements of 2000 human faces were used to determine the spacing between the mouth and ear pieces. After consulting with Bell System engineers about the layout of electronic components, 2500 sketches for possible designs were made. Numerous variations of the handgrip were considered until the familiar rounded-off rectangular cross section was adopted. Variations on dial and faceplate were tested till a four and one quarter inch diameter faceplate was selected to replace the older three-inch diameter version. Placement of the letters and numbers was studied, the angle of the dial was adjusted to reduce glare and the cradle was modified to minimize the receiver-off-the-hook problem. Accurate layout drawings were made for all the variations and finally clay and plaster models were built to compare the leading designs. Then testing began.

This process contrasts sharply with most interactive system development experiences where designs are hastily proposed and evaluated informally. Alternative command structures, error handling procedures, or screen formats rarely get implemented for pilot testing purposes. Dreyfuss devotes another entire chapter to emphasize the importance of testing. Tests and pilot studies should be more than the informal, biased opinion of a colleague or nearby secretary. A pilot test should involve actual users for sufficient time periods to get past initial learning problems and novelty. Competing designs should be evaluated in carefully controlled experimental conditions.

Experiments provide no guarantee of quality but are a useful supplement to informal guesswork. The process of developing an experimental comparison can itself be productive, often providing worthwhile insights. Statistical performance data and informal subjective commentary from participants can be valuable in fine-tuning proposed procedures. Experimental research can lead to fundamental insights which transcend specific systems. Nickerson (1969), Bennett (1972), Martin (1973), and Miller and Thomas (1977) provide broad ranging reviews of issues and references for designers and researchers of interactive systems.

This chapter is devoted to goals for the product and suggestions for the process of interactive systems design.

11.2 GOALS FOR INTERACTIVE SYSTEMS DESIGNERS

The diversity of situations in which interactive systems may be used makes it difficult to prescribe a universal set of goals. The attempts of several systems designers to define goals are shown in Figures 11-1 through 11-8.

Hansen's (1971) (Figure 11-1) First Principle should be the motto of every designer: *Know the User*. No qualifier or explanation is necessary. Hansen's sensitivity to human short-term memory limitations leads to his second category: minimizing memorization. Under optimization of operations, Hansen includes display inertia which suggests that when operations are applied, as little of the display should be changed as possible. This approach reduces disruptive movement and highlights the impact of the last operation. Muscle memory is the idea that users develop the feel for frequently used keypresses. Hansen recognizes the importance of engineering for errors by providing good error messages, reversible actions, and revisions to engineer out common errors.

Wasserman's (1973) (Figure 11-2) five design principles are reasonable, but the second and fifth ones may need qualification. Although it is usually good to minimize the user's need to learn about the computer system, sometimes restricting access to those who have acquired a certain knowledge level may be a good idea. The qualifying test, which works well for driver's licenses and college entrance, may be useful for complex and powerful systems. Naive users should be prevented from using a system which is too hard for them and would pro-

User engineering principles.

- First principle: Know the user.
- Minimize memorization.
  - Selection not entry.
  - Names not numbers.
  - Predictable behavior.
  - Access to system information.
- Optimize operations.
  - Rapid execution of common operations.
  - Display inertia.
  - Muscle memory.
  - Reorganize command parameters.
- Engineer for errors.
  - Good error messages.
  - Engineer out the common errors.
  - Reversible actions.
  - Redundancy.
  - Data structure integrity.

Figure 11-1: User engineering principles for interactive systems (W. J. Hansen, 1971).

Provide a program action for every possible type of user input.

Minimize the need for the user to learn about the computer system.

Provide a large number of explicit diagnostics, along with extensive online user assistance.

Provide program short-cuts for knowledgeable users.

Allow the user to express the same message in more than one way.

Figure 11-2: The design of idiot-proof interactive programs (Wasserman, 1973).

Know the user population.

Respond consistently and clearly.

Carry forward a representation of the user's knowledge base.

Adapt wordiness to user needs.

Provide the users with every opportunity to correct their own errors.

Promote the personal worth of the individual user.

Figure 11-3: Design guidelines for interactive systems (Pew and Rollins, 1975).

- Introduce through experience.
- Immediate feedback.
- Use the user's model.
- Consistency and uniformity.
- Avoid acausality.
- Query-in-depth (tutorial aids).
- Sequential – parallel tradeoff (allow choice of entry patterns).
- Observability and controllability.

Figure 11-4: Design guidelines for interactive systems (Gaines and Facey, 1975).

Simple. Project a "natural," uncomplicated "virtual" image of the system.

Responsive. Respond quickly and meaningfully to user commands.

User-controlled. All actions are initiated and controlled by the user.

Flexible. Flexibility in common structure and tolerance of errors.

Stable. Able to detect user difficulties and assist him in returning to correct dialog; never "deadending" the user (i.e., offering no recourse).

Protective. Protect the user from costly mistakes or accidents, (e.g., overwriting a file).

Self-documenting. The commands and system responses are self-explanatory and documentation, explanations or tutorial material are part of the environment.

Reliable. Not conducive to undetected errors in man-computer communication.

User-modifiable. Sophisticated users are able to personalize their environment.

Figure 11-5: Interface design for time-sharing systems (Cheriton, 1976).

duce an unpleasant experience. Wasserman's fifth principle about allowing the user to express the same message in more than one way may not always be good advice. Novices will prefer and do better with a system which has few choices and permits only limited forms of expression.

Pew and Rollins (1975) (Figure 11-3) echo Hansen's *Know the User* motto and add some of their own. Their 'adapt the wordiness to user needs' was probably intended to mean 'adapt the messages to the users level of syntactic and semantic knowledge.' Their last principle is a gem: 'promote the personal worth of the individual user.'

Gaines and Facey (1975) (Figure 11-4) emphasize the importance of the user being in control of the terminal, the pace of the interaction, the tutorial aids, and the execution process. Cheriton's (1976) (Figure 11-5) thorough list provides useful guidelines for interactive systems designers.

1. Simplicity
   - 1.1 Few keywords – few commands; few keywords; no extra commands or keywords special cases.
   - 1.2 Simplicity of input – fast input (with respect to keyboard layout); mnemotechnically sound abbreviations; simple input structure.
   - 1.3 Short commands – short keywords; little redundancy; avoidance of multiple input; use of default options.
   - 1.4 Simple commands – simple command structure; simple syntax of commands; correspondence between syntax and semantics; simple dialog structure.
2. Clarity
   - 2.1 Hierarchical structure – hierarchical structure of the language (commands and subcommands).
   - 2.2 Functionality – functional separation of commands; no multiple commands for (nearly) the same function; no command with multiple functions; clear elaboration of important special cases.
   - 2.3 Homogeneity – same structure for all commands; same meaning of keywords within all commands (where admissible); same capabilities in comparable contexts; uniform interpretation of missing parameters.
   - 2.4 Problem orientation – no avoidable technical restrictions or exceptions (caused by data structure, programming considerations, etc.); no avoidable separation into dialog branches; any command is admissible at any point of the dialog.
3. Uniqueness
   - 3.1 Determinism – every command is fully determined by its operands and preset options.
   - 3.2 No undefined states – all system states are always well defined (e.g., default options until the user sets new options).
4. Comfortable language
   - 4.1 Powerful commands – existence of powerful commands that do much in a single step.

Figure 11-6: Design criteria for documentation retrieval languages (Gebhardt and Stellmacher, 1978).

4.2 Flexibility – long and short forms of keywords; multilingual forms; direct and indirect operands; adjustment of the system to the user's knowledge and experience; commands adapted for casual, regular, and professional users; user control of system options (by parameters or presetting).

4.3 Short dialog – complete commands (including subcommands) and even command sequences can be input at once; new commands (or parts of commands) can be defined by a macro feature (renaming of strings).

4.4 Full use of data structure – all data structures can be displayed and utilized for searching and browsing.

5. Other comfort

5.1 Input comfort – rereading of previous input or output after corrections have been made; menutechnique.

5.2 Interruption – dialog can be interrupted at any time (stopped or continued subsequently).

5.3 Output language – clear, short, understandable system messages; output discernible from input; output reusable as input (where appropriate).

5.4 Additional comfort – various software and/or hardware provisions, as: function keys, acoustic signal after output transmission, highlighting and/or underlining, clear output arrangement, editing and clear display of tables, various techniques for browsing forwards and backwards; user's notebook.

6. Evidence and reusability

6.1 Evidence – evidence of the system state (waiting for input, input, waiting for output, output); acknowledgment of executed commands; periodic messages on delays; warnings about laborious commands.

6.2 Help functions – help functions providing information on the system state, the presently used function, all functions, structure and contents of data bases, past dialog, possible continuations; dialog protocol.

6.3 Reusability – former commands and output (or part of output) reusable for input; insertion of former commands into the present one (in particular, in query construction); saving commands for later execution.

7. Stability

7.1 Error handling – clear messages on severe input errors; error correction (wherever possible) on slight errors (but displaying to the user the system's interpretation); uniform error handling; no severe consequences of short input.

7.2 No compulsory situations – no compulsion to continue the dialog in a fixed way; dialog can be stopped at any point.

8. Data security – different passwords for data structure and data itself; missing passwords may be subsequently delivered to the system; on inadvertent trial to use secret data, the system must react as if this data did not exist; such situations must not lead to dialog discontinuation; security requirements for part of the data may not impede use of open data.

Figure 11-6 – *Cont.*

Gebhardt and Stellmacher (1978) (Figure 11-6) offer design criteria for documentation retrieval languages and Turoff, Whitescarver and Hiltz (1978) (Figure 11-7) describe human/machine interface characteristics in computerized conferencing systems. Kennedy (1974) (Figure 11-8) offers a list of items based on some experimental studies with data entry. Palme (1976) provides suggestions for interactive systems designers with a sensitivity to human needs.

The best detailed guide for design of interactive display systems was developed by Engel and Granda (1975). They make specific suggestions about display formats, frame contents, command language, recovery procedures, user entry techniques, general principles, and response time requirements.

Unfortunately, these lists are only crude guides to the designer. The entries are not independent and sometimes are in conflict. The lists contain contradictory recommendations and are incomplete. Finally, these design goals are largely unmeasurable. Can we assign a numerical value to the simplicity, stability, responsiveness, variety, etc. of a system? How can we compare the simplicity of two design proposals? How do we know what has been left out of the system design?

Experimental research can help to resolve some of these issues and

Forgiveness – ease in repairing errors
Segmentation – layered approach
Variety – choice of style
Escape – break out of danger
Guidance – direction and learning
Leverage – flexible, powerful features

Figure 11-7: The human-machine interface in a computerized conferencing environment (Turoff, Whitescarver, and Hiltz, 1978).

1. Use terse "natural" language, avoid codes, allow abbreviations.
2. Use short entries to facilitate error correction and maintain tempo.
3. Allow single or multiple entries to match user ability.
4. Maintain "social element" to the communication.
5. Permit user to control length of cues or error messages.
6. Error messages should be polite, meaningful and informative.
7. Give help when requested or when users are in difficulty.
8. Simple, logically consistent command language.
9. Control over all aspects of the system must appear to belong to the user.
10. Avoid redundancy in dialog.
11. Adapt to the user's ability.
12. Keep exchange rate in user's stress-free range; user can control rate.

Figure 11-8: Ground rules for a "well-behaved" system (Kennedy, 1974).

refine our capacity to measure system quality. Still, some aspects of designing will remain an art or intuitive science where esthetics and contemporary style determine success.

In spite of my desire to present experimental results, I felt that it was worthwhile to attempt an informal integration of the design principles offered by others. The next four sections present four, largely independent, hopefully thorough, design goals: simplicity, power, user satisfaction, and reasonable cost.

11.2.1 Simplicity

A primary virtue of design is simplicity: from the medieval rule of Occam's Razor which states that the best explanation of physical principles is the simplest one to the Bauhaus phrase 'less is more' to the contemporary 'small is beautiful.' With simple designs, the designer, implementer, and user are less likely to make mistakes. Simple systems are easy to learn, easy to remember, and easy to use, by the widest possible audience. Simple systems are easier to modify and fix if things go awry.

An interactive system is simple if it has few commands and if the commands have a consistent structure. Output should be readable and error messages should have a uniform format. Command structures should match the problem domain and the sequence of user thought processes.

11.2.2 Power

One of the joys of using computers is the power they offer. A good system provides powerful commands which enable users to easily accomplish their goals. The commands should facilitate problem-solving processes and provide all previously available manual functions. If a system carries out 19 of the 20 required functions, the users will complain about the missing 20th function. The computerized system must be better in every way than the manual system.

Experienced users should have especially powerful commands available. They should be able to create macros, extend the system, or tailor the system command structure and output formats to their needs. System operations should be rapid and convey a sense of power rather than a sense of lethargy. The hardware and software should be reliable, stable over time and secure with sufficient processing power and storage space. File integrity and privacy protection should be irreproachable.

11.2.3 User Satisfaction

User satisfaction is separate from effectiveness. A system may be effective but unpleasant to use or satisfying but ineffective. A bibliographic retrieval system may provide excellent results but be tedious to use or simple and satisfying to use but incapable of doing adequate searches through the literature.

A satisfying system gives the user the sense that he/she is in control. The system should respond to user commands rapidly, provide simple to understand messages, and offer adequate power. The computer should appear as a tool under the direction of the user. Gaines and Facey (1975) describe a reluctant novice who was finally convinced to try the interactive system. She began to use the system and gain some confidence when, while she was consulting a manual for several minutes, the terminal suddenly produced a nasty message and detached the terminal because of inactivity. This user refused to return.

Error messages should be constructive and supportive, not condemning and confrontive. Each command should produce feedback with meaningful acknowledgement. The system should never 'dead-end' leaving the user confused and without recourse. The system should be reliable and minimize fear of failure. There should be no way that files are inadvertently destroyed, and as much as possible it should be possible to undo undesirable commands. Users should have some way of finding out what they have done, what their current status is, and what options are open to them. Help commands should always be available. Users should be able to restart portions of a session or the entire session, to exit or abort, and to pause/resume at any point. The computer should appear as a helpful tool aiding users in the performance of their tasks.

11.2.4 Reasonable Cost

A system which costs too much is a failure. A good designer accurately estimates the cost of designing, implementing, and running the system. A good design may cost more time and money to develop, but can lead to enormous savings during implementation and in the productive life of the system. Good design can reduce hardware costs, improve reliability, reduce errors, and give users greater satisfaction. If a banking terminal system has a simpler and more powerful command structure that is easier to use, each transaction may take, say 20 percent, less time. This may mean that 20 percent fewer terminal operators, terminals, and telecommunication lines are necessary, central processor hardware needs are reduced, and operating systems demands are lowered. A 20 percent reduction in the transaction complexity and time can yield a 30 percent or more reduction in the system cost. A simpler and more powerful command structure may produce fewer costly and annoying errors, increase employee job satisfaction, reduce turnaround, facilitate hiring, and improve organizational morale.

11.3 DESIGN PROCESS FOR INTERACTIVE SYSTEMS

Establishing goals for interactive systems is the easy part. The hard part is doing the design. Designing requires the capacity to integrate multiple, complex, conflicting constraints, and produce the detailed specifications for each character of a display. These diverse requirements may be better met by a team rather than an individual designer. A closely knit team, with a competent leader and an open professional atmosphere, may be able to resolve design problems without the cluttered compromises generated by ad hoc committees.

It is impossible to provide an algorithm for designing, but the remainder of this chapter is an attempt at a design sequence. The neat linear presentation hides the dead-ends, jumps, iterations, and revisions that are part of every design experience. This design sequence is general and must be modified to suit specific project needs: hardware requirements might be set by the current environment, software development might be replaced by using available packages, and the schedule may be imposed.

11.3.1 Collect Information

The information collecting or pre-design stage involves getting organized and preparing for the job ahead. The design team should be formed and roles assigned. Participation from management is necessary so that surprises may be avoided. Since the success of many organizations will depend on their computer and information systems, it is vital that managers become involved in the design process. The experience with database systems has shown that, if the database administrator does not have a high enough organizational rank and if high-level managers do not participate, the project is likely to fail. Interactive systems also have a powerful organizational impact, restructuring communication patterns, and reassigning responsibilities. If critical decisions are left to technical personnel alone, those who oppose the new system will ensure its failure.

Users, managers, and customers whose activity will be impacted by the new system should be interviewed and sampled by questionnaires. The first goal is to understand current practice, even if the new system will require different procedures -- Know the User! Find out what procedures need improvement and give the users a chance to vent their displeasure to the design team. If you listen carefully you will learn something from the users and give them the feeling that they are part of the design process. Users want to improve their working environment themselves and resent being a pawn in a designer's technological chess game. Igersheim (1976) found, in a survey of 225 middle-level managers, that acceptance of an information system is positively related to involvement in the implementation and negatively related to the perception of the system as threatening.

No matter how original you think your project is, someone has done something like it before. Consult the professional literature about related projects and products. Study the academic literature for fundamental principles in psychology, information science, and computer science. The best advice can come from someone who has designed a similar system elsewhere. A few hours with someone who has done what you are doing can be extremely therapeutic for both parties.

Even at this early stage an attempt should be made to estimate costs and benefits from the new system. The costs of the design, implementation, and retraining of personnel should be determined. Tentative schedules should be prepared with observable milestones. Evolutionary progress is preferable to revolutionary discontinuity.

11.3.2 Design Semantic Structures

The first design task is to define goals and specify requirements. The design team must decide, for example, what banking operations will be available through the online system. Setting goals requires a close cooperation between management and technical staffs, because managerial decisions effect technical complexity and technical feasibility guides management goals. For example, reliable identification by signature or voiceprint analysis might encourage management to eliminate secret codewords and raise the maximum cash withdrawal amount at banking terminals.

Figure 11.9:

1. Collect information.
   - organize design team
   - obtain management participation
   - submit written questionnaires to users at all levels
   - conduct live interviews where possible
   - read practical and academic literature
   - speak with users and designers of similar systems
   - estimate costs and cost/benefit
   - prepare schedule with observable milestones

2. Design semantic structures.
   - define goals ánd establish a hierarchy of requirements
   - consider task flow sequence alternatives
   - organize operations into transaction units
   - create application domain data structures
   - develop application domain operators
   - specify privacy, security, and integrity constraints
   - obtain agreement on semantic design
3. Design syntactic structures.
   - compare alternative display formats
   - create syntax for operators
   - prepar system response formats
   - develop error diagnostics
   - specify response time requirements
   - plan user aids and help facilities
   - evaluate design specifications and revise where necessary
   - carry out paper and pencil experimental test
4. Specify physical devices.
   - choose hard or soft copy device
   - specify keyboard layout
   - select audio, graphics, or peripheral devices
   - establish requirements for communications lines
   - consider work environment (noise, lighting, etc.)
5. Develop software.
   - produce top-down modular design
   - consider modifiability, generality and portability
   - emphasize reliability and maintainability
   - provide extensive system documentation
   - conduct thorough test
6. Devise implementation plan.
   - assure user involvement at every stage
   - write and field test training manuals
   - implement a training subsystem or simulator
   - provide adequate training and consultation
   - apply spiral/layered/phased approach to implementation
   - aim to please the users
7. Nurture the user community.
   - provide onsite telephone or consultants
   - offer online consultant
   - develop online "gripe" command or suggestion box
   - make user news available online
   - publish newsletter for users
   - organize user group meetings for discussion
   - respond to user suggestions for improvements
8. Prepare evolutionary plan.
   - design for easy refinement or repair
   - measure user performance regularly
   - improve error handling
   - carry out experiments
   - sample feedback from users by questionnaires and interviews

Figure 11-9: Design process for interactive systems.

Semantic design, like semantic knowledge, should be level structured. High-level goals are set first, then refined into lower-level subgoals and tasks. Concurrent with the definition of tasks, the task sequence presented to the user is chosen. Since an interactive session proceeds linearly over time, the steps must be arranged in a complete ordering. The designer now faces the educator's problem of deciding which topics to cover first and discovering ways of decoupling dependent tasks. Tasks should be grouped into transaction units so users can satisfy their desire for closure.

Designers have developed special flowchart schemes to describe interaction sequences or have adapted graph theoretic schemes such as petri nets or state transition diagrams. The most appealing approach is the use of augmented transition networks where nodes are numbered states and edges have input/output events on them. Figure 11-9 shows a high level transition diagram for using an interactive programming facility (Feyock, 1977) with a subdiagram for the LOGON process. This hierarchical approach can show modular designs and hide low-level detail, but the diagrams can be confusing and do not assure completeness or consistency. Another approach is offered by Reisner (1979), who presents an 'action grammar,' based on Backus-Naur Form productions, to define the sequences of permissible operations in an interactive graphics system.

The application domain data structures often play a central role in shaping the system design. A personal calendar might be arranged bulletin board style with each entry having a day and time stamp; or entries may be arranged by topic and sorted by date; or the calendar may include date and day of the week notations, so that all Monday schedules could be displayed. Large files of information could be simply sorted or could be sectioned into pages, pages into chapters, and chapters into volumes. Several alternatives should be generated and justification presented for the one chosen.

The application domain operators on these structures are also crucial. Multiple low-level operations that would be easy to learn must be evaluated against complex powerful operations which would please more experienced users but challenge novices. The appropriateness of set theory, boolean algebra, predicate calculus, programming notation, or other mathematical approaches should be considered. Then application specific structures and operators should be studied. Chemical notation, architectural notation, editorial proof reading marks, or music symbols may fit for some applications.

Specify privacy requirements, security needs, and integrity constraints. Integrity constraints improve data quality and protection but can raise costs dramatically and increase response time. Management must make the decisions on these tradeoffs based on sound technical advice.

Once a set of decisions has been made and properly documented, the conclusions should be presented to managers and users for feedback to

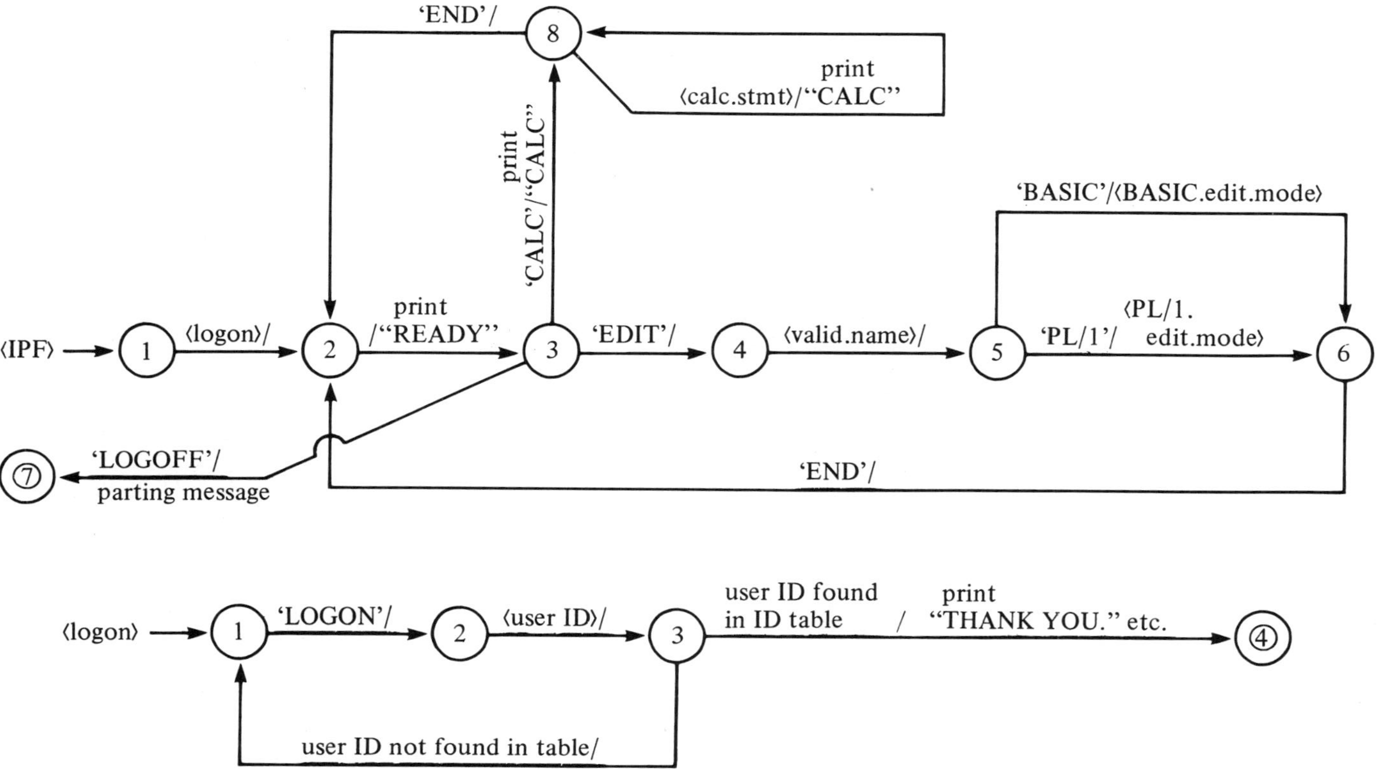

Figure 11-10: Transition diagram with LOGON subdiagram, for an interactive programming facility (Feyock, 1977).

improve the design and to stimulate participation. Such a presentation is a healthy milestone which raises enthusiasm for the project and gains acceptance for the design team.

11.3.3 Design Syntactic Structures

Once the user population characteristics and the semantic design requirements are clear, the syntax can be designed. If multiple user classes are expected, a range of syntactic styles may be adopted, including the menu selection, fill-in-the-blank, and parametric approaches. Design alternatives should be offered for output formats, split screen strategies (windows), detailed specification of operator syntax, error messages, tutorial aids, and help facilities. Response time requirements for each command type should be listed with means, minimums, and maximums. Competitive designs should be evaluated and justifications presented for the syntactic structures selected. Evaluation should be done first by colleagues, then by managers and users. Getting management and user representatives to sign-off on the semantic and syntactic designs forces more careful review and reduces the opportunity for misunderstanding. A sign-off is a protection for the design team.

Paper and pencil experimental tests can be conducted on at least portions of the interactive system design. Typewritten sheets can take the place of displays for evaluation of the task flow sequence, output formats, error messages, etc. These pilot studies are valuable since they can reveal design flaws at an early stage. If aircraft designers feel the need to build full-size plywood mockups, play directors feel the need to conduct dress rehearsals, spacecraft engineers feel the need to run elaborate simulations, then interactive system designers should feel the need to run paper and pencil pilot studies.

11.3.4 Specify Physical Devices

In many cases the interactive system designer may not have a choice over which terminals are used, but even in this case, specific terminal attributes should be kept out of the design process for as long as possible. Device independent requirement specifications, semantic design, and possibly syntactic design will yield easier to modify systems which can accommodate new terminal technologies.

When terminal hardware can be chosen by the designer, the choice can be overwhelming. Hundreds of terminals with dozens of features, an unlimited number of keyboard designs, and a variety of accessories make it a lengthy chore to select a terminal. Ample justification should be given for choosing esoteric features which limit system portability and produce dependence on a limited number of vendors.

Communication line requirements should be stated explicitly. The reliability in terms of error rates and mean-time-between-failures (MTBF) should be specified with the baud rate, coding scheme, etc. Backup communications strategies should be described if high reliability is necessary.

Guidelines should be established for the physical work environment of terminal users. Special air conditioning may be required, lighting levels should be considered (too little or too much light, or excessive glare can increase fatigue and error rates), noise levels should be mentioned (high noise levels may interfere with auditory cues from the terminal or terminal noise may disrupt nearby workers), and adequate desk space at the correct height should be specified.

11.3.5 Develop Software

Interactive system software, like all software, should be designed in a top-down modular fashion, with the usual concern for modifiability, generality, and portability. Greater attention should be devoted to reliability and maintainability since failures may effect thousands of users whose tolerance of errors may be low and whose capacity to cope with errors may be nonexistent.

The modular software design may follow the hierarchical semantic design. As always, use high-level languages where possible and adapt available packages if they suit your needs. Frame handling software which grew out of the computer-assisted instruction languages has been used successfully to speed implementation. Provide extensive system documentation material for those who must do maintenance. Testing is more challenging for interactive systems since so many decision paths must be explored and the real-time environment is difficult to establish during development. After testing single terminals, groups of terminals should be employed to measure response time degradation with increased load. If possible, the system should be tested to overload to find limitations and determine failure patterns.

11.3.6 Devise Implementation Plan

Even the best system can fail if the implementation plan is inadequate. Designing a successful implementation plan requires a sensitivity to human communication problems and has little of the technical content of earlier phases. Allow the system users to actively participate in the implementation planning. Solicit their advice about which sites should be first, which features should be taught first and when training sessions can be scheduled. Actively demonstrate that you are anxious to please them, interested in improving their work situation, and responsive to their suggestions.

Neither systems documentation nor design manuals are adequate for training purposes. A carefully designed training manual, that has been thoroughly tested and handsomely produced, is necessary. The spiral, layered, or phased approach should be used in training. A small subset of the facilities is taught and users receive positive reinforcement for success in learning to use the terminal features. The users gain a feeling of confidence and mastery which builds a positive image for the system. Then additional features can be explained. Designers should feel they have succeeded if users find the system simple and easy to use. Kennedy (1975) presents experimental results in the training of naive users in an interactive medical information system. Sondheimer (1979) reports on user resistance to adopting new facilities in an online editor. His results demonstrate how hard it is to get users to change work habits.

The system should provide a training mode in which novices can try out features without impacting sensitive data in the main file. The training system, possibly on a separate machine, should have a small version of the database and possibly additional tutorial aids. Consultants should be available to answer questions during training and the first days of system use.

11.3.7 Nurture the User Community

Once the system is in use, every attempt should be made to create an active user community. Onsite or telephone consultants can offer aid when difficulties arise. An online consultant can service many users at low cost. Both parties can view the same screen images and carry on a discussion using two lines of a display screen. An online 'gripe' facility or suggestion box gives users a feeling that they can provide useful input and an opportunity to vent their anger about unsatisfactory system components. The system maintenance staff should respond to user suggestions with appropriate action or an explanation. Keeping the user community active and involved will facilitate acceptance and provide suggestions for improvements.

For large communities of users a newsletter might be helpful. Occasional group meetings of user representatives might promote interchange of ideas. An independent user's organization, an effective source for product development in other areas, might be considered for widely used interactive systems.

11.3.8 Prepare Evolutionary Plan

No system is complete until it is obsolete. Large complex systems continuously evolve through improvements to current facilities, repair of errors, and modifications in system requirements. Good designers recognize this pattern and produce designs which are easy to maintain, modify, and improve. A good system contains software monitoring probes which provide statistics about performance and tabulate errors. This data can be used to change procedures, revise syntax, modify error messages, or develop automatic error handling. The monitoring probes can provide data for controlled experiments with the system. Experiments might be arranged to test new task flow sequences, improved syntax, altered error handling procedures, changed response time performance, new terminals, or a different class of users.

User satisfaction should be evaluated by interviews or questionnaires. A sample of users may be asked to respond to a set of questions at the end of a terminal session. Subjective questions can be misleading, but they do provide an indication of user satisfaction.

11.4 PRACTITIONER'S SUMMARY

Interactive system design is a difficult, challenging task which requires the capacity to integrate multiple complex requirements and pursue detailed specifications. Designers must be sensitive to manager and user feedback, technically sophisticated, and humble. Humility is important, because no complex system involving hundreds or thousands of people, can please all of the people all of the time. Try to see user complaints as stemming from a desire to participate rather than to attack.

The goals of system design are to produce a product which is simple, powerful, user-satisfying, and reasonable in cost. These goals can be in conflict, so be prepared to make some hard compromises. You can lessen criticism if you make your decisions explicit and provide written justification.

The interactive system design process should have observable milestones and numerous evaluation points. Informal reviews, pilot tests, and controlled experimental tests should be conducted. Involve users in the implementation plans, consciously create an active user community, and plan for evolutionary refinements.

11.5 RESEARCHER'S AGENDA

Interactive system design offers unlimited opportunity for research in a topic which has been poorly explored. An important first step would be to develop metrics of simplicity and power, on a feature by feature basis. Scales or questionnaires need to be tested, validated, and refined to evaluate user satisfaction. Standard accounting schemes are necessary to accurately measure costs and provide guidance for cost reduction.

The design process should be refined and tools to facilitate design should be developed. Packages or special languages for interactive systems development are an exciting opportunity. Decision tables, graph theoretic ideas, augmented transition networks, petri nets, specialized flowcharts, and other schemes need to be evaluated for their utility in aiding interactive system design. Finally, researchers in organizational behavior and dynamics might study the impact of interactive systems and suggest ways of improving user acceptance.

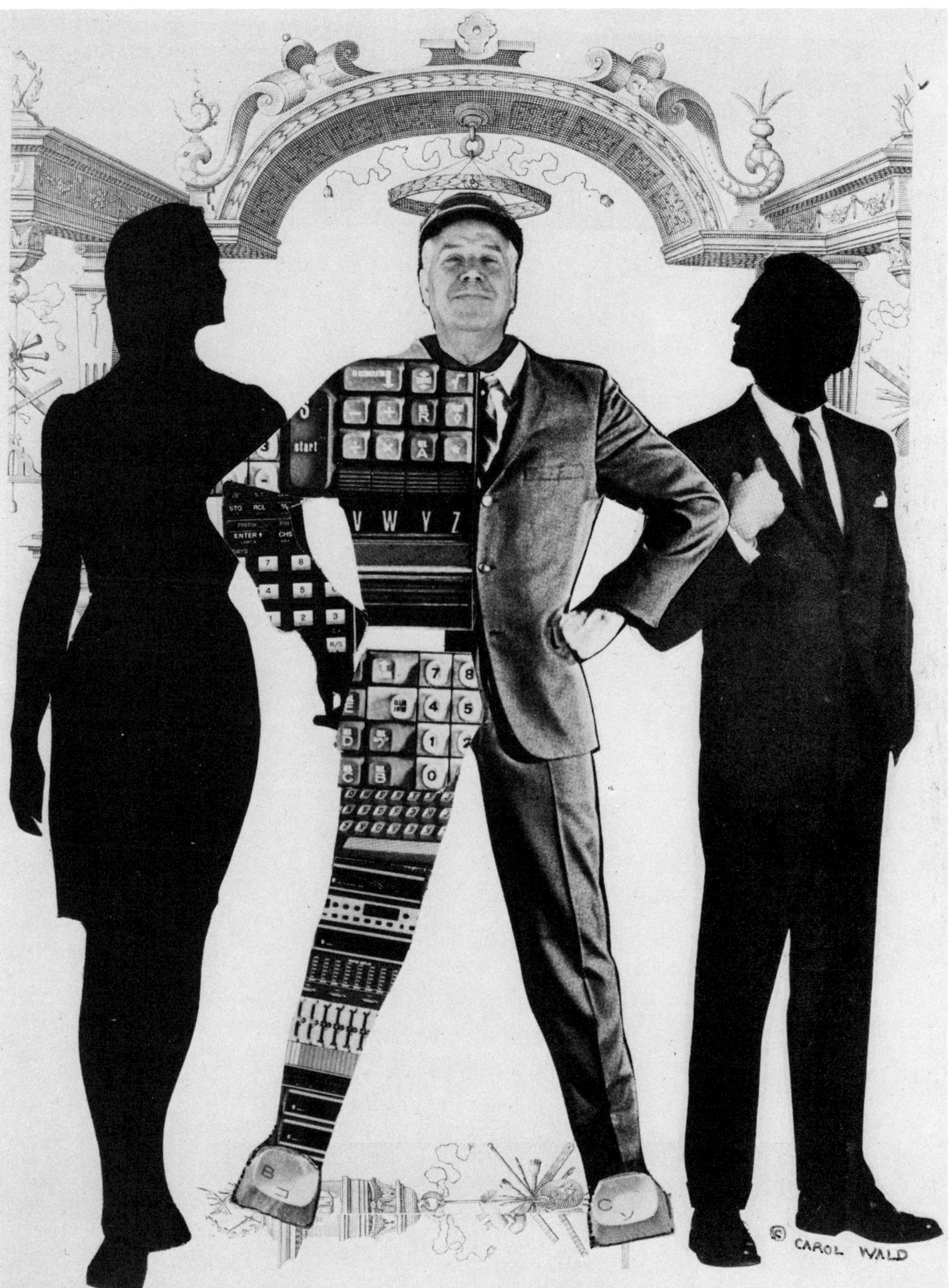
start
STO RCL
ENTER CHS
V W Y Z
© CAROL WALD

12

COMPUTER POWER TO, OF, AND BY THE PEOPLE

In the long run what may be important is the *texture* of a system. By texture we mean the *quality* the system has to evoke in users and participants a feeling that the system increases the kinship between men.

Theodor Sterling, 'Guidelines for Humanizing Computerized Information Systems (1974)

A broad view of the impact, dangers, promises of computer systems and some guidelines for building quality systems - impact of computer technology on individuals and society - fears of technological oppression - promises of miraculous computer systems - computers as tools - recognize human responsibility - consider the impact of new systems - treat people as individuals - strive for quality - increase kinship among people

In the first three decades of computer use, big corporations, government and universities controlled computer resources because they had the wealth and know-how. But the maturation of technology has reduced costs and simplified use enough so that every individual can benefit from computers and information systems directly. High technology can have a democratizing influence on society: the President and the average citizen have access to similar telephones, televisions, automobiles, stereos, or microwave ovens. The gap between high and low economic groups still exists, but the gap appears to be narrower than it has been in the past. Now, the gap in computational and informational resources between the haves and have-nots is beginning to decrease.

Hundreds of thousands of reliable, cheap microcomputers are being sold or embedded in consumer products. Banking terminals and plane, train, car, and hotel reservation systems contribute to bringing computer power to the people. Computer network utilities will bring information resources to many more people. The New York Times Information Bank makes current affairs research easier and paves the way to electronic newspapers. Online bibliographic search services enable researchers and students to scan millions of scientific journal articles in seconds and reduce months of research into minutes.

The terms teleconferencing, computer conferencing, and electronic mail describe systems which enable dispersed groups of people to cooperate and communicate conveniently (Hiltz and Turoff, 1978; Johansen, Vallee and Spangler, 1979). Each participant can send messages to one or more individuals in typewritten form, reducing disruptive phone calls and avoiding busy signals or no-answers. Each participant can carefully prepare and read their messages when convenient. The PLATO computer-based education system allows up to five users to sign on to TALK-O-MATIC. The screen is split into five sections and all five users can type simultaneously. These new communications media offer appealing alternatives to telephone conversations and physical meetings. Teleconferencing promoters claim that participants tend to measure their words more carefully, feel less threatened in making controversial remarks, behave more democratically, and appreciate the written record. For decision making, alternatives can be put to votes quickly and privacy protected. Use of electronic mail facilities is enjoyable and growing rapidly.

Word processing systems in offices are changing secretarial functions, requiring higher skill levels and increasing productivity. Daily correspondence, internal memos, legal documents, technical reports, and books can be developed more quickly and with fewer errors if these electronic tools are used. This book was produced with the help of computerized text editing, document processing, and computer photo-typesetting. Word processing coupled with electronic mail facilities can change organizational dynamics by restructuring communications patterns.

Home and office applications of computer and information systems are growing steadily. It is a challenge to keep up with the innovations and a greater challenge to understand where these changes will lead. Alvin Toffler catalogs the effect of rapid changes and suggests some ways of coping in *Future Shock* (1970). He defines 'future shock' as the 'dizzying disorientation brought about by the premature arrival of the future.'

A gaping chasm exists between social commentators who perceive technology, particularly computer technology, as dreadfully harmful and computer science researchers who feel that computer technology can lead to a better way of life. The antitechnologists, such as Jacques Ellul, are vocal and angry at technology which 'pursues its own course more and more independently of man.' He writes in *The Technological Society* (1965) that 'technique has become autonomous' and 'it has fashioned an omnivorous world which obeys its own laws.' Lewis Mumford who spent most of his prolific career describing technology with a sympathetic attitude wrote (1967) that 'not merely does technology claim priority in human affairs, it places the demand for constant technological change above considerations for its own efficiency, its own continuity, or even, ironically enough its own capacity to survive.' Charles Reich's popular, *The Greening of America* (1971) carries the theme further stating 'technology will dictate to man' and 'technology has its own reasons for removing things from the culture.' A final example comes from Theodore Roszak's *Where the Wasteland Ends* (1972), 'The treachery of technology...threatens to murder flora and fauna of the whole oceans.'

These vehement attacks contrast sharply with the dreamlike utopian visions offered by Allen Newell in an article entitled 'Fairytales' (1976):

> ...computer technology offers the possibility of incorporating intelligent behavior in all the nooks and crannies of our world. With it we could build an enchanted land.

Ecologically, computer technology itself is nearly magic.

> ...technology can be controlled, especially if it is saturated with intelligence to watch over how it goes, to keep accounts, prevent errors, and to provide *wisdom* (my italics) to each decision. And these guardians of our world, these magic informational dwarfs, need not extract too high a price.
>
> I wish to assert that computer science and technology are the stuff out of which the future fairy land can be built.

Newell and his collaborator, Herbet Simon, had earlier embraced computer technology (1958) and offered the hope that computers could and should be made to handle all of the problems that humans dealt with:

> There are now in the world machines that think, that learn and that create. Moreover, their ability to do these things is going to increase rapidly until -- in the visible future -- the range of problems they can handle will be coextensive with the range to which the human mind has been applied.

This extreme statement was based on Simon's belief that human capacities were 'quite simple' and could easily be emulated by machine (1969):

> A man, viewed as a behaving system, is quite simple. The apparent complexity of his behavior over time is largely a reflection of the complexity of the environment in which he finds himself... I myself believe that the hypothesis holds even for the whole man.

While most readers would be willing to choose a position somewhere between these extremist artificial intelligence researchers and social commentators, I feel that there is an alternative view of the conflict. Both extremes make the tacit assumption that humans and machines are competing for the same ecological niche. I argue that as time goes by, and even as we develop more sophisticated computer systems, the dichotomy between human creative skills and the computer's tool-like nature will become more clear. We will discern which tasks can be turned over to computers. We will see ever more clearly that computers are merely tools acting under human control and that computers have no more intelligence than a wooden pencil.

To help lead us to this healthy alternative position, which resolves the conflict by assigning tedious repetitious tasks to computers and reserving issues of creative judgment for humans, I propose five fundamental guidelines:

1) BUILD COMPUTER SYSTEMS THAT BEHAVE LIKE TOOLS

In the simple form this means avoiding interactive systems that begin with 'HELLO, I AM BETSY 307, WHAT IS YOUR NAME?' Don't assign human names or attributes to programs and systems. Don't attribute lifelike behavior or free will to computer systems. If something goes wrong, don't blame it on the machine or the program. Remember that tools never make mistakes, they do malfunction or break. These subtle changes produce significant differences in people's attitudes. Build tools that perform properly and efficiently. Create programs which work reliably and economically.

Fortunately, attitudes on these topics are changing in the right direction. Recent systems avoid using human names or attributes. The media is less attracted to phrases such as 'computer makes error' and recognizes manager, designer, programmer, and keypuncher errors or machine failures. Occasionally, even reputable papers such as the *New York Times* will publish outrageous counter-productive articles like 'When the Computer Procreates' (Bernstein, 1976). Occasionally computer manufacturers will talk about their 'brain' with its 'subconscious' parallel processor for error checking. Still my overall impression is that people are more clearly perceiving computers as tools.

Probably the best source for how to build systems which perform like tools is Sterling's excellent report on 'Guidelines for Humanizing Computerized Information Systems' (1974) which I would have liked better if it had been called 'Guidelines for Making Computerized Information Systems Which are Easy for People to Use.' The section headings from this report are listed in Figure 12-1.

2) RECOGNIZE THE DISTINCTIONS BETWEEN HUMAN REASON AND COMPUTER POWER

Weizenbaum's book *Computer Power, and Human Reason* (1976), in spite of its structural flaws and occasional extreme language, is a magnificent effort at discriminating between tools and people. He goes beyond the usual characterization of humans as creative, experienced, sensitive, empathic, responsive to new situations, and able to adapt old ideas; and machines as accurate, fast, and capable of storing large volumes of data. Weizenbaum details the distinctions:

> First (and least important), the ability of even the most advanced of currently existing computer systems to acquire information by means other than...'being spoon-fed' is still extremely limited...

A. Procedures for dealing with users.
   1. The language of a system should be easy to understand.
   2. Transactions with a system should be courteous.
   3. A system should be quick to react.
   4. A system should respond quickly to users (if it is unable to resolve its intended procedure).
   5. A system should relieve the user of unnecessary chores.
   6. A system should provide for human information interface.
   7. A system should include provisions for corrections.
   8. Management should be held responsible for mismanagement.

B. Procedures for dealing with exceptions.
   1. A system should recognize as much as possible that it deals with different classes of individuals.
   2. A system should recognize that special conditions might occur that could require special actions by it.
   3. A system must allow for alternatives in input and processing.
   4. A system should give individuals choices on how to deal with it.
   5. A procedure must exist to override the system.

C. Action of the system with respect to information.
   1. There should be provisions to permit individuals to inspect information about themselves.
   2. There should be provisions to correct errors.
   3. There should be provisions for evaluating information stored in the system.
   4. There should be provisions for individuals to add information that they consider important.
   5. It should be made known in general what information is stored in systems and what use will be made of that information.

D. The problem of privacy.
   1. In the design of a system, all procedures should be evaluated with respect to both privacy and humanization requirements.
   2. The decision to merge information from different files and systems should never occur automatically. Whenever information from one file is made available to another file, it should be examined first for its implications for privacy and humanization.

E. Guidelines for system design having a bearing on ethics.
   1. A system should not trick or deceive.
   2. A system should assist participants and users and not manipulate them.
   3. A system should not eliminate opportunities for employment without a careful examination of consequences to other available jobs.
   4. System designers should not participate in the creation or maintenance of secret data banks.
   5. A system should treat with consideration all individuals who come in contact with it.

Figure 12-1: Criteria for humanizing management information systems (Sterling, 1974).

> Second, it is not obvious that all human knowledge is encodable in 'information structures,' however complex. A human may know, for example, just what kind of emotional impact touching another person's hand will have both on the other person and on himself... There are, in other words, some things humans know by virtue of having a human body. No organism that does not have a human body can know these things in the same way humans know them. Every symbolic representation of them must lose some information that is essential for some human purposes.
>
> Third,...there are some things people come to know only as a consequence of having been treated as human beings by other human beings...
>
> Fourth, and finally, even the kinds of knowledge that appear superficially to be communicable from one human being to another in language alone are in fact not altogether so communicable. Claude Shannon showed that, even in abstract information theory, the 'information content' of a message is not a function of the message alone but depends crucially on the state of knowledge, on the expectations, and on the receiver...
>
> Human language in actual use is infinitely more problematical than those aspects of it that are amenable to treatment by information theory.

Critics argue that Weizenbaum is attacking current capacities of computer systems but shows no reason why computers should not be able to acquire human skills in the future. Godel's incompleteness proofs and the existence of recursively unsolvable problems offer some limitations, but the critical issue is our desire to preserve some concepts unformalized. The 'reasonable man (or woman)' theory of justice has served well, precisely because it is imprecise and subject to changing interpretation. It seems hardly possible and certainly not desirable to have machines decide on 'cruel or unusual punishment.' Tools have no capacity for wisdom and reason.

3) CONSIDER THE IMPACT OF SYSTEMS ON PEOPLE'S LIVES

Humans react emotionally to the meaning of information, while computers indiscriminately process binary digits. Systems designers should be sensitive to the impact that disclosure of information would have on individuals. Inside the computer, data from particle accelerators is treated in the same way as medical histories, psychiatric records, or credit ratings; but improper disclosure of personal information can disrupt people's lives. Crudely implemented hospital intensive-care systems can cause loss of life, poorly designed air traffic control systems can lead to disaster, and incorrectly entered credit or police data can ruin careers.

Legal precedents are beginning to place the responsibility for computer systems failures on the designers, implementers, and operators. When errors on a car loan repayment system led to hardship for an individual who had been properly paying, the courts awarded triple damages as a punitive measure and made it clear that responsibility for errors could not be assigned to computers, but must be accepted by the system implementers and operators. Malpractice insurance for software developers is available.

Systems designers must accept the burden of responsibility for their products. As time passes people will no longer be able to hide behind phrases such as 'the computer won't allow that' or 'the computer made a mistake.' Users will demand more reliable software, easier to use inquiry facilities, simpler interactive systems, and human accountability.

Users will also demand more protection of privacy. It is not clear that computer systems increase the number of violations of privacy. Paper filing systems are easy to compromise and violations are hard to detect. To obtain information improperly from computerized systems requires special knowledge and may result in a record of the access. However, the added danger from computer systems is that large numbers of people's privacy can be compromised. Computerized files can easily be searched for individuals satisfying certain traits. The computer amplifies the power to do good as well as evil.

Legislation for the protection of privacy in governmental files of personal data are beginning to have an impact. A Department of Health, Education and Welfare study commission report which laid the groundwork for the Federal Privacy Act of 1974 made five important recommendations:

- There must be no personal data record-keeping systems whose very existence is secret.

- There must be a way for an individual to find out what information about him is in a record and how it is used.

- There must be a way for an individual to prevent information about him that was obtained for one purpose from being used or made available for other purposes without his consent.

- There must be a way for an individual to correct or amend a record of identifiable information about him.

- Any organization creating, maintaining, using or disseminating records of identifiable personal data must assure the reliability of the data for their intended use and must take precautions to prevent misuse of the data.

4) TREAT PEOPLE AS INDIVIDUALS

Computerized systems are most appealing when the same rules can be applied to a large number of individuals, but an awareness of special cases is important. Systems designers must be sensitive to the needs of individuals and minorities and avoid creating dissatisfied minorities. Progress in this direction is encouraging. Organizations are producing Braille output for the blind, offering teletype inquiry services for the deaf, and providing special services for the elderly or infirm. For example, public utilities permit senior citizen and handicapped customers to register a second name (of a relative or friend) with an account, so that if bills are mislaid or forgotten the second name can be contacted before service is cut off.

For individuals who have difficulty in coping with an automated system, human consultants should be easily available. Banking terminals often indicate a telephone number for assistance, but too often a phone is not available. Simple facilities for recourse to supervisory personnel should be part of system design.

The immediate problems are easier to grasp than the long-range effects. It would have been difficult for designers of credit card systems to realize the dramatic impact of these systems on society. It is sometimes difficult to rent a car without a credit card because lack of credit cards is seen as an indication of financial instability or as a suggestion of criminal intent. Availabilty of complex automated systems encourages bureaucrats to create complex social systems dependent on computerized systems. Some critics argue that the tax laws, the welfare system, and governmental growth are partially a result of computer systems which permit and encourage complexity. A computerized system can spawn complexity and generate the need for further computerization. The response to these problems must be simpler systems, more attention to individual needs, and clear assignment of responsibility for failures.

5) STRIVE FOR QUALITY IN YOUR PERSONAL AND PROFESSIONAL LIVES

Zen and the Art of Motorcycle Maintenance by Robert Pirsig (1974) is possibly the best book on systems design that we have. Pirsig's autobiographical treatise describes his search for identity while on a cross-country motorcycle trip. Part of his work experience was as an author of computer programming manuals. Pirsig's understanding of harmonious interaction among system components and the need for modular functional design are coupled with his pursuit and profound interpretation of quality. Well over one hundred pages are devoted to defining 'Quality.' Quality cannot be measured or understood by machines yet every one of us knows Quality when we see it:

> What I mean (and everybody else means) by the word *quality* cannot be broken down into subjects and predicates. This is not because Quality is so mysterious but because Quality is so simple, immediate and direct.

In trying to measure Quality, Pirsig describes an evaluation of college students' English compositions. A consensus of Quality could be obtained by Pirsig and his students, but objective measures were never sufficient. The following paragraph discussing English composition could just as well be applied to computer programming where an outline is pseudo-code or a design specification and a footnote is a program comment:

> He singled out aspects of Quality such as unity, vividness, authority, economy, sensitivity, clarity, emphasis, flow, suspense, brilliance, precision, proportion, depth and so on; kept each of these as poorly defined as Quality itself, but demonstrated them by the same class reading techniques. He showed how the aspect of Quality called unity, the hanging-togetherness of a story, could be improved with a technique called an outline. The authority of an argument could be jacked up with a technique called footnotes, which gives authoritative reference. Outlines and footnotes are standard things taught in all freshman composition classes, but now as devices for improving Quality they had a purpose. And if a student turned in a bunch of dumb references or a sloppy outline that showed he was just fulfilling an assignment by rote, he could be told that while his paper may have fulfilled the letter of the assignment it obviously didn't fulfill the goal of Quality, and was therefore worthless.

Others have recognized the importance of an elusive sense of Quality which Pirsig was pursuing. Sterling, at the end of his detailed list of issues, wrote:

> In the long run what may be important is the 'texture' of a system. By texture we mean the 'quality' the system has to evoke in users and participants a feeling that the system increases the kinship between men... The texture of a system may lie in the choices it offers or in the courtesies it provides or in some of its outright inefficiencies. As we turn from a society of growth to a society of 'quality,' the texture of systems may well be the fundamental prerequisite on which is built the humanizing quality of our everyday life.

In a similar mood, Tomeski and Lazarus wrote (1975):

> The path to a healthier and more productive environment is through genuine concern and positive acts on behalf of people.

In summary, if we take the time and demonstrate a concern for quality when building computer systems or anything else, we will feel better about ourselves, improve the Quality of life for all those around us, and more clearly appreciate human capacities. Pirsig writes:

> A person who knows how to fix motorcycles -- with Quality -- is less likely to run short of friends than one who doesn't. And they aren't going to see him as some kind of object either. Quality destroys objectivity every time.
>
> Or if he takes whatever dull job he's stuck with - and they are all, sooner or later, dull - and, just to keep himself amused, starts to look for options of Quality, and secretly pursues these options, just for their own sake, thus making an art out of what he is doing, he's likely to discover that he becomes a much more interesting person and much less of an object to the people around him because his Quality decisions change him too. And not only the job and him, but others too because the Quality tends to fan out like waves. The Quality job he didn't think anyone was going to see is seen, and the person who sees it feels a little better because of it, and is likely to pass that feeling on to others, and in that way the Quality tends to keep on going.

> My personal feeling is that this is how any further improvement of the world will be done: by individuals making Quality decisions and that's all.

We can have a future with computers and information systems as intelligence amplifiers, aiding people in creative and productive work. The successful construction and widespread utilization of computer-based tools depends on the willingness of each designer and implementer to take responsibility for building in quality and increasing the kinship among people.

BIBLIOGRAPHY

ACM Curriculum Committee on Computer Education for Management, Curriculum recommendations for graduate professional programs in information systems, *Communications of the ACM*, 15, 5, (May 1972), 363-398.

ACM Curriculum Committee on Computer Science, Curriculum '68, recommendations for academic programs in computer science, *Communications of the ACM*, 11, 3, (March 1968), 151-197.

ACM Curriculum Committee on Computer Science, Curriculum '78, recommendations for the undergraduate program in computer science, *Communications of the ACM*, 22, 3, (March 1979), 147-166.

Alexander, Christopher, *Notes on the Synthesis of Form*, Harvard University Press, Cambridge, Massachusetts, (1973).

Anderson, J.R., and G.H. Bower, *Human Associative Memory*, Winston, Washington, D.C., (1973).

Anderson, N. and B. Shneiderman, Use of peer ratings in evaluating computer program quality, *Proceedings of the 15th Annual Conference of the ACM Special Interest Group on Computer Personnel Research*, (1977).

Aron, J., *The Program Development Process: The Individual Programmer*, Addison-Wesley, Reading, Massachusetts, (1974).

Atwood, Michael E. and H. Rudy Ramsey, Cognitive structures in the comprehension and memory of computer programs: An investigation of computer debugging, (Technical Report, T.R.-78-A21), U.S. Army Research Institute for the Behavioral and Social Sciences, Alexandria, Virginia (August 1978).

Ausubel, D.P., *Educational Psychology: A Cognitive Approach*, Holt, Rinehart and Winston, New York, (1968).

Bachman, Charles W., The programmer as navigator, *Communications of the ACM*, 16, 11, (November 1973), 653-658.

Bachman, Charles W., Trends in database management – 1975, *Proceedings of the National Computer Conference*, 44, AFIPS Press, Montvale, New Jersey, (1975), 569-576.

Backus, John, Can programming be liberated from the von Neumann style? A functional style and its algebra of programs, *Communications of the ACM*, 21, 8, (August 1978), 613-641.

Baker, F.T., System quality through structured programming, *Proceedings of the Fall Joint Computer Conference*, AFIPS Press, Montvale, New Jersey, (1972a), 339-343.

Baker, F.T., Chief programmer team mangement of production programming, *IBM Systems Journal*, 11, 1, (1972b), 56-73.

Barclay, J.R., The role of comprehension in remembering sentences, *Cognitive Psychology*, 4, (1973), 229-254.

Barnett, M.P., *Computer Programming in ENGLISH*, Harcourt Brace and World, Inc., New York, (1969).

Barnett, M.P. and W.M. Ruhsam, SNAP: An experiment in natural language programming, *AFIPS Conference Proceedings*, 34, Montvale, New Jersey, (1969), 75-87.

Bariff, M.L. and E.J. Lusk, Cognitive and personality test for the design of management information systems, *Management Science*, 23, 8, (April 1977), 820-829.

Bariff, M.L. and E.J. Lusk, Designing information systems for organizational control: The use of psychological tests, *Information and Management*, 1, 3, (May 1978), 113-121.

Basili, Victor R. and Marvin V. Zelkowitz, Analyzing medium-scale software development, *Proceedings of the 3rd International Conference on Software Engineering*, IEEE Catalog Number 78CH1317-7C, New York, (1978), 116-123.

Belady, L.A., Software complexity, *Software Phenomenology Working Papers of the Software Lifecycle Management Workshop*, U.S. Army Institute for Research in Management Information and Computer Science, (August 1977).

Bell, D., Programmer selection and programming errors, *The Computer Journal*, 19, 3, (1974), 202.

Bennett, J.L., The user interface in interactive systems, In C. Cuadra, (Ed.), *Annual Review of Information Science and Technology*, 7, American Society for Information Science, Washington, D.C., (1972), 159-196.

Berkebilio, L.A., Resource allocation program and productivity improvements, *5th Annual Conference Principles of Software Development*, Control Data Corporation, (November 1977), 9-32.

Bernstein, J., When the computer procreates, *The New York Times Magazine*, (February 15, 1976).

Bobrow, D., Natural language input for a computer problem solving system, In M. Minsky (Ed.), *Semantic Information Processing*, MIT Press, Cambridge, Massachusetts, (1972).

Boehm, B.W., Software and its impact: A quantitative assessment, *Datamation*, 19, 5, (1973), 49-59.

Boehm, B.W., J.R. Brown and M. Lipow, Quantitative evaluation of software quality, *Software Phenomenology Working Papers of the Software Lifecycle Management Workshop*, (August 1977), 81-94.

Boehm, B.W., R.K. McClean and D.B. Urfrig, Some experiences with automated aids to design of large-scale reliable software, *IEEE Transactions on Software Engineering*, 10, (1975), 125-133.

Boehm, B.W., M.J. Seven and R.A. Watson, Interactive problem-solving - An experimental study of 'lockout' effects, *Proceedings of the Spring Joint Computer Conference*, AFIPS Press, Montvale, New Jersey, (1971), 205-210.

Bohl, M., *Flowcharting Techniques*, Science Research Associates, Chicago, (1971).

Boies, S.J., User behavior on an interactive computer system, *IBM Systems Journal*, 13, 1, (1974), 1-18.

Boies, S.J. and J.D. Gould, Syntactic errors in computer programming, *Human Factors*, 16, (1974), 253-257.

Boillot, Michel, Computer communication modes and their effect on student attitudes towards programming, Nova University thesis, Available through ERIC ED 098 957, (April 1974).

Borman, W., The rating of individuals in organizations: An alternate approach, *Organizational Behavior and Human Performance* 12, (1974), 105-124.

Boyce, R.F., D.D. Chamberlin, W.F. King III and M.M. Hammer, Specifying queries as relational expressions: SQUARE, *Proceedings of the ACM SIGPLAN-SIGIR Interface Meeting*, Gaithersburg, Maryland, (November 4-6, 1973).

Bransford, J.D. and J.J. Franks., The abstraction of linguistic ideas, *Cognitive Psychology*, 2, (1971), 331-350.

Brooks, Jr., Frederick P., *The Mythical Man-Month*, Addison-Wesley Publishing Company, Reading, Massachusetts, (1975).

Brooks, R., A model of human cognitive behavior in writing code for computer programs (2 Vols.), Department of Computer Science, Carnegie-Mellon University, Pittsburgh, Pennsylvania, (May 1975). (AD A13582)

Brooks, R., Towards a theory of the cognitive processes in computer programming, *International Journal of Man-Machine Studies*, 9, (1977), 737-751.

Brooks, W.D. and P.W. Wilbur, Software reliability analysis, IBM Technical Report FSD 777-0009.

Brosey, M.K. and B. Shneiderman, Two experimental comparisons of relational and hierarchical database models, *International Journal of Man-Machine Studies*, 10, (1978), 625-637.

Brown, J.R. and M. Lipow, Testing for software reliability, *ACM SIGPLAN Notices*, 10, 6, (June 1977), 518-527.

Brown, T. and M. Klerer, The effect on language design of time-sharing operational efficiency, *International Journal of Man-Machine Studies*, 7, (1975), 233-247.

Brownell, W.A., Psychological considerations in the learning and teaching of arithmetic, *The Teaching of Arithmetic: Tenth Yearbook of the National Council of Teachers of Mathematics*, Bureau of Publications, Teachers College, Columbia University, New York, (1935), 1-35.

Bruner, J.S., *Toward a Theory of Instruction*, W.W. Norton and Company, New York, (1968).

Carbonell, J.R., On man-computer interaction: A model and some related issues, *IEEE Transactions on Systems Science and Cybernetics*, SSC-5, (January 1969), 16-26.

Carbonell, J.R., J.I. Elkind and R.S. Nickerson, Importance of time in a time sharing system, *Human Factors*, 10, 2, (1968).

Card, Stuart K., Studies in the psychology of computer text editing, Xerox Palo Alto Research Center, SSL-78-1, San Jose, California, (August 1978).

Card, Stuart K., Thomas P. Moran and Allen Newell, The keystroke-level model of user performance time with interactive systems, (submitted for publication), (1979a).

Card, Stuart K., Thomas P. Moran and Alan Newell, Computer text-editing: An information-processing analysis of a routine cognitive skill, *Cognitive Psychology*, (1979b to appear).

Carlisle, James H., Comparing behavior at various computer display consoles in time-shared legal information, Rand Corporation, Santa Monica, CA Report No. AD712695, (September 1970).

Carlson, Eric D., An approach for designing decision support systems, IBM Research Report RJ 1959, (March 1977).

Carlson, Eric D., Barbara F. Grace and Jimmy A. Sutton, Case studies of end user requirements for interactive problem-solving systems, *MIS Quarterly*, (March 1977), 51-63.

Chai, D.T., Language considerations for information management systems, *Proceedings of the ACM National Conference*, (1974), 443-450.

Chamberlin, D.D., et al, SEQUEL 2: A unified approach to data definition, manipulation, and control, *IBM Journal of Research and Development*, 20, 6, November (1976), 560-574.

Chapanis, A., Interpersonal dialogue: Interactive human communication, *Scientific American*, 232, 3, (March 1975), 36-42.

Chapin, N., New format for flowcharts, *Software: Practice and Experience*, 4, (1974), 341-357.

Chase, W.G. and H.A. Simon, Perception in chess, *Cognitive Psychology*, 4, (1973), 55-81.

Chen, P., The entity-relationship model – toward a unified view of data, *ACM Transactions on Database Systems*, 1, 1, (March 1976), 9-36.

Cheriton, D.R., Man-Machine interface design for time-sharing systems, *Proceedings of the ACM National Conference*, (1976), 362-380.

Chrysler, Earl, Some basic determinants of computer programming productivity, *Communications of the ACM*, 21, (1978a), 472-483.

Chrysler, Earl, The impact of program and programmer characteristics, *Proceedings of the National Computer Conference*, 47, AFIPS Press, Montvale, New Jersey, (1978b), 581-587.

Codd, E.F., A relational model of data for large shared data banks, *Communications of the ACM*, 13, 6, (June 1970), 377-387.

Codd, E.F., Relational completeness of data base sublanguages, In R. Rustin (Ed.), *Data Base Systems*, Prentice-Hall, Englewood Cliffs, New Jersey, (1971).

Codd, E.F., Seven steps to rendezvous with the casual user, *Proceedings of the IFIP TC-2 Working Conference on Data Base Management Systems*, Cargese, Corsica, (April 1-5, 1974), North-Holland, Amsterdam.

Codd, E.F., HOW ABOUT RECENTLY?(English dialogue with relational databases using RENDEZVOUS Version 1), In B. Shneiderman (Ed.), *Databases: Improving Usability and Responsiveness*, Academic Press, New York, (1978), 3-28.

Couger, J.D. and R.A. Zawacki, What motivates DP professionals?, *Datamation*, 24, 9, (September 1978), 116-123.

Cress, P., P. Dirksen and J.W. Graham, *FORTRAN IV with WATFOR and WATFIV*, Prentice-Hall, Inc., Englewood Cliffs, New Jersey, (1970).

Cronbach, L.J., *Essentials of Psychological Testing*, 3rd Edition, Harper and Row, New York, (1970).

Curtis, B., S.B. Sheppard, P. Milliman, M.A. Borst and T. Love, Measuring the psychological complexity of software maintenance tasks with Halstead and McCabe metrics, *IEEE Transactions on Software Engineering*, SE-5, 2, (March 1979), 96-104.

Dahl, O.J., E.W. Dijkstra and C.A.R. Hoare, *Structured Programming*, Academic Press, New York, (1972).

Date, C.J., *An Introduction to Database Systems*, 2nd Edition, Addison-Wesley, Reading, Massachusetts, (1977).

Dijkstra, E.W., Programming considered as a human activity, *Proceedings of the IFIP*, 1, (1965), 213-217.

Dijkstra, E.W., GO TO statement considered harmful, *Communications of the ACM*, 11, (1968), 147-148.

Dijkstra, E.W., The humble programmer, *Communications of the ACM*, 15, (1972), 859-866.

Dixon, W.J., *BMD: Biomedical Computer Programs*, University of California Press, Berkley, California, (1977).

Doktor, R., Cognitive style and the use of computers and management, *Management Datamatics*, 5, 2, (1976).

Doll, R. and A. Longo, Improving the predictive effectiveness of peer ratings, *Personnel Psychology*, 9, (1956), 215-220.

Dreyfuss, Henry, *Designing for People*, Simon and Schuster, New York, (1955).

Duncker, K., On problem solving, *Psychological Monographs*, 58, (1945), 270.

Dunsmore, H.E. and J.D. Gannon, Experimental investigation of programming complexity, *Proceedings of Sixteenth Annual ACM Technical Symposium: Systems and Software*, Washington, D.C., (June 1977), 1-14.

Dunsmore, H.E. and J.D. Gannon, Programming factors - language factors that help explain programming complexity, *Proceedings of the ACM National Conference*, (1978), 554-560.

Durding, B.M., C.A. Becker and J.D. Gould, Data organization, *Human Factors*, 19, 1, (1977), 1-14.

Eason, K.D., Understanding the naive computer user, *The Computer Journal*, 19, 1, (February 1976), 3-7.

Eason, K.D., L. Damordaran and T.F.M. Stewart, Interface problems in man-computer interaction, In E. Mumford and H. Sackman (Eds.), *Human Choice and Computer*, North-Holland Publishing Company, Amsterdam, The Netherlands, (1975), 91-105.

Edwards, A.L., *Experimental Design in Psychological Research*, Holt, Reinhart and Winston, New York, (1968).

Ellul, J., *The Technological Society*, Knopf, New York, (1965).

Elshoff, James L., An analysis of some commercial PL/1 programs, *IEEE Transactions on Software Engineering*, SE-2, (1976a), 113-121.

Elshoff, James L., A numerical profile of commercial PL/1 programs, *Software: Practice and Experience*, 6, (1976b), 505-525.

Elshoff, James L., Measuring commercial PL/I programs using Halstead's criteria, *ACM SIGPLAN Notices*, 7, 5, (May 1976c), 38-46.

Elshoff, James L., An investigation into the effects of the counting method used on software science measurements, *ACM SIGPLAN Notices*, 13, 2, (February 1978), 30-45.

Embley, D.W., Empirical and formal language design applied to a unified control structure, *International Journal of Man-Machine Studies*, 10, (1978), 197-216.

Endres, A., An analysis of errors and their causes in system programs, In Proceedings, 1975 International Conference on Reliable Software, *ACM SIGPLAN Notices*, 10, 6, (1975), 327-336.

Engel, Stephen E. and Richard E. Granda, Guidelines for Man/Display Interfaces, IBM Poughkeepsie Laboratory Technical Report TR 00.2720, (December 19, 1975).

Fagan, M., Design and code inspections, and process control in the development of programs, IBM Technical Report 21.572, (December 1974).

Farina, F., *Flowcharting*, Prentice-Hall, Englewood Cliffs, New Jersey, (1970).

Feyock, S., Transition diagram-based CAI/HELP systems, *International Journal of Man-Machine Studies*, 9, (1977), 399-413.

Fitter, Mike, Information systems and individual behaviour, In J. Banbury and R.K. Stamper, *Management Information Systems*, (1978).

Fitter, Mike, Towards more 'natural' interactive systems, *International Journal of Man-Machine Studies*, 11, (1979), 339-350.

Fitter, Mike and T.R.G. Green, When do diagrams make good computer languages?, *International Journal of Man-Machine Studies*, 11, (1979), 235-261.

Fitz-Enz, J., Who is the DP professional?, *Datamation*, 24, 9, (September 1978), 124-128.

Fitzsimmons, Ann and Tom Love, A review and evaluation of software metrics, *Computing Surveys* 10, 1, (March 1978), 3-18.

Foley, J.D. and V.L. Wallace, The art of graphic man-machine conversation, *Proceedings of the IEEE* ,62, 4, (April 1974).

Freedman, Daniel P., and Weinberg, Gerald M., *Ethnotechnical Review Handbook.* Ethnotech, Inc., Lincoln, Nebraska, 1977.

Frymire, W., Decision tables a basis for structured testing, *5th Annual Conference Principles of Software Development*, Control Data Corporation, (November 1977), 103-121.

Gagne, R.M., Human problem solving: Internal and external events, In B. Kleinmuntz (Ed.), *Problem Solving: Research, Method and Theory*, Wiley, New York, (1966).

Gaines, Brian R. and Peter V. Facey, Some experience in interactive system development and application, *Proceedings of the IEEE* , 63, 6, (June 1975), 894-911.

Gannon, John D., An experiment for the evaluation of language features, *International Journal of Man-Machine Studies*, 8, (1976), 61 73.

Gannon, John D., An experimental evaluation of data type conventions, *Communications of the ACM*, 20, 8, (August 1977), 584-595.

Gannon, John D., Characteristic errors in programming languages, *Proceedings of the ACM National Conference*, (1978), 570-575.

Gannon, John D., and J.J. Horning, The impact of language design on the production of reliable software, *IEEE Transactions on Software Engineering*, SE-1, 2, (1975), 179-191.

Gebhardt, F. and I. Stellmacher, Design criteria for documentation retrieval languages, *Journal of the American Society for Information Science*, 29, 4, (July 1978), 191-199.

Gilb, T., *Software Metrics*, Winthrop Publishers, Cambridge, Massachusetts, (1977).

Gilb, T. and G.M. Weinberg, *Humanized Input: Techniques for Reliable Keyed Input*, Winthrop Publishers, Cambridge, Massachusetts, (1977).

Gold, M.M., Time-Sharing and batch processing: An experimental comparison of their values in a problem-solving situation, *Communications of the ACM*, 12, 5, (May 1969), 249–259.

Goldberg, P.C., The future of programming for non-programmers, IBM Research Report RC 5975, (1975).

Goodman, T. and R. Spence, The effect of system response time on interactive computer aided problem solving, *ACM SIGGRAPH '78 Conference Proceedings*, (1978), 100–104.

Gordon, J.D., C.K. Capstick and A. Salvadori, An empirical study of COBOL programmers, *INFOR*, 15, 2, (June 1977), 229–241.

Gordon, R.D. and M.H. Halstead, An experiment comparing FORTRAN programming times with the software physics hypothesis, *Proceedings of the National Computer Conference*, 45, AFIPS Press, Montvale, New Jersey, (1976), 935–937.

Gould, J.D., Visual factors in the design of computer controlled CRT display, *Human Factors*, 10, 4, (1968).

Gould, J.D., Some psychological evidence on how people debug computer programs, *International Journal of Man-Machine Studies*, 7, (1975), 151-182.

Gould, J.D. and R.N. Ascher, Use of an IQF-like query language by non-programmers, IBM Research report RC 5279, (February 20, 1975).

Gould, J.D. and P. Drongowski, An exploratory study of computer program debugging, *Human Factors*, 16, (1974), 258–277.

Grace, B.F., A case study of man/computer problem-solving: observations on interactive formulation of school attendance boundaries, IBM Research Report RJ 1483, (February 1975).

Grace, B.F., Training users of a decision support system, IBM Research Report RJ 1790, (May 1976).

Grant, E.E. and H. Sackman, An exploratory investigation of programmer performance under on-line and off-line conditions, *IEEE Transactions on Human Factors in Electronics*, HFE-8, (1967).

Green, T.R.G., Conditional program statements and their comprehensibility to professional programmers, *Journal of Occupational Psychology*, 50, (1977), 93-109.

Greenblatt, D. and J. Waxman, A study of three database query languages, In B. Shneiderman (Ed.), *Databases: Improving Usability and Responsiveness*, Academic Press, (1978), 77–97.

Greeno, J.G., The structure of memory and the process of problem solving, University of Michigan: Human Performance Center Technical Report 37, (1972).

Grossberg, Mitchell, Raymond A. Wiesen and Douwe B. Yntema, An experiment on problem solving with delayed computer responses, *IEEE*

Transactions on Systems, Man, and Cybernetics, SMC-6, 3, (March 1976), 219-222.

Halstead, M., *Elements of Software Science*, Operating and Programming Systems Series, Elsevier Computer Science Library, New York, (1977).

Hansen, G., Measuring software reliability, *Mini-Micro Systems*, (August 1977), 54-57.

Hansen, J.V., Man-machine communication: An experimental analysis of heuristic problem-solving under on-line and batch-processing conditions, *IEEE Transactions on Systems, Man and Cybernetics*, 6, 11, (November 1976), 746-752.

Hansen, W.J., User engineering principles for interactive systems, *Proceedings of the Fall Joint Computer Conference*, 39, AFIPS Press, Montvale, New Jersey, (1971), 523-532.

Hansen, W.J., Measurement of program complexity by the pair (cyclomatic number, operator count), *ACM SIGPLAN Notices*, 13, 3, (March 1978), 29-33.

Harris, L.R., User oriented data base query with the ROBOT natural language query system, *International Journal of Man-Machine Studies*, 9, (1977), 697-713.

Hart, D.J., The human aspects of working with visual display terminals, INCA-FIEJ Research Report No. 76/02, Washingtonplatz, Darmstadt, West Germany, (1976), 1-61.

Heath, I.J., Unacceptable file operations in a relational data base, *ACM-SIGMOD Proceedings*, (1972).

Heidorn, G.E., Automatic programming through natural language dialogue: A survey, *IBM Journal of Research and Development*, 20, 4, (July 1976), 302-313.

Held, G.D., M.R. Stonebraker and E. Wong, INGRES: A relational database system, *Proceedings of the National Computer Conference*, AFIPS Press, Montvale, New Jersey, (1975).

Hill, I.D., Wouldn't it be nice if we could write computer programs in ordinary English -- or would it? *Honeywell Computer Journal*, 6, 2, (1972), 76-83.

Hiltz, S.R. and M. Turoff, *The Network Nation: Human Communication via Computer*, Addison-Wesley, Reading, Massachusetts, (1978).

HIPO - A Design Aid and Documentation Technique, Order GC 20-185, IBM Corporation.

Hirsch, Richard S., Human factors in man-computer interfaces, IBM Human Factors Center, San Jose, California, (1976).

Hollander, E.P., Reliability of peer nomination under various conditions of administration, *Journal of Applied Psychology*, 41, (1957), 85-90.

Holt, H.O. and F.L. Stevenson, Human performance considerations in complex systems, *Science*, 195, (March 18, 1977), 1205-1209.

IBM, Structured walk-throughs: A project management tool, IBM Corporation, Armonk, N.Y., (August 1973).

Igersheim, Roy H., Managerial response to an information system, *Proceedings of the National Computer Conference*, 45, AFIPS Press, Montvale, New Jersey, (1976), 877–882.

Johansen, Robert, Jacques Vallee and Kathleen Spangler, *Electronic Meetings: Technical Alternatives and Social Choices*, Addison-Wesley Publishing Company, Reading Massachusetts, (1979).

Kammann, R., The comprehensibility of printed instructions and flow-chart alternative, *Human Factors*, 17, (1975), 183-191.

Kane, J. and E. Lawler, Methods of peer assessment, *Psychological Bulletin*, 85, 3, (1978), 555–586.

Keen, Peter G.W. and Michael S. Scott Morton, *Decision Support Systems: An Organizational Perspective*, Addison–Wesley Publishing Company, Reading, Massachusetts, (1978).

Kennedy, T.C.S., The design of interactive procedures for man–machine communication, *International Journal of Man–Machine Studies*, 6, (1974), 309-334.

Kennedy, T.C.S., Some behavioural factors affecting the training of naive users of a interactive computer system, *International Journal of Man-Machine Studies*, 7, (1975), 817–834.

Kerschberg, L., E.A. Ozkarahan, and J.E.S. Pacheco, A synthetic english query language for a relational associative processor, *Proceedings Second International Conference on Software Engineering*, San Francisco, (1976), 505-519.

Knuth, D.E., An empirical study of FORTRAN programs, *Software – Practice and Experience*, 1, (1972), 105–133.

Kroemer, K.H. Eberhard, Human engineering the keyboard, *Human Factors*, 14, 1, (1972).

Leavenworth, B.M. and J.E. Sammet, An overview of nonprocedural languages, *ACM SIGPLAN Notices*, 9, 4, (April 1974), 1-12.

Ledgard, H. and L. Chmura, *COBOL with Style*, Hayden, Rochelle Park, New Jersey, (1976).

Lee, Jeanne M. and B. Shneiderman, Personality and programming: Time-sharing vs. batch processing, *Proceedings of the ACM National Conference*, (1978), 561-569.

Lemos, Ronald S., The cost–effectiveness of team debugging in teaching COBOL programing, *ACM SIGCSE Bulletin*, 10, 1, (February 1978), 193-196.

Lemos, Ronald S., An implementation of structured walk-throughs in teaching COBOL programming, *Communications of the ACM*, 22, 6, (June 1979), 335-340.

Lewin, A. and A. Zwany, Peer nominations: A model, literature critique and a paradigm for research, *Personnel Psychology*, 29, (1976), 423-447.

Licklider, J.C.R., Man-computer symbiosis, *IEEE Transactions on Human Factors in Electronics*, HFE-1, (March 1960), 4-11.

Litecky, C.R. and G.D. Davis, A study of errors, error-proneness and error diagnosis in COBOL, *Communications of the ACM*, 19, 1, (January 1976), 33-37.

Littlewood, B., Software reliability measurements: Some criticisms and suggestions, *Software Phenomenology Working Papers of the Software Lifecycle Management Workshop*, U.S. Army Institute for Research in Management Information and Computer Science, (August 1977), 473-487.

Lochovsky, F., Database management system user performance, Ph.D. Dissertation, University of Toronto, (1978).

Lochovsky, F. and Tsichritzis, User performance considerations in DBMS selection, *ACM-SIGMOD Proceedings*, (1977), 128-134.

Love, Tom, Relating individual differences in computer programming performance to human information processing abilities, Ph.D. Dissertation, University of Washington, (1977).

Love, Tom, and Ann B. Bowman, An independent test of the theory of software physics, *ACM SIGPLAN Notices*, 7, 10, (November 1976), 42-49.

Lowerre, B.T., The HARPY speech recognition system, Ph.D. Dissertation, Department of Computer Science, Carnegie-Mellon University, Pittsburgh, Pennsylvania, (1976).

Lucas, H.C. and R.B. Kaplan, A structured programming experiment, *The Computer Journal*, 19, 2, (1976), 136-138.

Malhotra, A. and P. Sheridan, Experimental determination of design system requirements for a program explanation system, IBM Technical Report RC-5739.

Mandler, G., Organization and recognition, In E. Tulving and W. Donaldson (Eds.), *Organization of Memory*, Academic Press, New York, (1972).

Martin, A., A new keyboard layout, *Applied Ergonomics*, 3, 1, (1972).

Martin, J., *Design of Man-Computer Dialogues*, Prentice-Hall, Englewood Cliffs, New Jersey, (1973).

Mayer, R.E., Different problem-solving competencies established in learning computer programming with and without meaningful models, *Journal of Educational Psychology*, 67, (1975), 725-734.

Mayer, R.E., Comprehension as affected by structure of problem representation, *Memory and Cognition*, 4, (1976a), 249-255.

Mayer, R.E., Some condition of meaningful learning for computer programming, advance organizers and subject control of frame order, *Journal of Educational Psychology*, 68, (1976b), 143-150.

Mayer, R.E., *Thinking and Problem Solving: An Introduction to Human Cognition and Learning*, Scott, Foresman Company, Glenview, Illinois, (1977).

McCabe, T., A complexity measure, *IEEE Transactions on Software Engineering* , SE-2, 6, (December 1976), 308-320.

McCormick, Ernest J., *Human Factors in Engineering and Design* (Fourth Edition), McGraw-Hill Book Company, New York, (1976).

McCue, Gerald M., IBM Santa Teresa Laboratory - Architectural design for program development, *IBM Systems Journal*, 17, 1, (1978), 4-25.

McDonald, N. and M. Stonebraker, CUPID: The friendly query language, *Proceedings of the ACM Pacific Conference*, San Francisco, (April 17-18, 1975).

McGee, W.C., On user criteria for data model evaluation, *ACM Transactions on Database Systems*, 1, 4, (December 1976), 370-387.

McHenry, R.C., Notes on software reliability and quality, *Software Phenomenology Working Papers of the Software Lifecycle Management Workshop* , U.S. Army Institute for Research in Management Information and Computer Science, (August 1977), 401-417.

McLuhan, Marshall, *Understanding Media: The Extensions of the Man*, McGraw Hill, New York, (1965).

Metzger, Phillip W., *Managing a Programming Project*, Prentice-Hall, Inc., Englewood Cliffs, New Jersey, (1973).

Miller, G.A., The magical number seven, plus or minus two: Some limits on our capacity for processing information, *Psychological Reveiw*, 63, (1956), 81-97.

Miller, G.A., Needed: A better theory of cognitive organization, *IEEE Transactions on Systems, Man, and Cybernetics*, SMC-4, 1, (January 1974), 95-97.

Miller, L.A., Programming by non-programmers, *International Journal of Man-Machine Studies*, 6, (1974), 237-260.

Miller, L.A., Naive programmer problems with specification of transfer-of-control, *Proceedings of the National Computer Conference*, 44, AFIPS Press, Montvale, New Jersey (1975), 657-663.

Miller, L.A. and C.A. Becker, Programming in natural English, IBM Technical Report RC 5137, (November 1974).

Miller, L.A. and J.C. Thomas, Jr., Behavioral issues in the use of interactive systems, *International Journal of Man-Machine Studies*, 9, (1977), 509-536.

Miller, L.H., A study in man-machine interaction, *Proceedings of the National Computer Conference*, 46, AFIPS Press, Montvale, New Jersey, (1977), 409-421.

Miller, Robert B., Response time in man-computer conversational transactions, *Proceedings Spring Joint Computer Conference 1968*, 33, AFIPS Press, Montvale, New Jersey, 267-277.

Mills, H., Top down programming in large systems, In R. Rustin (Ed.), *Debugging Techniques in Large Systems*, Prentice-Hall, Englewood Cliffs, New Jersey, (1971).

Mills, H., How to write correct programs and know it, Gaithersburg, Maryland, IBM-FSD Report, (1972a).

Mills, H., Mathematical foundations for structured programming, Gaithersburg, Maryland, IBM-FSD Report No. FSC-72b-6012, (1972b).

Model 204 User Language Reference Manual, Computer Corporation of America, (1977).

Montgomery, C.A., Is natural language an unnatural query language?, *Proceedings of the ACM National Conference*, ACM, New York, (1972), 1075-1078.

Moulton, P.G. and M.E. Muller, DITRAN -- a compiler emphasizing diagnostics, *Communications of the ACM*, 10, (1967), 45-52.

Musa, J.D., A theory of software reliability and its application, *IEEE Transactions on Software Engineering*, SE-1, 3, (September 1975), 312-327.

Musa, J.D., Software reliability measurement, *Software Phenomenology Working Papers of the Software Lifecycle Management Workshop*, U.S. Army Institute for Research in Management Information and Computer Science, (August 1977), 427-451.

Mumford, E. and H. Sackman (Eds.), *Human Choice and Computers*, North-Holland Publishing Company, Amsterdam, The Netherlands, (1975).

Mumford, L., *The Myth of the Machine*, Harcourt Brace Jovanovich, Inc., New York, (1967).

Myers, G.J., A controlled experiment in program testing and code walkthroughs/inspections, *Communications of the ACM*, 21, 9, (September 1978), 760-768.

Myers, Isabel Briggs, *The Myers-Briggs Type Indicator*, Consulting Psychologists Press, Incorporated, Palo Alto, California, (1962).

Nagy, G. and M.C. Pennebaker, A step toward automatic analysis of student programming errors in a batch environment, *International Journal of Man-Machine Studies*, 6, (1974), 563-578.

Nassi, I. and B. Shneiderman, Flowcharting techniques for structured programming, *ACM SIGPLAN Notices*, 8, 8, (1973), 12-26.

Nelson, T., A conceptual framework for man-machine everything, *Proceedings of the National Computer Conference*, 42, AFIPS Press, Montvale, New Jersey, (1973).

Newell, A., Fairytales, *ACM SIGART Bulletin*, 57, (November 1976).

Newell, A., and H.A. Simon, Heuristic problem solving: The next advance in operations research, *Operations Research*, 6, (January-February 1958).

Newell, A. and H.A. Simon, *Human Problem Solving*, Prentice-Hall, Englewood Cliffs, New Jersey, (1972).

Newman, Julian, The processing of two types of command statement: A contribution to cognitive ergonomics, *IEEE Transactions of System, Man and Cybernetics*, SMC-7, 12, (December 1977), 871-875.

Newman, W.M. and R.F. Sproull, *Principles of Interactive Computer Graphics*, (Second Edition), McGraw-Hill, New York, (1978).

Newsted, P.R., FORTRAN program comprehension as a function of documentation, School of Business Administration, University of Wisconsin, Milwaukee, Wisconsin, undated.

Newsted, P.R., Grade and ability prediction in an introductory programming course, *ACM SIGCSE Bulletin*, 7, 2, (June 1975), 87-91.

Nickerson, R.S., Man-computer interaction: A challenge for human factors research, *IEEE Transactions on Man-Machine Studies*, MMS-10, (1969), 164.

Nickerson, R.S., J.I. Elkind and J.R. Carbonell, Human factors and the design of time sharing computer systems, *Human Factors*, 10, 2, (1968), 127-137.

Nie, N.H., C.H. Hull, J.G. Jenkins, K. Steinbrenner, and D.H. Bent, *Statistical Package for the Social Sciences* (Second Edition), McGraw-Hill Book Company, New York (1975).

Norman, D.A. and D.E. Rummelhart, A system for perception and memory, In D.A. Norman (Ed.), *Models of Human Memory*, Academic Press, New York, (1970).

Norman, D.A. and D.E. Rummelhart, *Explorations in Cognition*, W.H. Freeman, San Francisco, (1975).

Okimoto, G.H., The effectiveness of comments: A pilot study, IBM SDD Technical Report TR 01.1347, (July 27, 1970).

Palme, Jacob, Interactive software for humans, *Management Datamatics*, 5, 4, (1976), 139-154.

Parnas, D.L., A technique for software module specifications with examples, *Communications of the ACM*, 15, 5, (May 1972a), 330-336.

Parnas, D.L., On the criteria to be used in decomposing systems into modules, *Communications of the ACM*, 15, 12, (December 1972b), 1053-1058.

Parr, F.N., Error counting models of software reliability, *Software Phenomenology Working Papers of the Software Lifecycle Management Workshop*, U.S. Army Institute for Research in Management Information and Computer Science, (August 1977), 453-471.

Petrick, S.R., On natural language based computer systems, *IBM Journal of Research and Development*, 20, 4, (July 1976), 314-325.

Pew, R.W. and A.M. Rollins, Dialog Specification Procedure, Bolt Beranek and Newman, Report No. 3129, Revised Edition, Cambridge, Massachusetts, 02138, (1975).

Piaget, J., *Science of Education and the Psychology of the Child*, Orion Press, New York, (1970).

Pirsig, R., *Zen and the Art of Motorcycle Maintenance*, Morrow and Co., (1974).

Plath, W.J., REQUEST: A natural language question answering system, *IBM Journal of Research and Development*, 20, (1976).

Polya, G., *How to Solve It*, Doubleday Anchor, Garden City, New York, (1957).

Polya, G., *Mathematical Discovery: On Understanding, Learning and Teaching Problem Solving*, Wiley, New York, (1968).

Ramamoorthy, C.V. and S.F. Ho, Testing large software with automated software evaluation systems, *ACM SIGPLAN Notices*, 10, 6, 382–394.

Ramsey, H. Rudy, Michael E. Atwood and Gary D. Campbell, A behavioral analysis of software design methodologies, U.S. Army Research Institute for the Behavioral and Social Sciences, Alexandria, Virginia, (August 1978).

Ramsgard, William C., *Making Systems Work: The Psychology of Business Systems*, John Wiley and Sons, Inc., New York, (1977).

Reddy, D.R., (Ed.) *Speech Recognition*, Academic Press, New York, (1975).

Rehling, W., Experiences with HIPO, *5th Annual Conference Principles of Software Development*, Control Data Corporation, (November 1977), 123-154.

Reich, C., *The Greening of America*, Bantam Books, Inc., New York, (1971).

Reifer, D., Automated aids for reliable software, *ACM SIGPLAN Notices*, 10, 6, (June 1975), 131–142.

Reisner, Phyllis, Use of psychological experimentation as an aid to development of a query language, *IEEE Transactions on Software Engineering*, SE-3, 3, (1977), 218–229.

Reisner, Phyllis, Using a formal grammar in human factors design of an interactive graphics system, IBM Research Report RJ2505, San Jose, California, (April 11, 1979).

Reisner, P., R.F. Boyce and D.D. Chamberlin, Human factors evaluation of two data base query languages: SQUARE and SEQUEL, *Proceedings of the National Computer Conference*, AFIPS Press, Montvale, New Jersey, (1975).

Reitman, W.R., *Cognition and Thought: An Information Processing Approach*, Wiley, New York, (1965).

Roadman, H., An industrial use of peer ratings, *Journal of Applied Psychology*, 48, 4, (1964), 211-214.

Robertson, G., A. Newell and K. Ramakrishna, ZOG: A man-machine communication philosophy, Department of Computer Sience, Carnegie Mellon University, Pittsburgh, Pennsylvania, (August 4, 1977).

Roszak, T., *Where the Wasteland Ends*, Doubleday and Co., Inc., New York, (1972).

Rouse, W.B., Design of man-computer interfaces for on-line interactive systems, *Proceedings of the IEEE, Special Issue on Interactive Computer Systems*, 63, 6, (June 1975), 847–857.

Rouse, W.B., Human-Computer interaction in multitask situations, *IEEE Transactions on Systems, Man, and Cybernetics*, SMC-7, 5, (May 1977), 384-392.

Rupp, Bruce A. and Richard S. Hirsch, Human factors of workstations with display terminals, IBM Human Factors Center, HFC-ss(G320-6102-0), San Jose, California, (November 15, 1977).

Rustin, R., (Editor), *Proceedings of the ACM SIGMOD Conference*, (1974), ACM, New York.

SAS Institute, *SAS Programmers Guide*, SAS Institute, Raleigh, California, (1979).

Saal, H.J. and Z. Weiss, An empirical study of APL programs, *Computer Languages*, 2, 3, (1977), 47-60.

Sachs, J., Recognition memory for syntactic and semantic aspects of connected discourse, *Perception and Psychophysics*, 2, (1967), 437-442.

Sackman, H., Experimental analysis of man-computer problem-solving, *Human Factors*, 12, (1970a), 187-201.

Sackman, H., *Man-Computer Problem Solving*, Auerbach Publishers Inc., Princeton, New Jersey, (1970b).

Sammet, J.E., Roster of programming languages for 1976-77, *ACM SIGPLAN Notices*, 13, 11, (November 1978), 56-85.

Schatzoff, M., R. Tsao and R. Wiig, An experimental comparison of time sharing and batch processing, *Communications of the ACM*, 10, 5, (May 1967), 261-265.

Schick, G.J., and R.W. Wolverton, An analysis of competing software reliability models, *IEEE Transactions on Software Engineering*, SE-4, 2, (March 1978), 104-120.

Schneidewind, N.F., An approach to software reliability prediction and quality control, *Proceedings of the Fall Joint Computer Conference*, 41, AFIPS Press, Montvale, New Jersey, (1972), 837-838.

Schneidewind, N.F., Analysis of error processes in computer software, *ACM SIGPLAN Notices*, 10, 6, (June 1975), 337-346.

Schneidewind, N.F. and H.M. Hoffman, An experiment in software error data collection and analysis, *Proceedings of the Sixth Texas Conference on Computing Systems*, (November 14-15, 1977).

Scowen, R.S. and B.A. Wichmann, The definition of comments in programming languages, *Software - Practice and Experience*, 4, (1974), 181-188.

Segal, Barr Zion, Effects of method of error interruption on student performance at interactive terminals, University of Illinois Department of Computer Science Technical Report UIUCDCS-R-75-727, (May 1975).

Senko M.E., The DDL in the context of a multilevel structured description: DIAM II with FORAL, *Data Base Description, Proceedings of the IFIP-TC-2 Working Conference*, Wepion, Belgium, January 1975, B.C.M. Douque and G. M. Nijssen, (Eds.), North-Holland Publishing Co., Amsterdam, the Netherlands, (1975), 239-258.

Senko M.E., DIAM II with FORAL LP: Making pointed queries with light pen, *Proceedings of the IFIP Congress* 77, North Holland Publishers, Amsterdam, the Netherlands, (1977).

Senko M.E., E.B. Altman, M.M. Astrahan, and P.L. Fehder, Data structures and accessing in database systems, *IBM Systems Journal*, 12, 1, (1973), 30-93.

Sheppard, S.B., M.A. Borst and L.T. Love, Predicting software comprehensibility, (Technical Report, T.R.-77-388100-1), General Electric Information Systems Programs, Arlington, Va., (February 1978).

Sheppard, S.B., B. Curtis, P. Milliman, M.A. Borst, and T. Love, First year results from a research program on human factors in software engineering, *Proceedings of the National Computer Conference*, 48, AFIPS Press, Montvale, New Jersey, (1979), 73-79.

Sheridan, Thomas B. and William R. Ferrell, *Man-Machine Systems: Information, Control, and Decision Models of Human Performance*, The MIT Press, Cambridge, Massachusetts, (1974).

Shneiderman, B., Experimental testing in programming languages, stylistic considerations and design techniques, *Proceedings of the National Computer Conference*, 44, AFIPS Press, Montvale, New Jersey, (1975), 653-656.

Shneiderman, B., Exploratory experiments in programmer behavior, *International Journal of Computer and Information Sciences*, 5, 2, (June 1976a), 123-143.

Shneiderman, B. (Ed.), *Database Management Systems*, Information Technology Series, 1, AFIPS Press, Montvale, New Jersey, (1976b), 59-61.

Shneiderman, B., Measuring computer program quality and comprehension, *International Journal of Man-Machine Studies*, 9, (1977a).

Shneiderman, B., Teaching programming: A spiral approach to syntax and semantics, *Computers and Education*, 1, (1977b), 193-197.

Shneiderman, B., Improving the human factors aspect of database interactions, *ACM Transactions on Database Systems*, 3, 4, (December 1978a), 417-439.

Shneiderman, B., Perceptual and cognitive issues in the syntactic/semantic model of programmer behavior, *Proceedings of Symposium on Human Factors and Computer Science*, Human Factors Society, Santa Monica, California, (1978b).

Shneiderman, B. and R. Mayer, Syntactic/semantic interactions in programmer behavior: A model and experimental results, *International Journal of Computer and Information Sciences*, 7, (1979), 219-239.

Shneiderman, B., R. Mayer, D. McKay and P. Heller, Experimental investigations of the utility of detailed flowcharts in programming, *Communications of the ACM*, 20, (1977), 373-381.

Shneiderman, B. and D. McKay, Experimental investigations of computer program debugging and modification, *Proceedings of the 6th International Congress of the International Ergonomics Association*, (July 1976).

Shooman, M., A summary of software reliability models and measurement, *Software Phenomenology Working Papers of the Software Lifecycle Management Workshop*, U.S. Army Institute for Research in Management Information and Computer Science, (August 1977), 419-426.

Shooman, M.L. and M.I. Bolsky, Types, distribution, and test and correction times for programming errors, In Proceedings, 1975 International Conference on Reliable Software, *ACM SIGPLAN Notices*, 10, 6, (August 1975), 347–357.

Sime, M.E., T.R.G. Green and D.J. Guest, Psychological evaluation of two conditional constructions used in computer languages, *International Journal of Man-Machine Studies*, 5, 1, (1973), 123–143.

Sime, M.E., T.R.G. Green and D.J. Guest, Scope marking in computer conditionals - a psychological evaluation, *International Journal of Man-Machine Studies*, 9, (1977), 107–118.

Simon, H.A., *The Science of the Artificial*, MIT Press, Cambridge, Massachusetts, (1969).

Singleton, W.T., Theoretical approaches to human errors, *Ergonomics*, 16, 6, (November 1973), 727–737.

Small, D.W. and L.J. Weldon, The efficiency of retrieving information from computers using natural and structured query languages, Science Applications Incorporated. Report SAI–78–655–WA, Arlington Va., (September 1977).

Smith, J.M. and D.C.P. Smith, Database abstractions: Aggregation and generalization, *ACM Transactions on Database Systems*, 2, 2, (June 1977), 105-133.

Smith, L.B., A comparison of batch processing and instant turnaround, *Communications of the ACM*, 10, 8, (August 1967), 495–500.

Sondheimer, Norman, On the fate of software enhancements, *Proceedings of the National Computer Conference*, 48, AFIPS Press, Montvale, New Jersey, (1979).

Sowa, J.F., Conceptual graphs for a data base interface, *IBM Journal of Research and Development*, 20, 4, (July 1976), 336–357.

Standish, Thomas A., Observations and hypotheses about program synthesis mechanisms, Automatic Programming Memo 9, Report No. 2780, Bolt Beranek and Newman, Cambridge, MA 021318 (December 19, 1973)

Stay, J.F., HIPO and integrated program design, *IBM Systems Journal*, 2, 143-154.

Sterling, T.D., Guidelines for humanizing computerized information systems: A Report from Stanley House, *Communications of the ACM*, 17, 11, (November 1974), 609–613.

Stevens, W.P. and G.J. Myers and L.L. Constantine, Structured design, *IBM System Journal*, 13, 2, (1974), 115–139.

Stewart, T.F.M., Ergonomic aspects of man-computer problem solving, *Applied Ergonomics*, 5, 4, (1974), 209-212.

Stewart, T.F.M., Display and software interface, *Applied Ergonomics*, 7, (1976), 137-147.

Stewart, T.F.M., O. Ostberg and C.J. Mackay, Computer terminal ergonomics, University of Loughborough, United Kingdom, (1974).

Stucki, R. and G. Foshee, New assertion concepts For self-metric software validation, *ACM SIGPLAN Notices*, 10, 6, (June 1975), 59-65.

Symington, J. and T. Kramer, Does peer review work, *American Scientist*, 65, Hearings Held in July 1975 Before a House Subcommittee, 17-20.

System 2000 Referènce Manual, MRI Systems Corporation, (1973).

Tharp, Alan L. and Woodrow E. Robbins, Using computers in a natural language mode for elementary education, *International Journal of Man-Machine Studies*, 7, (1975), 703-725.

Thomas, J.C., Quantifiers and question-asking, IBM Research Report RC 5866, (February 18, 1976a).

Thomas, J.C., A method for studying natural language dialogue, IBM Technical Report RC 5882, (February 1976b).

Thomas, J.C., Psychological issues in database management, *Proceedings of the International Conference on Very Large Data Bases* IV, Tokyo, (1977).

Thomas, J.C. and J.D. Gould, A psychological study of query by example, *Proceedings of the National Computer Conference*, 44, AFIPS Press, Montvale, New Jersey, (1975).

Toffler, Alvin, *Future Shock* , Random House, New York, (1970).

Tomeski, E. and H. Lazarus, *People-Oriented Computer Systems*, Van Nostrand Reinhold Co., New York, (1975).

Tracz, W.J., Programming and the human thought process, *Software: Practice & Experience*, 9, 2, (February 1979), 127-138.

Treu, S., Interactive command language design based on required mental work, *International Journal of Man-Machine Studies*, 7, (1975), 135-149.

Turoff, M., An on-line intellectual community or MEMEX revisited, *Technological Forecasting and Social Change*, 10, 4, (1977).

Turoff, M. and Starr Roxanne Hiltz, Computerized conferencing: Meeting through your computer, *IEEE Spectrum Magazine*, (May 1977).

Turoff, M.W., J. Whitescarver and S.R. Hiltz, The human machine interface in a computerized conferencing environment, *Proceedings of the IEEE Conference on Interactive Systems, Man, and Cybernetics*, (1978), 145-157.

Walston, C.E. and C.P. Felix, A method of programming measurement and estimation, *IBM Systems Journal*, 16, 1, (1977), 54-73.

Walther, G.H. and H.F. O'Neil Jr, On-line user-computer interface the effects of interface flexibility, terminal type, and experience on performance, *Proceedings of the National Computer Conference*, 43, AFIPS Press, Montvale, New Jersey, (1974).

Waltz, D., An English language question answering system for a large relational database, *Communications of the ACM*, 21, 7, (July 1978), 526-539.

Wason, P.C. and P.N. Johnson-Laird, *Psychology of Reasoning: Structure and Content*, Harvard University Press, Cambridge, MA, (1972).

Wasserman, T., The design of idiot-proof interactive systems, *Proceedings of the National Computer Conference*, 42, AFIPS Press, Montvale, New Jersey, (1973).

Watson, R.W., User interfaces design issues for a large interactive system, *Proceedings of the National Computer Conference*, 45, AFIPS Press, Montvale, New Jersey, (1976), 357-364.

Weinberg, G.M., *The Psychology of Computer Programming*, Van Nostrand Reinhold, New York, (1971).

Weinberg, G.M., D.P. Geller and T.W.S. Plum, IF-THEN-ELSE considered harmful, *ACM SIGPLAN Notices*, 10, 8, (August 1975), 34-44.

Weinberg, G.M. and E.L. Schulman, Goals and performance in computer programming, *Human Factors*, 16, 1, (1974), 70-77.

Weissman, L., A methodology for studying the psychological complexity of computer programs, Ph.D. Thesis, University of Toronto, (1974a).

Weissman, L., Psychological complexity of computer programs: An experimental methodology, *ACM SIGPLAN Notices*, 9, (1974b).

Weizenbaum, J., ELIZA -- A computer program for the study of natural language communication between man and machine, *Communications of the ACM*, 9, 1, (January 1966), 36-45.

Weizenbaum, J., *Computer Power and Human Reason*, W.H. Freeman and Company, San Francisco, California, (1976).

Welty, Charles, A comparison of a procedural and a nonprocedural query language: Syntactic metrics and human factors, Ph.D. Dissertation, Computer and Information Science Department, University of Massachusetts, (1979).

Wertheimer, M., *Productive Thinking*, Harper and Row, New York, (1959).

Wickelgren, W., *How To Solve Problems,* W. H. Freeman, San Francisco, 1974.

Winograd, T., *Understanding Natural Language*, Academic Press, New York, (1972).

Winship, B.J. and J.D. Kelly, A verbal response model of assertiveness, *Journal of Counseling Psychology*, 23, 3, (1976), 215-220.

Wirth, N., Program development by stepwise refinement, *Communications of the ACM*, 14, (1971).

Woods, W.A., Transition network grammars for natural language analysis, *Communications of the ACM*, 13, 10, (1970), 591-606.

Woods, W.A., Progress in natural language understanding – an application to lunar geology, *Proceedings of the National Computer Conference*, 42, AFIPS Press, Montvale, New Jersey, (1973), 441–450.

Woods, W.A., R.M. Kaplan and B. Nash-Webber, The Lunar Sciences Natural Language Information System, Bolt Beranek and Newman, Cambridge, Massachusetts, (June 1972).

Wright, P. and F. Reid, Written information: Some alternatives to prose for expressing the outcomes of complex contingencies, *Journal of Applied Psychology*, 57, (1973), 160–166.

Wulf, W.A. and M. Shaw, Global variables considered harmful, *ACM SIGPLAN Notices*, 8, 2, (February 1973), 28–34.

Wynne, B.E. and G.W. Dickson, Experienced managers' performance in experimental man-machine decision system simulation, *Academy of Management Journal*, 18, 1, (1976), 25–40.

Youngs, E.A., Human errors in programming, *International Journal of Man-Machine Studies*, 6, (1974), 361-376.

Yourdon, Edward, *Structured Walkthroughs* (2nd edition), Yourdon Press, New York, (1978).

Zak, D., Initial experiences in programming productivity realized using implementation language, *5th Annual Conference Principles of Software Development*, Control Data Corporation, (November 1977), 191–219.

Zloof, M.M., Query-by-Example, *Proceedings of the National Computer Conference*, AFIPS Press, Montvale, New Jersey, (1975a).

Zloof, M.M., Query-by-Example, the invocation and definition of tables and forms, *Proceedings of the International Conference on Very Large Data Bases*, Boston, Massachusetts, (September 22–24, 1975b), 1–24.

Zloof, M.M., Query-by-Example: Operations on the transitive closure, Research Report RC 5526, (1975c).

Zloof, M.M., Query-by-Example: Operations on hierarchical data bases, *Proceedings of the National Computer Conference*, 45, AFIPS Press, Montvale, New Jersey, (1976), 845–853. 845–853.

Zloof, M.M., Query-by-Example: A data base language, *IBM Systems Journal*, 16, 4, (1977), 321-343.

Zloof, M.M., Design aspects of the Query-by-Example data base language, In B. Shneiderman (Ed.), *Databases: Improving Usability and Responsiveness*, Academic Press, New York, (1978), 29–54.

Zmud, R., Behavioral considerations for decision support system design, Department of Management, School of Business, Auburn University, (1977a), (to be published).

Zmud, R., Performance with and appreciation of interactive information systems: The effects of think-time and cognitive style, Department of Management, School of Business, Auburn University, (1977b).

Zmud, R., Perceptual investigation of the cognitive implications of decision style theory, *Journal of Management*, 4, 1, (Spring 1979).

SUGGESTED PROJECTS AND EXERCISES

I. COURSE LENGTH EXPERIMENTAL PROJECT

When this text is used for a typical 15-week university-level course, students may be required to design, administer, evaluate and write up a complete experiment. I have found this approach extremely productive in that it makes the issues more realistic and is highly motivating for students. Since the students may not be experienced in experimental design, precise guidance is essential to ensure success.

I encourage students to work in teams of two, hopefully composed of a computer/information-science oriented and a psychology oriented major. Having a partner is useful to split the workload and increase the diversity of skills within a team. I allow students to choose their partners and do allow one-person teams.

The teams make their experimental proposals and I provide feedback for revisions. Then the experimental materials are submitted for review and revision. Next a pilot study with 3–6 subjects is required to test out the experimental materials and to gauge the difficulty of the task for the intended subjects. Students and professional researchers are notoriously bad in judging how long it will take subjects to perform a task or how difficult they will find it. A report on the pilot describing what happened and what changes have been made is required.

Administering the experiment turns out to be a great moment in the course. I encourage students to make contact with instructors of courses which have students with the right background to be subjects. If necessary I will contact the instructor to answer questions, but generally instructors and students are intrigued by the novelty of being involved in an experiment. Instructors should be shown the experimental materials and told how much time is needed when they are asked to permit use of their course. We have found that fixed-time experiments work best, but subjects should be told that they must stay till the end of the experiment. We use the experimental consent form described in Section 2.6. Student subjects are usually interested in the experiment, but can become unhappy if the task is completely unrelated to their course work, extremely difficult or extremely time-consuming. Many student-run experiments are completed in 15 or 20 minutes but others have taken 45 minutes or an hour. When the experiment is administered the team members should be present to answer questions and demonstrate the importance of the research effort. In about ten percent of our experiments something went wrong during the administration which required a new set of subjects and a new administration.

Project teams should turn in their experimental data in compact form and conduct their statistical analyses by hand or with available statistical program packages. The format for the final report is (the figures in parentheses indicated estimated length in double-space typewritten pages):

1. Introduction (3–6)

   State the area of research and why it is interesting.

   Describe relevant previous research.
2. Experimental procedures (1–2)

   State the hypotheses and briefly outline the experiment.

   2.1 Subjects (1): Describe subjects, their background and assignment to experimental groups.

   2.2 Materials (1–2): Describe the materials so that the knowledgeable reader has a clear picture of what they were like.

   2.3 Administration (1–2): Describe the test conditions, time, protection of anonymity.
3. Results (2–3): Uninterpreted results with tables, graphs, histograms, etc. This is a simple report of what happened.
4. Discussion (2–3): Explanations, conjectures, interpretations and suggestions for future experiments.
5. Conclusions (1): Summary and statement of most important findings.
6. References.
7. Appendix: Complete set of experimental materials.

I require a first draft of sections 1 and 2 of the final writeup to be turned in early for review and evaluation. When the final reports are turned in, students make 5–10-minute presentations about their findings.

Several student projects have led to published results or have been combined with other work to form a publishable paper. In other cases student projects have become the basis for larger experiments. In any case the goal for the students is merely to gain experience with experimentation.

I've used the following schedule:

2nd week – brief description of topic area and team member names

3rd week – statement of the hypothesis, independent and dependent variables, experimental design and background of subjects

5th week – first draft of experimental materials for review and identification of subjects to be used (contact should have been made with the course instructor or the manager if professional subjects are used)

7th week – one page description of pilot experiment and intended revisions

10th week – after actual administration, submit raw data in compact form

11th week – first draft of sections 1 and 2 of final report

12th week – tables, graphs or histograms of results

14th week – final report and class presentations

Directing a large number of student experiments can be time-consuming for the instructor, but it is exciting and rewarding.

II. DISCUSSION QUESTIONS

1. Describe the features of a controlled experiment.
2. Why is a controlled experiment better/worse than introspection/field studies?
3. Describe one experiment in detail using the terminology of a controlled experiment.
4. Describe one experiment briefly and suggest how it might have been improved.
5. Mention three personality features that you feel would be an asset to programmers and say why.
6. As personnel director of a large software firm, you have been asked to criticize/defend the use of standard psychological tests such as the SVIB or MMPI for incoming programmers.
7. Describe an ideal physical/social environment for programming.
8. Why is memorization–reconstruction a good/bad method for evaluating program quality or programmer ability?
9. Describe the syntactic/semantic model of programming behavior.

10. A programming organization manager has proposed a standard for all programs:
    (1) indentation must be used
    (2) comments are permitted only at the beginning of a module
    (3) mnemonic names must all be five characters in length because the compiler handles this length well
    (4) Boolean expressions can be no longer than 3 ANDs, ORs or NOTs
    (5) GOTOs may not be used in COBOL

    You should say
    (a) why this might be a good idea
    (b) why this might be a bad idea
    (c) design at least one experiment to test the proposed standard

11. Defend/attack the use of lines of code as a measure of programming productivity.

12. Describe a technique (objective automatable/human performance/subjective) for evaluating program quality and indicate its strengths and weaknesses.

13. Compare and contrast two (group processes/team organizations).

14. What are the advantages/disadvantages of peer rating of programs?

15. You have been appointed the director of a national commission organized by all manufacturers of computer hardware and software. You have been charged with proving the superiority of high-level programming languages over assembly languages. Describe your plan of attack and details of the three experiments you wish to run. Be precise and use the terminology of experimental design.

16. Describe one technique for evaluating program quality from each of the following categories and give its advantages and disadvantages.
    (a) objective automatable
    (b) human performance based objective measures
    (c) subjective

17. Describe in precise detail the structured walkthrough approach to design evaluation, then give the advantages and disadvantages of this group process.

18. A new control structure has been proposed for inclusion in a programming language being developed by your organization. Describe your plan for evaluating the effectiveness of this control structure from a human factors point of view, by designing three controlled experiments.

19. Describe the egoless-democratic team or the chief programmer team organization and then give the advantages and disadvantages.
20. Describe the idea behind Halstead's software science or McCabe's cyclomatic complexity metric and then give the advantages and disadvantages.
21. Compare the network and hierarchical data models in terms of the complexity of the allowable structures.
22. Why is the relational model thought to be easier for people to use? What disadvantages does it have?
23. Make arguments for the presence and absence of keywords in database query languages.
24. Describe a set of procedures for evaluating a database query language that is being considered for purchase by a large organization.
25. Describe methods for comparing the ease of use of two schemas that have been proposed for the same database.
26. What are the advantages/disadvantages of natural language query systems for large databases?
27. Describe an evaluation plan for a natural language query system being offered to replace a currently working query language system.
28. Describe an experiment to compare the effectiveness of time-sharing to batch program development.
29. What are the advantages/disadvantages of fixing response time at two seconds for every command?
30. Make a case for adding/eliminating a HELP facility on a working interactive system.
31. Set up guidelines for pilot testing a proposed interactive system.
32. What are the opportunities/dangers of expanded computer usage?
33. Under what conditions should a professional programmer decide not to perform the implementation of a system?

THE t DISTRIBUTION

ν	$\alpha = 0.20$	$\alpha = 0.10$	$\alpha = 0.05$	$\alpha = 0.02$	$\alpha = 0.01$	ν
1	3.078	6.314	12.706	31.821	63.657	1
2	1.886	2.920	4.303	6.965	9.925	2
3	1.638	2.353	3.182	4.541	5.841	3
4	1.533	2.132	2.776	3.474	4.604	4
5	1.476	2.015	2.571	3.365	4.032	5
6	1.440	1.943	2.447	3.143	3.707	6
7	1.415	1.895	2.365	2.998	3.499	7
8	1.397	1.860	2.306	2.896	3.355	8
9	1.383	1.833	2.262	2.821	3.250	9
10	1.372	1.812	2.228	2.764	3.169	10
11	1.363	1.796	2.201	2.718	3.106	11
12	1.356	1.782	2.179	2.681	3.055	12
13	1.350	1.771	2.160	2.650	3.012	13
14	1.345	1.761	2.145	2.624	2.977	14
15	1.341	1.753	2.131	2.602	2.947	15
16	1.337	1.746	2.120	2.583	2.921	16
17	1.333	1.740	2.110	2.567	2.898	17
18	1.330	1.734	2.101	2.552	2.878	18
19	1.328	1.729	2.093	2.539	2.861	19
20	1.325	1.725	2.086	2.528	2.845	20
21	1.323	1.721	2.080	2.518	2.831	21
22	1.321	1.717	2.074	2.508	2.819	22
23	1.319	1.714	2.069	2.500	2.807	23
24	1.318	1.711	2.064	2.492	2.797	24
25	1.316	1.708	2.060	2.485	2.787	25
26	1.315	1.706	2.056	2.479	2.779	26
27	1.314	1.703	2.052	2.473	2.771	27
28	1.313	1.701	2.048	2.467	2.763	28
29	1.311	1.699	2.045	2.462	2.756	29
inf	1.282	1.645	1.960	2.326	2.576	inf.

Adapted from Table IV of R. A. Fisher, *Statistical Methods for Research Workers*, 14th edition, (copyright© 1970, University of Adelaide), by permission of Macmillan Publishing Co., Inc., Hafner Press.

NAME INDEX

SUBJECT INDEX